advanced Praise

"Having invested a lifetime in developing others, Byron Thompson brings a wealth of information and experience in this enriching fable that is certain to put you on the path to a purposeful, engaging, and fulfilling retirement. This book is perfect for anyone who is on the precipice of their next chapter, in the midst of retirement, or simply hungers for a richer life."

—Kimberly Davis, author of *Brave Leadership: Unleash Your Most Confident, Powerful and Authentic Self to Get the Results You Need*

"Unsure of your retirement or reluctant to embrace change? Read this book aimed at boomers seeking purpose and fulfillment."

—Douglas R. Carter; author of *Clients Forever*

"Pulling from his forty-plus years in helping people to reach their full potential, Byron trained the trainers . . . He is a master at what he knows and the way he imparts his knowledge to others. A witty, high energy, storyteller, Byron brings to life in this book ways the reader will not only be entertained, but also ways they can learn the lessons that the characters learn—realizing their retirement dreams as well."

—Pati Hope, author of *GPS for Living, A Year in a Suitcase, and Everybody Wants to Go to Heaven; Just Not Now*

"Byron has a passion for helping people, especially those approaching or already at retirement. This book is the culmination of lessons learned from a life being well lived. It serves as a template for the rest of us as we navigate the unfamiliar waters of the second chapter of our lives."

— Greg Berg, PhD, author of *A Therapy Primer*

To Gayle
With much appreciation
for who you are!

sea CHanGe

a STORY aBOUT ReaLIZING YOUR DReams In ReTIReMenT

Byron Thompson

BYRON E. THOMPSON

Author of *Build Your Dream:
12 Essential Tools for Successful Living

Sea Change: A Story About Realizing Your Dreams in Retirement

Copyright © 2019 Byron E. Thompson. All rights reserved. No part of this book may be reproduced or retransmitted in any form or by any means without the written permission of the publisher.

Published by Wheatmark®
2030 East Speedway Boulevard, Suite 106
Tucson, Arizona 85719 USA
www.wheatmark.com

ISBN: 978-1-62787-640-7 (paperback)
ISBN: 978-1-62787-641-4 (ebook)
LCCN: 2018910234

INTRODUCTION

If you are anywhere near the age of retirement, this book is for you. At this time in your life you have a unique set of circumstances, concerns, and opportunities. All of these issues center around the critical question you and other baby boomers are asking: "How do I spend the rest of my life in order to consider it a life well lived?"

You are the only one who can answer that question, but there are a great many men and women who have gone before you who can provide some helpful guidelines to assist you in coming up with your unique solution. You'll find them in the story you are about to read.

This is not another self-help book that outlines what you should do, because there is no one-size-fits-all answer to that question. Saying that, I invite you to join the eight characters in this parable as they search for their own answers. In so doing, you can expect to redefine your own journey toward a life well lived.

PROLOGUE

Six Months Before

"Good morning!" boomed the impeccably dressed McKenzie "Mac" Katz when he came bouncing into the richly furnished, walnut-paneled boardroom of Seminar Solutions. "Who's the boss?" he yelled.

"The customer!" his equally enthusiastic management team shouted back at him as they jumped up from their leather chairs gathered around the expensive oak conference table.

"This morning we're going to hear a progress report on our next exciting seminar," the graying but youthful-looking CEO and founder of the successful training company said. "Here to present the details are our own VP of operations, Doug Carson, and Cruise Director Pat Higgins of Imperial Cruise Lines."

The two presenters, dressed for showmanship in all-white cruise uniforms, sprang to their feet and took turns announcing the details of the program. Doug Carson kicked off the presentation, saying, "You're receiving a detailed handout of the program and a copy of the sales brochure that we'll be sending out to one million carefully-selected prospects, all of whom have the needs, desires, and financial capability to participate in the seminar. We will gross one million and net three hundred thousand.

"The market is huge. There are ten thousand baby boomers retiring every day. That gives us a market of over three hundred thousand every year. We can run the program on an annual basis and add significantly to our bottom line. The program design is based on the research and conclusions of a well-being theory developed by Martin Seligman and others at the University of Pennsylvania. It is designed to be a practical application of his principles for the layperson to achieve a life worth living.

"A key component of this program is that through the use of analytics, we will be able to select six hundred participants, dividing them into seventy-five teams of eight, each with matching characteristics enabling them to make optimum progress during the two weeks of the training. We'll have the entire ship to ourselves, and some crew members will be trained to work as group leaders. Take a few minutes to review it, and Pat will answer any questions."

"What about cost? Aren't cruises expensive?" asked CFO Rob Mezner.

"They can be," Doug responded. "But here's the part that's got me excited. We've worked the pricing out with Imperial Cruise Lines. They want this seminar to be a success every bit as much as we do. So since it is a repositioning cruise, meaning they have to get the ship back to Europe in order to accommodate their summer Mediterranean guests, they've developed a sliding scale of prices so that anyone who can afford a vacation will be able to participate."

"That's it," said Mac. "Any questions or concerns?"

A buzz of excitement filled the room. The Seminar Solutions team could tell they had another winner on their hands.

"I have a question and a concern," said Dr. Craig Burk, the company's psychologist. "That's a lot of heavy, intense data for such a short time frame. It could put a lot of pressure on any participants who are unusually vulnerable due to their anticipation about major life changes. Have you considered the psychological strain on participants?"

"Good question, Craig," said Doug. "We had a respected independent psych team evaluate the curriculum for potential problems. They've reassured us there is less than 1.7 percent chance of that happening. Thus, our liability is limited. This is no fire walk or sweat lodge type of program, but it could happen." Doug's comment drew a laugh from the team. "Besides, Craig, you are going to be on the cruise doing a presentation and keeping an eye out for any potential problems. The comprehensive questionnaire the participants complete will throw up any red flags, so you'll know who might be at risk."

"Any more questions?" asked Mac Katz. "No? We're dismissed. Let's get back to work."

With that, the rest of the Seminar Solutions team left, excitedly talking among themselves about the new program and leaving Dr. Craig Burk sitting by himself with a look of consternation on his face.

January 6
Three Months Before

8:00 a.m., 1264 Fifth Street, Muncie, Indiana

Eddie Townsend sat, elbows on his desk, holding his face in his hands, staring at the computer. It seemed to be mocking him, daring him to write something, anything. But it sat there, blank. When he saw his reflection in the screen, he did not see the smiling, happy-go-lucky Eddie everyone was used to seeing. Instead he saw a worried-looking, frowning image. He saw a hack of a wannabe writer who had dug a hole he wasn't sure he could dig himself out of. As he looked around his home office, even the decorations seemed to underscore and mock his failed attempts to succeed. His diploma from Indiana State University hung above a row of citations and awards he'd received from his former employer. Next to the floor-to-ceiling bookcase with all his favorite books was his prized treasure map on a three-by-three corkboard. Pictures and icons representing his dreams and goals were pinned to it. A life-long positive thinker, he believed these images would program his subconscious mind and eventually become a reality: a facsimile of a one-million-dollar bill, a golf trophy that said "club champion," a physically fit man with Eddie's face from a much earlier photo. So far it hadn't worked. "Not yet," he thought.

Then he turned back and glared at that blank computer screen as he had for over a year. Well, he didn't glare nonstop. He'd only stare until he thought of a distraction—check his email, read the news online, go to the kitchen to refill his coffee cup for the umpteenth time, or straighten the mess on his desk. He couldn't wait to get away from the accusing screen that reinforced his self-doubt. After checking to be sure that Melissa wasn't anywhere near, he reached over and opened his bottom desk drawer and took out the pint of Old Crow he kept behind a file folder. He took a healthy swig from the bottle, noting that it was almost empty. He reminded himself that writers frequently needed to loosen up and relax in order to be productive. He smiled as he looked at the picture of Hemingway he kept on his desk for inspiration.

———————

The phone rang, jarring him from his reverie. Recognizing his best friend's number on caller ID, he answered enthusiastically, "Hey, Charlie, what's up?"

"Where've you been? We've been looking for you at the club to get you out on the golf course so that we can take some of your pension money away from you. I thought you were looking forward to playing a lot."

Eddie smiled as he swiveled his leather chair around and propped his feet up on the chair next to his. "To be honest with you, Charlie, I was, but it hasn't turned out that way, not for me or a lot of the other guys I've talked to at the club. After a year and a half, golf has gotten boring. I've been enjoying it less and less. I even found myself almost missing work."

"Are you thinking about going back?"

"No, I don't miss the stress and the long hours, but I do miss the sense of being productive and worthwhile. I miss the bull sessions with my colleagues, talking about the important issues in the company and the industry. I tried to keep in touch with them, but they're busy and don't always have time to talk. I'm out of the loop too. The changes taking place have been too rapid for me to keep up with, and I'm feeling increasingly irrelevant."

"You had plans to spend more time with Melissa," Charlie said. "How's that working out?"

"Melissa has her schedule. She's still active in her law practice, and she hasn't had the time to spend with me that I thought she would."

"Eddie, we've been friends since grade school. I'm concerned. You told me when we had lunch last year that you needed a new challenge, something that would enable you to use your knowledge and years of experience in helping people grow and become more successful. What are you doing about that?"

"You know damn well. It's *not* working out," he said angrily. "When I took up writing, I made the mistake of bragging to you, the rest of the guys, and Melissa about it. I said I'd knock out a soon-to-be *New York Times* best-selling book in no time. It was going to be so good that it would set the reading world on its tail. But after over a year of trying, I don't have even one chapter that I'd be willing to show anyone, especially Melissa. She has no idea that I haven't made any progress. I told her that it was coming along right on schedule. So now you know."

"Bummer, buddy, I'm sorry you're having so much trouble with it. Can I do anything to help you?"

Eddie hesitated a few minutes, and then he said, "Actually, there is. I could use a good sounding board. Can you meet me for a drink this afternoon?"

"Of course. What time and where?"

"How about Gino's? Say four o'clock?"

"You got it. Are you going to bring that hot wife of yours?"

"No, I want to talk to you alone."

"Sounds really serious. Are you sure I can't do something?"

"No, no. I'll be all right. Sorry, I didn't mean to go off on you like that. I'm just a little discouraged right now and feel like a failure. Thanks for the call. I'll see you at four o'clock. And, Charlie, tell the guys not to start counting the money you think you'll win off of me. I still got plenty of game."

"Yeah, right," he said, laughing. "Let me know when you're ready to get your butt kicked. In the meantime, why don't you try to figure out what's holding you back? See you at Gino's."

After hanging up, Eddie smiled, thinking about his friend and what he said. "What is holding me back?"

It wasn't writer's block. He wished that it were. He had plenty to say. He'd thought about his subject for a long time. He'd even kept a journal with ideas for the book for five years before retiring. He just didn't know how to organize his material. He kept editing and reediting as he wrote, never satisfied with what he'd written. He'd submitted a few things but got some very negative, terse rejection letters that confirmed his self-doubts. He took one last look at the computer, slammed the lid down, got up, and went to the kitchen to fill his coffee cup.

———

"Hi, Dad!" he heard his son say as he entered the bright, cheery kitchen. ⋯ of sunshine shone through the open window, letting the ⸱⸱⸱eeze gently sway the polka-dotted curtain.

⸱⸱⸱nile as he saw his two children sitting at the ⸱⸱⸱at gives?" he asked. "Hey, don't you two have ⸱⸱⸱ey haven't moved back in, have they, my love?" ⸱⸱⸱his wife on the cheek.

The truth was that he loved his two young-adult children and missed them now that they had moved out and had lives of their own. He wished he could see them more often, but even though they still lived in Muncie, they weren't as close as they used to be. They had their own lives, friends, and activities. He thought of the old Harry Chapin song, "Cat's in the Cradle." Life was moving too fast.

"No," Melissa said. "Brad has the day off, and Courtney is going in late, so we decided to all have breakfast together before I go to the office."

"It wasn't that way when I was working," his family chorused in unison, anticipating Eddie's predictable response. He believed his children did not have the total commitment to their careers that he once had. Courtney gave him a hug and a kiss.

"Oh, good," he said, laughing. He gave Brad a punch on the arm on his way to his usual seat at the head of the table. "I'm counting on them to support me in my old age."

"How's the book coming along, Dad?" asked his son.

"Great!" he said, grinning. "I think it's coming around now. I just need to rework a couple of the key ideas, and then you can look for it on the *New York Times* best-seller list."

"How's your new job son," he asked as he filled his coffee cup.

"Well, it could be better. I still don't have the hang of it. It seems more complicated than I thought it would be."

Eddie listened as Brad went into detail about his work and sympathized with him as he talked about the challenges he was facing. He hoped to himself that this job, unlike the last two, would last. He had concerns that he would end up supporting both his children. The world was changing so fast that things didn't seem to be as stable as they were in earlier days.

When he asked Courtney about her work, he got a brighter picture but she still didn't seem to be in a good solid work environme This caused a brief knot of anxiety in his stomach over his uns concern about his family's financial future.

Still, he put on a positive face and enjoyed the next thirty minutes of chatter with his kids.

"Well, back to the grindstone," he said. He hugged the kids and went back upstairs to his office.

9:00 a.m.

The kids left for work and as Melissa cleaned up the kitchen she shook her head thinking, "He's been saying 'great' since he started writing this alleged book, and so far there's no evidence of any progress. In the meantime, he's going through our retirement savings. Mister positive, mister personality," she thought. "Everybody loves Eddie Townsend. Sometimes he frustrates me with his over-the-top enthusiasm. He's not willing to admit that he's not a writer. I wish he hadn't taken that early retirement. He's so impractical."

Melissa went out to pick up the mail and the *Muncie Indiana Star Press*. She opened the brochure from Imperial Cruise Lines and gasped. Eddie was trying to write a book on the same subject they were covering in their seminar. Here was the perfect opportunity for him to get away, get some fresh ideas and make some money with his writing. She had been secretly reading what he'd written, and his stuff was tending toward the trite. It was definitely not his best thinking and, in her opinion, not salable.

The timing was right for them. Besides, cruise ships had casinos. Gambling was something she enjoyed. A little too much, according to Eddie, and he could be right. She made good money as a divorce attorney but not much found its way home at the end of the year, thanks to her hobby. "But," she thought, "This could be a great opportunity to recover some of the money I lost on my last 'business trip' to Atlantic City."

They had never taken a cruise, although they talked about it several times. She was hooked, and she knew Eddie would be a pushover for an adventure like this. "I just have to pick the right time to bring this up," she thought.

She found him hunched over his computer at the kitchen table and asked, "Would you like another cup of coffee?"

"Sure," he said.

She knew that, as with most writers, any opportunity to be diverted was a welcome one, so she filled his cup. Before she could speak, he enthusiastically launched into a description of how much progress he was making and how well it was going.

"I've got to go to Office Depot to buy some more paper and an ink cartridge. Then I'll be back to write up a storm for the rest of the day," he said as he pushed his half-empty cup away and stood up. "I'll see you later this afternoon. Oh, I almost forgot. Charlie called and wants to get together," he said. "So I'm going to meet him later for a cup of coffee, so I'll be a little late getting home."

She realized that this was not the right time. "Okay, my love. See you later then." She gave him a kiss on the cheek.

———————

Eddie didn't go right home after he finished his shopping at Office Depot. He went for a long walk and then ended up going to Gino's an hour before he was going to meet Charlie.

Right on schedule Charlie walked in the door and found Eddie in his favorite booth in the back, drinking Dewar's and water. He signaled Joyce on the way by to bring him a Seven and Seven.

"Hey, buddy," he said as he slid into the booth across from Eddie. "What's going on?"

"Oh, nothing. I just felt like getting together with my best friend for a drink."

"Eddie, I know you too well. Your suggestion that we meet for a drink was more serious than that. Tell me."

"Like I said on the phone, I'm a little stuck with my writing."

"You're not going to stonewall me, are you?"

"What do you mean?"

"Eddie, you're my best friend. You know I'm here to help, but you've got to let me in. Let's talk."

Eddie signaled Joyce for another drink, and when she brought it, Charlie could see that it was a double.

"Whoa, that's your second double." (Actually, it was his third.) "Isn't it a little early?"

"OK, Charlie, here's the deal. You know that time when I didn't get the promotion at work and I went into a blue funk?"

"Yeah. I remember. You were depressed."

"No, no. I've never been depressed in a clinical sense. I was just a little down and I'm feeling that way now. I just needed someone to talk to. I'll be all right now."

Changing the subject, he said, "Bring me up to date with what's going on, buddy."

The two friends talked for another forty-five minutes about Charlie's family, his golf game, the rest of the gang and the weekly poker game at the club.

Charlie looked at his watch and said, "I gotta get moving. I told Marie I'd pick her up after work. You sure you're alright?"

"Oh yeah. I'll be fine. You helped me a lot just by being here for me. Thanks."

"Okay, buddy, if you say so. I'm here for you. Joyce, let me have the check."

"No, no I've got it," said Eddie. "I'll get it before I go. I want to do a little more writing before I leave." In reality, even though he would have liked him to pay, he didn't want Charlie to see how many drinks were on the check.

They both got up and punched one another on the arm, the way guys do who really love one another but don't dare put it into words. Charlie's punch was lighter than his frustrated buddy's as they said goodbye.

Feeling a little woozy, Eddie signaled Joyce and asked her for a cup of black coffee, hoping to sober up sufficiently before going home to face Melissa.

———————

9:00 a.m., 1570 Polk Street, San Francisco, California
As soon as Phil Butler tore open the envelope, he knew what he wanted to do. The brochure was from Imperial Cruise Lines, announcing a retirement seminar cruise. The dates coincided with their twenty-fifth wedding anniversary, and Carol had been a little unhappy lately. They'd had many discussions about their retirement, and he thought this would be a great surprise.

"Anything in the mail, Phil?" she called from upstairs.

"No, just a couple of bills and a catalogue from Chico's," he said, stuffing the envelope in his pocket. "I'm off to work. I'll see you this afternoon."

"Do you want to meet me at the club for lunch?" she asked.

"No can do. I have a ton of stuff on my plate, and I'm meeting Everett for lunch to talk over some contracts."

When she heard the door slam, she thought, "Damn, he got away again. I thought today was the day I would muster up the courage to have the conversation with him. I've got to tell him sometime. The sooner the better."

Phil slid behind the wheel of his new midnight-blue Jaguar XJ12 and drove down California Street to his corner office on the twelfth floor of a building with a view of the Golden Gate Bridge. He took the envelope from his suit jacket and scanned the announcement in detail, allowing his mind to drift back over the past twenty-five years.

He'd worked hard to build the salvage business he inherited when his parents died. He'd married way above his class to a smart, gorgeous, educated beauty who came from a wealthy family. They'd had three great kids, now all out on their own, beginning their lives and their careers or still in college. He'd done well financially and had given the kids the kind of direction and parenting that ensured they were headed in the right direction. But, and this was a big one, his marriage was in trouble, and he knew it.

Carol hadn't said anything specific, but the signs were there; her coolness and lack of intimacy toward him. The meaningful conversations they once had, working together to build a successful business, no longer happened. "Desperate times call for desperate measures," he thought. That's why the seminar was such a good idea.

He called Cathy into his office and asked her to make all the arrangements by four o'clock, before he left for the day.

———

9:45 a.m., 237 University Avenue, Des Moines, Iowa
Dr. Arthur Alden Gibson III leafed through the stack of mail on his desk, one boring piece of correspondence after another. Something from his Rotary club about a board of directors meeting; a request from one of the members of the Des Moines Golf and Country Club to bring up at the next board meeting; something from city hall relating to his just-completed term as mayor, requiring his signature. "What has my life become since I retired from my practice?" he mused. "Just one mind-numbing event after another."

He came to the envelope from Imperial Cruise Lines. Opening it, his eyes lit up, and a smile creased his face. "Nicole would absolutely love this," he thought. "I'll just clean up these details and find her to see if she's up for it."

10:45 a.m.
"Nicole, I'd like to talk to you about something," said Arthur. Slim and tanned, she was lounging on their indoor pool deck.

She saw the brochure in his hand. "Is it the cruise to Barcelona?"

"Yes, how did you know?"

"I saw it earlier and put it back in the envelope so you'd say, 'Hey, honey, here's a neat cruise that we can take,' and I'd pretend it was something I had to think about and finally give in and say okay." Nicole said all this playfully, in her sweet Louisiana accent, which became more pronounced when she wanted something from him. Fortunately, this was something he wanted too, so there was no conflict. He did have a concern about the subject matter.

His girlfriend was a former flight attendant whom he introduced as his wife. She was not particularly astute when it came to money matters. In fact, she spent little time pursuing anything but the latest styles, fashions, and comings and goings of the Kardashians as reported in *People Magazine*. She made up for those intellectual deficiencies with her sweet personality, her drop-dead-gorgeous looks, and a figure that made her look ten years younger than her forty-nine years.

"Okay, I'll book it, then?"

"Well, all right, if it's something you want to do." She smiled with mock reluctance.

9:30 a.m., Executive Apartments, #1247, Alexandria, Virginia
Donald M. Conway, PhD, leisurely looked over the morning mail, which Inga had already read. She took care of all their important matters, as she had done for the forty-five years of their married life. One envelope, though, had a handwritten note penciled on it that read, "Please read this and discuss with me this afternoon, *Schatze*." This pet name was their German term of endearment for one another, so he knew this must be something special. He picked up the Imperial Cruise Line brochure and read it.

1:00 p.m.

When he walked into the living room, Inga was sitting on the couch, knitting.

"*Was ist los, Schatze?*" asked Don, putting the brochure down in front of his wife.

She said, "We haven't taken a real vacation in some time, and this is a trip that promises to be especially interesting because of the topic."

"Can we afford it?" he asked. Inga handled their money, so he genuinely did not know the answer to his question.

"*Ja,*" she said. They frequently lapsed into German with one another. "There will probably be some intellectually stimulating people on this cruise, and it will be a chance for us to make some new friends."

"It sounds good to me," said Don. "Let's do it."

————

7:30 p.m., the Fairmont Hotel
San Francisco, California

Carol pulled up in front of the hotel in her Mercedes and received an admiring look from the valet as he held open the door for the stylishly dressed, attractive blonde.

"Good evening, Mrs. Butler," he said.

She flashed him a beautiful smile as she took her claim check and passed through the revolving door into the historic, grand hotel. Kyle and Beatrice were waiting for her in the lobby with its antiques and gold ornaments, which spoke of wealth and opulence. They walked into the dining room together, and a few minutes later, Phil rushed in.

When they were seated in the dining room and had ordered drinks, Phil took an envelope out of his pocket and dropped it on the table in front of Carol.

"What's this?" she asked.

"Your twenty-fifth wedding anniversary gift. We're going on a luxury cruise and make a plan for our retirement, all in one 'swell foop,'" he said. He took the Imperial Cruises brochure from his pocket and excitedly read it to the group.

"That's great!" said Kyle. "You two deserve a getaway like that. You've worked hard, and now it's time to reap some rewards."

"Yes, you have and do!" said Beatrice, excitedly hugging Carol.

Carol's mind went into a swirl. "I can't back out of this," she thought. "He's put me in a corner. I'll just have to wait until this cruise ordeal is over to tell him."

"What?" asked Carol.

Beatrice was speaking to her, "I said, aren't you excited?"

"Oh, yes, I'm ... ah, ah, speechless. Who wouldn't be excited?"

The conversation moved on to Kyle's business and what Beatrice was doing with her volunteer work.

————

8:00 p.m. 1264 Fifth Street, Muncie, Indiana

That evening Eddie finished his favorite dinner: filet mignon, french fries, green beans, and Parker House rolls, accompanied by a good bottle of Bordeaux. Melissa poured him another cup of coffee. "Wow! That was a great dinner. What's the special occasion?"

"You. You're the special occasion," she replied.

"What do you mean?"

"You've been working on this new book for quite a while, and I'm sensing you're feeling some frustration. Am I right?"

"Yeah, I'm a little stuck, my love, but I'll think of something clever and get it handled."

"I know you will. You always do. But something came along today that was like an omen."

She handed him the brochure and waited as he read it. He raised an eyebrow. "I don't know, that's a lot of money."

"We've got the money. Besides, I checked with Adam, and he said we can justify it as a business expense and deduct it. Plus, I want to go. Can we do it? Please, please?"

He knew when she adopted a playful tone, with the "please, please" act, that it was no longer up for discussion. She'd made up her mind and that was that.

"Well, okay, but you'll have to grant me special favors," he leered.

She ignored that and said, "I'll register us in the morning. You'll probably want to lose a few pounds before we go, but don't get too buff. I don't want to spend the whole cruise fighting off all the super-models that will no doubt be making moves on you."

"Sarcasm?" he asked.

"You think?" she quipped in response.

He kissed her and started clearing the table.

Later that night he felt elated, thinking about the cruise. He could see it as a real opportunity to write his book in a fresh, supportive environment. This would cause Melissa, he thought with satisfaction, to finally appreciate him for his talent.

———

April 6
Three Months Later

The four couples, along with several hundred other people, packed their bags and flew to Miami, eager for their great adventure.

———

Day One

Miami, Florida
April 7

9:30 a.m., Port of Miami, Cruise Terminal J
Phil and Carol Butler climbed out of the hotel shuttle that Imperial Cruise Lines provided for them and began the early boarding check-in process that came as a bonus with their luxury suite accommodation. They had flown in from San Francisco the day before and spent the night at the Marriott Harbor Hotel. After a good night's sleep, they woke up refreshed and ordered a continental breakfast. "I'm so glad we didn't take the red-eye," said Carol for the third time. "We'd be so jet-lagged if we had."

Joe, the overly enthusiastic van driver, overheard her and said, "You were wise. When I pick up people who have to rush to the ship, they are so wiped out and cranky. I know they're just going to sleep for the first couple of days and miss a lot." Then, without waiting for a reply but hoping for a tip, he started his tour-guide speech, pointing out such unmemorable landmarks as warehouses and freighters along the way.

After showing their passports at the gate, they climbed the gangway to board the ship on deck four. They were given their

Serendipity identification cards as they entered the luxuriously appointed lobby.

A crew member directed them to the elevator, which took them up to the eleventh deck to executive suite #1. It was one of only four spacious, elegantly appointed, luxury suites and it was prepared for their arrival. Phil and Carol were no strangers to luxury. They were accustomed to the sophistication of San Francisco and traveled first class on many occasions. Nonetheless, they were impressed with the décor of their suite.

Entering, they heard the soft sounds of instrumental music from the stereo and the gentle trickling of a small fountain and smelled the fragrance of a lavender-scented diffuser that permeated the air. A welcoming note from the captain sat by the bowl of fresh fruit, and a bottle of Dom Perignon champagne was nestled in an ice bucket. The large sliding glass door opened onto their private veranda. There was a large-screen TV on the wall next to the desk. They walked past the guest bathroom and through the living and dining rooms into their bedroom.

The first thing they noticed was the king-sized bed with a fluffy duvet that promised a comfortable night's sleep. A spacious walk-in closet was situated discreetly in the corner. The bath boasted both a shower and a Jacuzzi tub, promising many relaxing soaks after working out in the fitness center.

Just then, a young man knocked on the door, introducing himself as their butler, Violin. (He pronounced it *vee-o-lin* but spelled it like the instrument.) "I'm from Bulgaria, and my father is a musician," he explained, in answer to Phil's question. "Is everything to your satisfaction, Mr. and Mrs. Butler?" he asked.

Phil looked around with satisfaction and thought, "This is exactly the kind of luxury environment that will bring our love back to life."

"Yes, thank you. It's perfect," said Phil. "What do you think, honey?"

"I wouldn't change a thing," she said, smiling.

Violin let himself out, and Carol giggled.

"What?" asked Phil, looking at her quizzically.

"I just think it's funny we have a butler, and our name is Butler." She giggled again.

He laughed. "Let me help you with the unpacking."

"No, that's all right," she said. She had experienced his idea of packing and unpacking in the past. "I'll do it. Why don't you open that wine, and we'll have a glass while I put everything away?"

As she busied herself, she observed, "This may be the best thing about taking a cruise vacation. You don't have to be constantly packing and unpacking every few days."

After an hour she exclaimed, "There! I'm done. We're settled in for the next two weeks. Let's go explore the ship and then have a bite of lunch."

"Actually," Phil said, reading, "We are scheduled to have lunch in the Grand Dining Room any time after twelve o'clock. Our orientation meeting for the seminar, according to this instruction sheet, is in the Celebrity Theater at two o'clock."

They decided to check out the pool deck first. Already people were taking advantage of the warm Florida sunshine, stretched out on the lounges, and a couple of early topers bellied up to the bar, drinking Bloody Marys.

Phil felt the elation he always experienced the first day of any vacation but especially on a cruise ship. He looked at Carol, and his overflowing happiness caused him to laugh. He reached for her hand, but she didn't take it; she merely gave him a tight little smile.

A little confused by her reserve, he looked at his directory and said, "Let's go up to the next deck and check out the library." Once there, they browsed around, and Carol identified half a dozen books she wanted to read. Now she would have the time.

"It's a quarter to twelve. We should be getting down to the dining room," he said.

———

Stateroom 735

Eddie opened the door to their stateroom and fell in love with it immediately. "I'm going to get a lot of work done on the book here."

Melissa noticed that he referred to the book as though it were a living entity rather than a vague idea in his mind. However, she let it pass because she was as thrilled with their stateroom as her husband was.

The first thing she noticed when she entered was the comfortable queen-sized bed with a duvet such as she'd only seen in Macy's back in Muncie. There were extra pillows on the bed, something Melissa always wanted at home but never felt they could afford. The small desk against the wall just under the small television held an ice bucket with a bottle of Korbel champagne and two crystal water glasses with a welcome card signed by the general manager propped next to them. Immediately to their right as they entered was a bathroom with a shower.

They looked at one another and Eddie said, "How did we get so lucky?"

She smiled at him and said, "We earned it, and we deserve it."

Just then there was a knock on the door and a crew member brought their suitcases in. As Eddie started to tip him, he backed away and said, "All your gratuities are included in your fare, sir."

"Thank you," Eddie said, as the man eased his way out the door.

"Isn't that great?" he exclaimed to Melissa. "I love this whole experience already. Let's go look around the ship before we have lunch."

"We don't have too much time. Why don't you go have a quick look while I unpack? Come back in a half hour, and then we'll go."

"Great! Thanks!" he said. When he exited the elevator and walked onto the pool deck, he was greeted by the sight of guests dressed in light casual clothing or bathing suits. They seemed to range in age from forty to eighty years old, with the majority in their midfifties to midsixties.

Eddie saw some overweight men flexing their muscles in bathing suits that were at least two sizes too small, and he theorized that they must have played football back in the day, and they imagined they were still the same studs.

There were some sixtyish women wearing two-piece bathing suits, some who should, most who shouldn't. Others were reading novels or knitting endless pairs of booties or bonnets for their grandchildren back home. Many of the women were wearing expensive-looking leisure clothes, obviously purchased for the cruise.

Many men sat on their lounges reading Kindles and paperback books, mostly Lee Childs and Tom Clancy novels. There was little evidence of serious reading, as Eddie liked to think of his master-piece-in-waiting to be.

All these activities were being assisted by a stream of crew members handing out towels and delivering cold drinks to the happy group.

A stream of walkers circled the oval track on the deck above the pool. Others were visiting the spa and fitness center or having coffee at Barista, the coffee shop.

In the days ahead, Eddie was to observe that the nearby pool bar was usually peopled in midmorning with heavy partiers from the night before, drinking Bloody Marys.

Eddie noticed the clock on the wall, and seeing that it was time to meet Melissa for lunch, he headed back to the cabin.

12:00 p.m., the Grand Dining Room

The doors opened promptly at twelve, and Phil and Carol were at the front of the line.

"Would you like to join a table with others or dine alone?" asked the maître d'.

"Alone," answered Carol, before Phil could speak.

He looked at her quizzically. As they were escorted to a table for two by a window, he asked, "Why?"

"I don't feel like interacting with new people right now," she answered. They ate in silence, finished rather quickly, and left the room.

————————

As Eddie and Melissa Townsend arrived in the Grand Dining Room, they found themselves at the end of a line of guests. When they reached the maître d', Eddie jokingly said, "Reservation for Dr. Townsend."

The man didn't miss a beat. "Of course, Dr. Townsend. We've been expecting you. Turning to the next waiter in line, he said, "Table thirty-seven for Dr. Townsend and his daughter." He winked at Melissa.

They were seated at a table for six where two other couples were already scanning the menu. Eddie shook hands with the nearest man and said, "Eddie Townsend, my wife, Melissa. We're from Muncie, Indiana."

Not looking up, the scowling, balding man wearing wire-rimmed glasses, said, "Bill McClosky." The neatly dressed woman next to him said, "I'm his wife, Terri, from LA, and this is Mike and Brenda Murphy from Boston."

The waiters brought salads and a basket of bread. Bill exclaimed, "What the hell! Don't you get a choice of what you want for lunch here?"

Eddie took out his instruction sheet and read: "A limited menu will be served on the first day only, prior to the orientation meeting. This will ensure that everyone will be able to be at the meeting on time. If you have any special request, please let your server know, and we'll be able to accommodate you. Chef Angelo Baretti."

"So we can special order if we want to," said Mike.

"For what we're paying for this trip, we ought to be able to have anything we want without their telling us what we have to eat," said Bill angrily.

"It'll be all right, Bill," said Terri, obviously embarrassed by his outburst.

"I don't know," he said. "First, we had that god-awful, all-night flight and rushed around to just barely get here on time. Now we've got to rush through lunch and go to some damn meeting."

The waiters brought delicious New Orleans muffulettas, accompanied by macaroni salad.

Bill pushed his plate back and groused, "We didn't get anything decent to eat on that damn flight, and now we get a weird sandwich of some kind."

"Wow," Eddie thought. "That is one negative guy. I wonder if he's like that all the time or if he's just having a bad day. That kind of negative attitude would not only spoil his day but the rest of the cruise and if he persists, his whole life. There's a lesson for me. I wonder if that's the attitude I have toward writing."

They spent the rest of the meal talking about where they were from and how many cruises each had taken before. They took the obligatory look at the photos of each other's grandchildren and oohed and aahed over them.

When it was time to leave, everyone except Bill said sincerely how much they enjoyed meeting each other and hoped they were seated together again before the cruise was over.

Eddie and Melissa, smiling at one another, walked out of the dining room and headed for the orientation meeting.

———————

Arthur and Nicole Gibson arrived at the dining room at one thirty. The room was only about half full, as most of the guests had finished eating and left for the seminar. The maître d' seated them at a table for two and signaled the waiter to bring their food right away.

Arthur was upset with Nicole for taking so long to get unpacked and then insisting on taking a shower before deciding what to wear. As always, Nicole was oblivious to how her behavior affected Arthur or anyone else.

At five minutes before two, Arthur finally said, "We have to go! We're supposed to be in the Celebrity Theater at two o'clock for the meeting."

"Well," she drawled, "if we're a little late, it won't be the end of the world." She took one last swig of coffee and followed him out.

———

Day One: Getting Acquainted

The placard outside the Celebrity Theater read:

WELCOME
Orientation Meeting
Imperial Cruise Lines Retirement Seminar

April 8, 2:00 to 4:00 p.m.

———

1:45 p.m.

Phil and Carol were ushered by a crew member to seats in the first row. Only a few other guests were seated, so Carol read the meeting outline she'd been handed at the door.

When Eddie and Melissa arrived at the theater, a crew member ushered them to seats in the third row. Eddie read the program he'd been handed at the entrance.

Program
Welcome: Captain Luca Manzini

Orientation: Pat Higgins, Cruise Director

Ice breaker warm-up

Announcements

Purpose: learning and fun

Explanation of how you might benefit

Format of seminar schedule: get as much or as little as you want

The matching process: algorithms and analytics

Teams

Discussion groups

Presenters

Questions

2:00 p.m., Celebrity Theater stage

A distinguished man in a white naval uniform and with a decidedly Italian accent took the microphone and said, "Welcome, everybody; itsa my pleasure to be your captain on this cruise. My nama is Luca Manzini, and my crew and I are dedicated to a-makin' this an unforgettable, enjoyable, and safe experience for you. If you-a have any questions or need anything during the cruise, ask any crew member and they-a will see to it that you are taken care of.

"Now, I'll pass you over to your cruise director, Pat Higgins. Please sit back and enjoy yourselves. I gotta go drive this thing while you have a great trip."

This comment brought an appreciative round of laughter and applause.

"Good afternoon, everyone. I'd like to add my welcome. I'm Pat Higgins, your cruise director. Is everyone getting comfortably settled and enjoying our hospitality so far?"

The audience responded with a round of applause.

"Before we get started, let's break the ice and get acquainted with the people around us. There are over six hundred people in this seminar, and you can't meet them all today, but you can meet the people nearest you. When I say go, say hello to the people on both sides and in front and back of you. Tell them your name and where you are from, unless of course you are one of the people in the witness protection program."

This brought a laughing response.

"Ready? Go!"

The room became a jumble of talk, laughter, and pandemonium as people began getting acquainted. After fifteen minutes, Pat picked up the microphone again and said, "Who met someone you didn't like?"

"No one!" yelled the crowd, laughing.

"Well, these are the kind of people you'll be interacting with for the next two weeks. Let me tell you what to expect from here on out. I know you all received the program and the advance information, but I'd like to expand on it a bit more.

"First of all, the overall purpose of the next two weeks is to make your retirement years fulfilling, satisfying, and rewarding. We also want to make sure you have fun and enjoy the best cruise experience of your life.

"Let's look at the ways you can expect to benefit from being here. The format of the seminar schedule allows you to benefit as much or as little as you want. There are no tests or exams. There is no pass/fail except by your own determination. No two people are exactly alike, and each of you is in a unique place, so you'll have different reasons for being here.

"Saying that, we all have a lot in common, and we can learn from one another. We'll explore together what it means to live a rich, full, satisfying life in retirement.

"Let's begin by sharing with others your expectations of the seminar and why you enrolled. Under your seat, you'll find pencils and cards. Print your name on the card. Witness protection people, stay with your aliases for this exercise.

Another outburst of laughter from the appreciative audience.

"Please take five minutes to complete the questions, and when I call time, we'll take the next step."

After five minutes, Pat directed, "Form yourselves into groups of eight. Front row, stand, turn around, and face the second row. Third row, turn around, and face the fourth row, and so forth until you are in groups of eight.

"You'll have three minutes to share what you've written on your card. There are blank spaces for you to fill in any additional ideas you hear in your group. You'll hear a bell at the end of three minutes. When you hear the bell, the person to your right will share what he or she has written. No right or wrong answers here. We're here to learn from one another. The tallest person in each group will go first. In case of a tie, the ugliest person will break the tie."

Now already waiting for Pat's humor, laughter broke out again.

"Ready? Go!"

After the sharing, Pat said, "Please pass the cards to your right, where the group leaders will pick them up.

"Here's how the rest of the seminar will work. During the two weeks of the cruise, you'll hear presentations from top people in their fields, who will provide you with information on topics vital to successfully navigating the waters of retirement.

"These presentations are not going to be data dumps. You'll have an opportunity to meet many of the other participants during the seminar to discuss and individualize the material. Each day we meet, you'll be assigned to a different discussion group to get a greater interpretation of the subject.

"You don't need to take notes. This information is included in your seminar packet, which is in your stateroom or suite. The most important aspect of the seminar is your assigned team. You'll be having dinner together each evening starting tomorrow to discuss the topic of the day or anything else you want to discuss.

"What's that? Did I see an expression of concern on that gentleman's face over there? Just kidding. Someone might be thinking, what if I don't like the people on my team? Not to worry, that is not going to happen. If you do find that to be true, just tell the captain, and he'll have the scoundrel thrown overboard."

Now already waiting for Pat's humor, laughter broke out again.

"Not true. The reason we know that you'll be compatible with the people on your team is because of the way you were each assigned to your teams.

"That elaborate questionnaire you completed as part of your application to participate in the seminar was scrutinized and evaluated by our team of psychologists and training experts. They then entered all of the data into a computer and, using algorithms and the science of analytics, they matched each of you with the people who are most compatible with you and, more importantly, have the most to teach you.

"That is all explained in detail in your seminar packet being delivered to your stateroom or suite. A journal is also included, which will allow you to capture the parts of the seminar that are most meaningful to you. In addition, you'll receive handouts from some of the presenters covering their material.

"That's it for today. Who has a question? Hearing none, we're done for today.

"A reminder, the captain's reception will be here in the Celebrity at four p.m. today. It is an opportunity for you all to meet the captain, the other officers, and the seminar presenters. Enjoy a glass of champagne and some light hors d'oeuvres.

"After that, you'll be on your own for dinner this evening. Have a good one.

"See you tomorrow at two o'clock, right here."

The room was buzzing as the group filed out, chatting and getting acquainted.

———

Eddie and Melissa listened with great interest to Pat's presentation, nodding and poking one another at various times as they heard the points they thought most applied to them. "This is going to pay off big time for me," said Eddie. "I can see how it will help me with my writing."

"I think it's going to be good for both of us and for our relationship going forward," agreed Melissa. "Our lives will be different in retirement than they were when we were both working. We'll need to make some adjustments that we haven't made so far."

"I agree, and I believe this is true for most couples at this stage of their lives. I think retirement requires a new contract for living."

———

4:00 p.m.
The Celebrity Theater

The Captain's Reception

The long line to enter the Celebrity started at three thirty, and it took almost an hour for everyone to get in. All the important members of the crew and the seminar presenters smiled, greeted, and shook everyone's hand. There were twenty in all. A musical quartet played a selection of upbeat popular tunes. In the meantime, white-coated servers circulated with glasses of champagne and hors d'oeuvres.

Pat Higgins took the microphone, welcomed the crowd, then introduced the officers and all the presenters and lastly Captain Manzini. The captain took the microphone and welcomed the participants with a toast.

"Thank you all for being here. We are ready to depart in thirty minutes, so it's probably a good idea if I'm up there to be sure we don't run into another ship."

A smattering of laughter rippled through the audience.

Shortly after, the room emptied. The ship's horn blasted, announcing its departure from the dock. The decks and suite verandas were lined with guests. Most were drinking champagne, wine, or a soft drink to celebrate the beginning of their two-week adventure.

———

6:00 p.m., the *Serendipity*

Phil and Carol watched the scene on the dock below from the spacious veranda of their suite and felt the euphoria that came with savoring the elegance of the moment. They lifted their champagne glasses and toasted each other. "Happy anniversary," Phil said.

She smiled as he leaned over and kissed her cheek. "Happy anniversary to you," she said.

———

Arthur looked appreciatively at Nicole in her white short shorts and tight-fitting tank top. She still had the energy, enthusiasm, and looks of the college cheerleader she'd been during her lone year at Tulane thirty years earlier. He thought, "I'm a lucky guy. This trip is going to be fun and hopefully an opportunity for us to clarify our relationship."

———

"We're off on our first cruise," said Eddie to Melissa as they stood on the small deck of their stateroom and watched the activity below. "Thank you for encouraging me to do this. I'd never have spent the money or done this on my own." He kissed her and said, lifting his glass of sparkling wine, "Here's to a wonderful time together."

"Another wonderful time together like so many over the past forty years," she said. She took his glass, set them both down on the cocktail table, and gave him a serious kiss on the mouth.

"What was that for?" he asked.

"Because you're you," she said, smiling.

The ship turned away from the dock and headed out to sea, and they were off. The adventure was about to begin for all of them.

7:00 p.m., the Grand Dining Room

The maître d' greeted Arthur and Nicole as they entered. He ushered them to a window table for two, passing another couple on the way to their table. The man was carrying a Manhattan he'd picked up on his way past the Porthole Bar.

When they were seated and handed their menus, Nicole leaned over to Arthur and said, "It's moments like this that I realize how lucky I am to have you in my life."

"Is that the champagne or Nickie talking?" he asked with a smile.

"A little of both," she said. "I always feel this way, but sometimes I'm too shy to say it."

"What? You, shy?" he said. "I would think that's the last thing anyone would say about you."

"For a doctor, you don't know much about people. Many times, people who appear to be confident by actin' up and bein', you know, all out there and everythin', are basically shy and a little fragile. We're just puttin' on an act to cover that up."

He kissed her hand and said, "Thank you for reminding me. I forget that everybody needs love and understanding."

She smiled sweetly at him and said, "Now you gotta feed me, dahlin'."

———

Don Conway walked in with a Manhattan in his hand that he'd picked up on his way through the Porthole Bar. When he and Inga approached their table, he stuck out his hand and said, "I'm Don Conway, and this is my wife, Inga."

"Sister Mary Catherine," said the first woman they met.

"Sister Mary Elizabeth," the woman next to her said with a smile. "Just call us Liz and Cathy."

"Bert Hennessey, and this is my wife, Joyce," said the man seated to the sisters' left.

"Where are you all from?" asked Don.

Answering for both of them, Sister Liz, as Don referred to her the rest of the evening, said, "We're from Baltimore."

"Cleveland," said Bert. "How about you?"

"Well, just a minute," he said. He held up his empty glass and pointed at it, signaling the waiter. "We're from the Washington, DC, area now. We've only lived there for three years. I retired from New York University, where I was a history, German, and music professor. I was born in Brooklyn, and we lived there for the past forty years. Inga is from Germany and ..."

"Excuse me, sir," interrupted the waiter. "Your menu."

"I don't need to see it," said Don. "Just bring me a steak, medium rare. I haven't eaten all day, and I'm famished. Inga, how about you?"

"I'll have a tossed salad and a piece of white fish."

"Will sea bass be all right, madam?" asked the waiter.

She nodded.

"We've already ordered," said Bert.

"After today's meeting, I'm looking forward to the seminar," said Sister Liz, hoping she could keep Don from continuing with the nonstop story of his life. "I'm curious about this whole experience."

"It was good then?" asked Inga.

"It was great. You weren't there? I thought everybody was required to attend," said Sister Liz.

"Ah, no," said Inga. "We were late getting to the ship."

"Did your flight get in late?" asked Bert.

"No, we just didn't do a good job of planning, did we, Schatze?" Don said, winking at her.

"No, I guess we didn't." She smiled.

"Forgive me for asking," said Inga, "but isn't it unusual for people in your profession to be taking a retirement seminar? Aren't you pretty much provided for?"

"You really need to talk to the monsignor to get forgiven," said Sister Catherine, with a twinkle in her eye. "But no, it is not all that unusual. We don't have any considerations about the afterlife, but we do need to provide for ourselves while we're still here."

———————

The conversation shifted to the reasons each of them had registered for the unique seminar. The common reason seemed to be their desire to get more enrichment from the "next chapter of their lives," as Sister Cathy put it.

Finally, Bert stood and said, "We should be going. The first meeting starts at one o'clock tomorrow, and I want to be well rested." The others nodded in agreement, and they left the dining room together.

———————

DAY TWO

April 8

The knock on the door signaled the arrival of their continental breakfast, right on time. Melissa opened the door and let the waiter in. He greeted them warmly, laid a tablecloth, and served their juice, coffee, and croissants. As they ate, Melissa asked, "What are your plans for this morning, my love?"

"I'm going to write up a storm," Eddie said, smiling. "This change of scenery is just what I need to get this project back on track. You mentioned that you thought I might be a little stuck, and I think you're right."

"That's good news," she said. "I'll get out of your hair and give you some privacy. I'll go to the pool and read my book."

"Great, come back around eleven, my love, and we'll have some lunch before the meeting."

She dressed for the pool and gave him a peck on the cheek. "Ciao," she said from the doorway.

Eddie sat down in front of his laptop and with great expectation typed at the top of the page:

Fulfillment after Fifty: How to Retire Happy

Then he stared at the screen, waiting for a lightning bolt of inspiration to come through the open sliding door to the veranda. Nothing.

"I'd better have another cup of coffee before I get started," he thought.

After a twenty-minute break, during which time he watched Pat Higgins give the morning report of the day's activities on the television and read *Currents*, the onboard newspaper, he once again sat down in front of the computer. Another fifteen minutes passed without a single word, and his confidence in himself as a writer evaporated. The euphoric feeling he'd had the evening before completely disappeared.

"I need a change of pace," he said to himself. "This room is too small. I'll take my computer and go up to the library. It'll be quiet there."

In the library, he found a comfortable easy chair and settled in. Barista, the coffee shop, was adjacent to the library, so a cappuccino was definitely called for. On his way back to his chair, he looked at the books on the shelf, and Anne Lamott's *Bird by Bird* jumped out at him. "Wow!" he said to himself. "Coincidence? I think not. This has got to be an omen. Just when you need the right tool at the right time, it comes along."

He closed his laptop, opened the book, and began to read. When he went to Baristas for another cappuccino, he realized it was ten after eleven and he needed to meet Melissa. She was waiting for him in the stateroom. "How did it go?" she asked.

"Great. I got some good ideas on the direction I want to take with it."

"I see you've got a book."

"Yeah, it's one I've read before, but I need to reread it to get the guidance I need to move things along to the next phase."

She smiled and said, "We'd better get ready if we're going to have any lunch before the afternoon meeting."

"Right," he said, as he put his book down.

"Where is your laptop?" she asked.

"Oh my God! I must have left it in the coffee shop. I'll run up and get it. Be right back," he said, as he sprinted out the door.

After retrieving the laptop, they went to Wave's café on the pool deck for a fast burger before the meeting.

———————

8:00 a.m., Executive Suite #1

The smell of fresh, brewing coffee greeted Phil as he stepped out of the shower. With a big smile, he called out, "Good morning!" and joined his wife on the veranda. Carol was stretched out on a lounge, drinking a cup of coffee. She was wearing a white bikini, which accented her bronzed, shapely body.

Phil had just come back from a three-mile run on the track, and his morning workout at the fitness center. While he was toweling off his hair with another towel around his waist, she admired his fit body, which reminded her of why she fell in love with him in the first place. She felt a tinge of sadness about her decision to divorce him.

"Coffee?" she asked, leaning toward the tray of juice, fresh fruit, croissants, and coffee that Violin had delivered a few minutes earlier.

"Yes, thanks. Stay put, I'll get it," he said, helping himself at the breakfast table.

"There, that's it," she thought. "The reason I can't stay. We used to do everything together: raise the kids, build the business, and now I can't even serve him breakfast. He doesn't need me anymore. He's got a whole bunch of people assisting him, doing the things I used to do."

As he sipped his coffee, Phil relaxed on a lounge and appreciated the extra-large veranda that was a part of the executive suites—the best Imperial Cruise Lines offered. With the spacious deck, comfortable lounges, and small tables, like the rest of the suite, it left little to be desired in comfort and luxury.

"Are you ready for today's meeting?" he asked.

"It should be interesting," she replied, with no emotion.

Phil thought, "I hope there is enough good stuff this afternoon to get her excited about this trip."

"Do you think we should talk about our expectations before the meeting?" he asked.

"No," she said. "They probably have it organized, so we'll know what to do when we get there."

Before he could lead the conversation any further, she stood up. "I think I'll go to the pool to get some sun and read until it's time to go."

She picked up her book and the fluffy white robe with the Imperial insignia and left him with his thoughts.

———

The Seminar

Day Two
Identifying the Challenges of Retirement

———

They Meet

6:15 p.m., the Porthole Piano Bar
Arthur nervously approached the group around the table in the bar with the placard BCGT#1, the team name given to them for the seminar, made up of the first initials of their last names. "Hi, my name is Arthur Gibson, and this is my wife, Nickie," he said. This was their first get-together as a team, and they were supposed to meet at six o'clock. A barrage of names assaulted him as the other six people

introduced themselves, too fast for him to keep up. "Don Conway, Carol Butler, Melissa Townsend, Inga Conway, Phil Butler, Eddie Townsend."

Arthur immediately felt the panic that welled up every time he met more than two people at once. He couldn't remember which one was Carol and which one was Melinda (if her name was Melinda), or which one was Bill or if there was a Bill. "Damn!" he thought. "Why did Nicole have to sit in front of that vanity mirror so long? If we had been here early, I wouldn't be so embarrassed. Why didn't Imperial Cruise Lines send us the names of the other people in our group?"

Arthur's thoughts were interrupted when Eddie Townsend said, almost as though he was reading Arthur's mind, "Hi! Welcome to the group, Arthur and Nicole. We were just talking about how hard it is to remember people's names. We meet so many new people all at once. Champagne?" Eddie signaled the waiter.

Phil Butler, a sharply dressed businessman wearing tailor-made gray slacks and a blue blazer covering a crisp, white linen shirt was obviously comfortable in group settings. He turned out to be the jokester of the group. "The only other Nickie I knew played right guard on our football team, and he didn't look anything like you."

She smiled at the obvious compliment in a way that made her look even cuter to Phil's way of thinking.

"It's Nicole, but my family always called me Nickie," she drawled.

"What part of the south are you from, Nickie?" asked Carol.

"Luziana, just outside N'awlins. A little town called French Settlement." It sounded to Phil as though the words were made of honey.

"*Salut*," said Don Conway, a heavyset grandfather who had already had two Manhattans and couldn't wait for the third.

"I normally don't drink when I'm out to sea, but I guess you can get just as drunk on water as you can on land." A few of the group groaned at Phil's lame joke, but Nicole laughed and took note of Phil's rugged good looks.

"Wait," said Melissa. "If we toast ourselves, then none of us can drink. So let's drink to absent friends."

Everybody smiled except Arthur, who didn't get it. They lifted their glasses for the toast, and Inga Conway conspicuously raised her sparkling water glass. They chatted idly about the ship, the crew, the bar, and their overall experiences. The waiter brought more drinks for those who wanted them.

As they chatted, Sonny Beranski played a medley of popular songs on the piano, which contributed to the Porthole's atmosphere of relaxation and casual elegance. Soon the maître d' announced their dinner reservation and escorted them to their table.

7:00 p.m., the Grand Dining Room

Phil Butler picked up the conversation about names. "It *is* embarrassing when you meet so many people at once and you can't remember who is who."

"Yes," agreed Carol, whose low-cut neckline showed off a beautiful necklace, strong enough to hold up what must have been at least a three-carat diamond. "It's especially difficult for people when they retire and move to a new community. My aunt and uncle moved to Florida last year and have had more trouble trying to remember all the new people they've met. She said it's hard for them to fit in because of that."

Phil went on. "You spend your whole time trying to remember the name of the person you've just met when the next person is introduced."

"It's no better for my brother," said Don. "He said that since he retired, there are so many new people moving into his hometown that keeping them all straight is a big problem for him and a lot of his friends. It's just plain embarrassing when you meet someone and five minutes later you can't remember their name."

"It's probably happened to all of us at one time or another," said Phil.

"I can relate to that with the worst experience I've ever had," chimed in Nicole. Her long brown hair cascaded over her shoulders. She looked much younger than her forty-nine years, thanks to the time she spent at the spa and health club. She wore a tight-fitting Vera Wang original, a Tiffany diamond necklace, a diamond ring that weighed at least five carats, and a pair of Manolo Blahnik shoes.

Phil noticed her big, brown eyes and perfect teeth, and he thought, "That's what I'd call a knockout.

"It happened when Arthur took me to one of his class reunions."

Arthur winced. "I know which one you're talking about. My thirtieth medical school reunion, right?"

"Yes," she said, smiling. "You don't mind, do you?"

"If I said I *do* mind, do you think the group would let it drop now?"

She laughed and said, "Then it's okay?"

"Go ahead." Everybody turned to Nicole, who loved being the center of attention. They waited expectantly for her to go on.

"Well, as Arthur said, it was his thirtieth reunion but my first. I hadn't met any of these people before. So as we started to circulate at the welcome cocktail party, a beautiful woman approached us and enthusiastically said, 'Arthur!'"

Arthur interrupted. "She was mildly attractive."

"Hah! Mildly attractive, my eye. She had to be poured into her dress, and she was downright drop-dead gorgeous. She hung onto Arthur the whole time we stood there."

Arthur took another sip of his prosecco, took off his glasses, and nervously cleaned them with his pocket hankie, feeling his face begin to flush.

Nicole went on in an exaggerated, enthusiastic voice. "Arthur said, 'Clarissa Johnson, it's been a long time.' She gave him a big hug and held on a little too long. She smiled and looked at me, and Arthur said, 'Er, this is Clarissa Johnson,' which I already knew by the enthusiastic greeting she got from my husband. 'Uh, Clarissa and I went to school together.' I knew that too, since we were at a class reunion."

She laughingly went on. "Next, he said, 'We graduated the same year.' Which I assumed, since we were still at the same reunion. In the meantime, Clarissa kept looking at me expectantly. Arthur babbled on about how Clarissa had been grossed out when they had to cut open a kidney."

Everyone, especially Phil, could see how much Nicole was enjoying the spotlight. "She looks good on stage," he thought, and was hanging on her every word. This did not go unnoticed by Carol, feeling a rush of jealousy. She'd seen Phil's wandering eye often during the twenty-five years of their marriage.

Nicole continued. "That's when I realized that Arthur was blathering on and on about this inane topic because he'd *forgotten* my name."

At this, everyone burst out laughing. Arthur said, "It's true. I just drew a blank."

Nicole jumped back in. "We'd only been together for five years at the time, so I thought it was reasonable that he should have had some idea of who I was."

The group was rolling with laughter at Nicole's dramatic recounting of her experience, but Carol seemed to be especially enjoying it, perhaps because she could see a little of herself in Clarissa and understood Nicole's underlying jealousy in her telling of the story.

"It's true. I just panicked. I knew that I knew her, but I couldn't remember her name."

"Yes, I sensed that, and I wasn't going to let him off the hook. I would have if she wasn't still standing way too close to him. Finally, Clarissa stuck out her hand and said, 'I'm Clarissa Johnson.' I smiled, shook her hand, and said, 'Lovely to meet you,' without giving her my name. I knew she wanted to ease Arthur's embarrassment, but I wasn't going to give either one of them the satisfaction of being bailed out. She could have asked my name, or Arthur could have fished around in his wallet and found something with my name on it, but nooo."

All this time, the group, with the exception of Arthur, was

laughing. "Finally, Clarissa looked across the room and said, 'Oh, excuse me, I see my husband, Fred, looking for me. I must go.'"

While the group was wiping tears of laughter from their eyes, Arthur stood up and said, "Hey, everybody, this is Nicole, my wife." Everyone broke out in a new round of laughter. The ice had definitely been broken.

At this point, the waiters brought Caesar salads and a basket of fresh-baked baguettes, along with chilled bottles of a Napa Valley chardonnay. Everyone oohed and aahed in their enjoyment of them.

"Well, we all know why we're here and what the stakes are, so let's get acquainted. Where's everybody from, and what do you do— or did you do if you are no longer doing it?" asked Phil to the table in general.

"Well, I'm from San Francisco, and I work with my husband in his business," said Carol, her voice dripping with sarcasm.

"I know that," said Phil, with a laugh. "You're my wife."

"I know *you* know that," she replied. "But the rest of the group doesn't."

"Oh, right," he said. "Well, since Carol started it, I'm Phil Butler. I worked in the salvage business."

Turning to Melissa, who was seated on Carol's right, he said, "How about you, Melissa?"

She said, "Eddie and I have lived in Muncie, Indiana, all our lives. I practice law, and Eddie is, uh, what do you do exactly, honey?" She smiled, turning to her husband, on her right.

Eddie laughed and said, "As little as possible. But I was in human resources and training until I retired, and now I do a little writing."

Everyone turned to look at Inga, on Eddie's right. "Well," she said slowly, with a pronounced German accent, "I was an office manager for an insurance agency for many years when I wasn't at home with the children."

When it became obvious she wasn't going to say more, Phil turned to Don and laughingly said, "And now for the rest of the story, Don."

"I am Don Conway, actually Dr. Donald L. Conway." The booze freed his normally loquacious personality even more than usual. "I'm not a medical doctor, although I considered medicine at one point, but I have a PhD in philosophy and taught for a number of years in the New York area. We lived in Brooklyn during my teaching years. Our children—we have three of them—all live in and around the New York area. I met and married Inga in Germany when I was there doing some advanced studies in German and music. When I retired, we moved to the Washington, DC, area, specifically Alexandria, Virginia, because I started lecturing at the Smithsonian. We like it there, and it's close enough that we can easily get back up to New York to see our five grandchildren."

Before he could go on, Phil, sensing that he had a lot more to say, interrupted him and turned to Arthur Gibson. "Arthur, tell us about yourself."

"We live in Des Moines, Iowa, and I'm retired now, but I was an actual doctor," he said, throwing a barb at Don. "I practiced surgery at Des Moines General for thirty-five years. I love that city, served one term as mayor, and am still involved. I'm serving as president of both the Rotary Club and the Des Moines Country Club."

It occurred to Phil that the atmosphere was getting a little tense. To lighten things up he said, "You are busy and involved; that's better than being a hermit. Although the advantage of being a hermit is, you'd have no peer pressure."

Everybody laughed, including Arthur, who didn't laugh often.

"Well, Nicole, that leaves you. Other than attending amusing class reunions, what else do you do?" asked Phil, smiling at her.

"I'm a socialist."

"What?" asked Phil, confused. "What does a socialist do?"

"Oh," she said, "I go to a lot of parties and I throw a lot of parties and I go out to lunch with my friends a lot."

"Are your friends socialists too?" asked Don.

"Yes, we pretty much spend all of our time socializing."

Arthur, after nearly ten years with her, had become used to her malapropisms. He jumped in, hoping to keep Nicole from embarrassing herself further. "Yes, Nickie and her friends do a lot of socializing." Nicole smiled prettily and nodded.

———————

Just then the waiters cleared the salad plates, brought new cutlery, and served the soup course, a delicious lobster bisque laced with brandy. The sommelier refilled their wine glasses. Inga put her hand over the top of her glass, indicating that she didn't want any more. As they ate, they talked politely about the food, the service, the table settings, and the dining room itself, which was quite ornate. When the soup course was finished, the waiters again reset the table and brought new cutlery. Then they brought the mouth-watering filet mignon steaks with asparagus, baby carrots, and little potatoes accompanied by bottles of a 2009 burgundy. The group exchanged more small talk until coffee arrived, along with delicious little chocolate cakes with the Imperial Cruise Line logo drawn on top.

———————

8:30 p.m., the After-Dinner Conversation

Don, who obviously enjoyed his food as much as his booze and had eaten everything with relish, exclaimed, "Wow, this is truly a feast for a king. It reminds me of the Swedish film from about twenty years ago, *Babette's Feast*. Do any of you remember that?"

"Yes, I loved it," said, Inga, surprising the others. She hadn't said much during the meal.

"Why did you like it?" asked Don. Before she could answer, he began to tell the others his somewhat flawed version of the story of the film. How the protagonist, Babette, had been a chef in Paris and was now living in a poor village in Denmark. She won the lottery and used her winnings to buy and prepare a gourmet dinner for the people who had befriended her and who never had, nor would they ever be able to have, a feast like it.

Eddie thought that Don's insensitivity to Inga was probably indicative of the way he typically behaved. He jumped into the conversation and asked Inga, "Do you see a lot of movies?"

"Yes," she said. "When I met Don, we spoke only in German, so in order to learn English, I went to the movies and practiced speaking with my neighbor. It took some time, but little by little I learned."

"What was your biggest benefit from mastering English? You are absolutely fluent now," said Eddie.

Inga laughed, the first time any of them had seen her that relaxed. "Thank you, but I still don't consider myself to be fluent," she said. "English is the easiest language to learn fundamentally, but there are so many idioms that mastering the language is a lifetime endeavor for most foreign-born people."

Just then a laughing group approached their table and, recognizing Eddie, stopped to say hello. He greeted them enthusiastically and said to his dinner companions, "I'd like you to meet some nice people. This is Frank and his wife, Lee Hardaway." Laughing and shaking hands with the next man, he said, "This handsome guy in the bow tie is Les Ledbetter, and the person that makes him tolerable to be around is his wife, Debbie.

"This is Stan and Ginnie Hall from Tennessee. If it wasn't for them, this group of scoundrels wouldn't have any class at all. Finally, meet Al and Cathy Smith from Vancouver, British Columbia. They tell me that if you want authentic English fish and chips, you have to stop by their pub in downtown Vancouver. I have to take Cathy's word for it. She seems honest to me. Al, not so much." The whole group was having a great time laughing at Eddie's introductions. He then introduced his team at the table; they shook hands, excused themselves, and left.

"Are those people you knew from before the cruise?" asked Carol.

"No, I just met them standing in line when we went to lunch today."

"How do you do that? I mean, remember people's names like that? It takes me three or four times to remember them," she said.

"Well, it's a skill I learned and one I used to teach in our company leadership training classes."

"I'd like to know how to do that," said Nicole.

"Me too," chimed in Inga.

"I think we all would," said Phil. "Could you teach us?"

"Sure," said Eddie, whose mission in life was to assist people in using all of their latent abilities. He would gladly share his knowledge with anyone who was interested. "I'll be happy to. Let's give everybody an opportunity to take a restroom break, then we can do it in thirty minutes or less." The compliments and the interest of the group in a topic in which he was expert gave Eddie a burst of enthusiasm and confidence he hadn't felt in a long time.

———————

9:00 p.m., the Name-Remembering Lesson

When they settled back into their seats, Eddie asked, "Everyone ready?"

"Do we have to write anything down?" asked Don.

"No, it's better if you don't because we're going to use our minds in a different way than we're ordinarily accustomed to."

"So let's get started. Here's a question for you. Do we think in words or do we think in pictures? Before you answer, tell me, when I say the word 'car,' do you see the letters C-A-R in your mind, or do you see an actual car?"

"I guess we see a car," said Don, who had sobered up after two cups of coffee and a restroom visit.

"What car?"

"I see Nickie's Mercedes," said Arthur with a smirk.

"I see my Lamborghini," said Phil, laughing. "Not one that I own but one I've always wanted."

"Exactly," said Eddie. "That's why we have difficulty remembering names. We think in pictures not in words, so in order to remember a person's name, we need to convert it into a picture. That's what I do to remember names. I know the mind is essentially an associating mechanism, so I make picture associations with their names."

"So those people you just introduced us to were pictures in your head, right?" laughed Carol.

"Right. I use a simple formula. What's that tax-deferred instrument we invest in to save for the future?"

"It's an IRA," said Inga.

"Correct. I use those letters to remind me. *I*—get a clear image of the person. *R*—repeat the name several times, either aloud or to myself. And *A*—associate the name to something with which I'm familiar."

"Can you give us an example?" Don asked.

"Yes. When I met Frank Hardaway, I pictured him at a craps table, rolling not dice but hot dogs, yelling, 'Eight the hard way.' *Leaning* on his arm was his wife, *Lee*. So I see this absurd picture when I see them together or separately."

"So the hot dogs or franks remind you of his first name and trying to make eight the hard way reminds you of Hardaway and his wife leaning reminds you of Lee, is that it?" asked Inga.

"Yes," laughed Eddie. "For a person who has not played craps that might not work for them, so they'd need a different picture. That's the whole system; just convert names into pictures. With a little practice, a person can become quite good at it. People like to have their names remembered."

"That's great," said Nicole. "Can we do it with our names here?"

"Let's try it," said Arthur. He was becoming enthusiastic about the idea of overcoming one of his major weaknesses.

"Ooh, ooh, do me first," said Nicole, excitedly waving her hand in the air like a third-grader who knows the answer.

"Okay," said Eddie. "Who has an idea for Nicole?"

"I do," said Don. "I see her with a large martini glass in her hand with an oversized onion in it. You know, a Gibson." He sat back, pleased with himself.

"Yes," said Carol. "And she is holding a lump of coal and alternately picking her teeth and nicking the coal with the toothpick from her Gibson."

"Great!" said Eddie. "Another useful technique for remembering is to rhyme the name if you can. So we have Nicole drinking an oversized Gibson. Let's have her spilling it all over her elegant evening gown. That brings the element of exaggeration into the picture. The more absurd, ridiculous, and exaggerated we can make it, the better the odds we'll recall the picture and hence the name."

Nicole did not want to relinquish the stage just yet, so she jumped to her feet and pretended to be holding the oversized martini glass in both hands while doing her impression of a tooth-picking, coal-nicking, and slightly tipsy lady guzzling her drink.

"This is great stuff," said Phil. "I suppose then we can also have Arthur doing the same thing."

"We could," said Eddie, "but why not give him a little individuality? Let's have him badly playing a Gibson guitar. In other words, he is an awful or 'arthful' Gibson guitar player. So much so that his face is distorted, and he is grimacing at the terrible sounds he is producing. So we know that he is an 'arthful' Gibson guitar player."

Don and Carol let out a groan at the pun. "I'd like to see that," laughed Melissa.

"Okay," said Arthur, and to everyone's surprise he stood up, loosened his tie, and began to play an air guitar with his version of a grimace. Everybody was roaring with laughter except Nicole, who was shocked. She'd never seen Arthur behave with such a lack of self-consciousness.

"I've got a great idea for mine," said Phil, jumping to his feet. "I see myself standing next to Mr. Carson, the butler from Downton Abbey, filling his coffee cup."

"Great," said Eddie. "Who has an idea to make that more dramatic and memorable?"

Melissa said, "I'd have Phil punching Carson with one fist and overfilling his cup so that it is spilling all over the floor, disgusting Carson and causing him to dance out of the way to keep it off his shoes."

"We've got it then," said Eddie. "Phil Butler is filling Carson the butler's coffee cup to overflowing."

"Act it out, Phil," said Don, getting into the spirit of the game. Phil was not the least bit shy, so he pulled Don to his feet, shoved an empty coffee cup in his hand, and said, "Don, you be Carson." He proceeded to do an exaggerated charade of pretending to punch Don while bowing like a butler and pouring an imaginary cup of coffee. Don, played his part to the hilt, doing his best impression of a butler while dancing away from the spilling coffee, all the while with a disgusted look on his face.

Everybody was laughing and getting into the spirit now, even Inga, who had held back more than anyone to this point. She jumped up, pushing Don back down in his seat when her husband tried to get up. "I'm at the entrance to the penitentiary, and it's my job to weigh the prisoners when they check in. I have to know the answer when the warden asks me, 'How much does the con weigh?' Get it, *con weigh*—Conway?" she asked. This brought a new chorus of groans from Arthur and Melissa.

Phil said, "I knew another Inga from work, so I see her helping you lift a heavy guy in striped convict clothes onto the scales."

"That'll work," said Eddie, thoroughly enjoying the active participation of his dinner companions/students. "That's always a sure-fire way to remember someone, if you know someone else with the same name. If you don't, you can just repeat the name silently over and over until you've got it. It is also a good idea to call the person by name in your conversation with them, as long as you don't overdo it. You can ask the person to spell their name if it is particularly unusual, and you may even want to write it down. They won't mind. After all, you are talking about them, and people like to feel important."

He glanced directly at Nicole, and she smiled back, but his meaning went over her head.

Now Don leapt to his feet before anyone else could beat him to the punch. "Mine is really simple," he said, grinning. "I am playing the piano, which is not a Steinway, but a Conway, and I'm putting on or 'donning' my tuxedo jacket at the same time."

"I like that," said Melissa, "and I'm going to have Inga helping you put on your jacket."

Inga said, "I'm going to have him without his pants on, just his boxer shorts."

Everybody laughed at that, and Carol said, "Now we've got some information we didn't have before."

"Yes, and I would say TMI," said Melissa. More laughter from around the table. The group's enjoyment was clearly evident.

"How about you, Carol?" asked Eddie. "Do you have an idea that we can use to remember your name?"

She slowly got up and said, "Well, I can see myself singing Christmas carols for my first name, but I don't know about my last name, unless I use the Carson thing that Phil used."

"What if you butt Phil with your head down as though you were a billy goat while you are singing?" asked Arthur.

"Hey," said Phil in mock protest. "Why does she have to butt me?"

"Because you are the one who deserves to be butted," said Carol.

"Okay, so we've got it," said Eddie. "Carol Butter or Butler."

"Wait, I want to see that acted out," said Arthur.

Carol sang *"We Wish You a Merry Christmas"* as she put her head down with her fingers above her ears, pointing at Phil and looking more like an imitation of a bull than a billy goat, but everyone laughed and got the idea.

"I guess it's my turn," said Melissa as she stood. "All I can think of is a sign at the city limits that says 'Town's End.'"

"Sure," said Don. "I see you waving an oversized banner while holding up your hand to direct traffic back into town, but you're missing or 'Melissa-ing' a lot of the cars."

"We need action," said Inga.

"I don't think so," protested Melissa.

"Action ... action ... action ..." chanted Don, Inga, and Phil in unison.

"Okay," said Melissa. She used both hands to simulate waving the heavy, oversized banner and pretending to curse the speeding motorists who were ignoring her.

Cheers from the crowd for being such a good sport. "Well, that's it then," said Eddie. "We've—"

Before he could finish, Melissa said, "Not so fast, buster. You're not getting off the hook. You had us all making fools of ourselves. It's your turn."

"I don't have one," he said in mock jest.

"Boo, boo, hiss, hiss," teased Carol, with her hands around her mouth making like she had a megaphone. "Let's see what you got."

"I know I'm doomed to failure. You're all going to be expecting something spectacular, so I can't win."

"Good. Fail then, but fail mightily," said Don in a theatrical voice.

"All right. I'm Mr. Ed, the talking horse, going to the edge of town."

"What?" said Nicole in confusion.

"Well, Mr. Ed was a popular TV character about thirty years ago, and he is going to *leave town*," Eddie said. "Get it? 'Town's end,' the end of town? Townsend." They all stared at him.

Phil said, "That's terrible. As hard as you tried to prepare us for disappointment, you didn't try hard enough. That was the worst name association of the evening."

While the group was laughing, Eddie said, "Do you want to see me clippity-clopping out of town?"

"No!" the group cried in unison.

———

9:50 p.m., Good Night

By now they had been together for nearly four hours, and the dining room had emptied. The waiters were hovering around the table, waiting for them to leave.

"I guess it's time," said Phil. "We'd better get out of here before they kick us out."

"Or bar us from ever coming back," quipped Don.

In the corridor, Inga said, "I'm sorry to see the evening end. It was so much fun, and the time passed so quickly."

"Yes," said Phil. "But we get to do it again tomorrow night."

"Right," said Eddie. "Same time in the Porthole Bar and then dinner in the Italian restaurant." Everyone hugged warmly, a little too warmly in the case of Phil and Nicole, a fact that did not go unnoticed by Carol.

When they started for the elevators, Melissa said to Eddie, "Why don't you go ahead, honey? I just want to check out the music in the piano bar." He knew she wanted to go into the casino and gamble, but he didn't want to start that argument again, so he kissed her on the cheek and said, "I'll just read until you come up."

She said, "Oh, don't wait up for me. I want to think about the memory stuff from this evening, so I'll be a while. You don't mind, do you?" In fact, he did mind, but she made her own money, so as usual, he didn't respond and went on to bed.

———

"Well, you took a shine to her, didn't you?" said Carol icily, when they left Nicole and Arthur in the hall.

"Oh, she seems nice enough," said Phil.

"Nice enough to stare at her all night and give her a prolonged hug."

They got on the elevator, walked to their suite, and went to bed without another word.

———

"You didn't have to tell everybody that reunion story," said Arthur in a flat voice.

"Oh, it was funny, and everybody enjoyed hearing it," said Nicole.

"Yes," he said. "Funny at my expense."

"Oh, I'm sorry, darlin'. I didn't mean to embarrass you. I won't do it again."

"Okay." He knew it had happened before and it would happen again, but he was long past caring.

———

"Nice people," said Inga as she linked her arm with Don's and smiled at him.

Don couldn't remember the last time she'd been that warm and loving toward him. They got on the elevator and went happily up to their suite.

———

DaY THRee

April 9

Eddie was sitting by himself in the café when Phil walked up to his table. "Hi. Mind if I join you?"

"Not at all. Have a seat," said Eddie. "That was a fun evening last night."

"It sure was; that name remembering technique you taught us was great. Carol and I had a chance to use it this morning."

"Thanks. I'm glad I ran into you. We didn't get much of a chance to talk one-on-one in the group. Melissa went to the spa, so I'm on my own for lunch."

"Me, too," Phil said, sitting down. "I'm supposed to take a sandwich to Carol when I finish. How did you happen to sign up for this gig?" asked Phil.

"I was glaring at a blank computer screen one day, trying to write a book."

"You said last night that you are a writer."

"A wannabe writer. I've been at it for over a year." Eddie went on to tell Phil about his frustration and failure. "Ever written anything?"

"Me? No, I'm more of a doer. Not the intellectual type at all."

"What do you do exactly?"

"A couple of things. I've got a little scrap business, and I dabble in real estate," said Phil. "What was your career?"

"Well, I was always a talker until I retired two years ago. I was VP of training for an insurance company, and when the company offered me early retirement, I jumped on it. Since the seminar is about retirement, we thought it would be timely. How about you?" asked Eddie.

"The reason I signed us up for this seminar is because Carol and I are celebrating our twenty-fifth wedding anniversary, and we've been talking about our future. A retirement seminar seemed like just the ticket."

"You seem kind of young to be thinking about retirement," said Eddie.

"Well, yeah, we are, but I've got good people running the salvage business, and it doesn't require much of my time. I'll always have the real estate stuff, which is interesting to me, but Carol would like me to pay more attention to her, so ... What's your book about?"

"It's about an interest of mine: helping people to experience well-being in retirement. I've thought about it for a long time. For five years before I retired, I interviewed many of our clients on what was working for them, or not, and kept a journal with my findings."

"What's the holdup? It sounds as though you've got plenty of material."

"I do. I just haven't figured how to organize my material. I don't know why I'm having such a problem with it."

"I guess we're both taking this seminar for answers to the questions, 'What do we do next?' and 'How do we do it?'" said Phil. "I'm looking forward to the next two weeks. The topics sound real interesting."

"Yeah, they do. I'm hoping that this'll get me off my duff and get me to writing. I actually brought my laptop so that when I get unstuck, it will come pouring out of me like Old Faithful."

"I didn't bring any work with me because Carol is always accusing me of being a workaholic. Instead, there's a first-rate fitness center on the ship, and I'm going to get plenty of use out of it."

"Yeah, I like that too. There's also a walking deck."

"Tell me about retirement," said Phil. "What do I have to look forward to?"

"You sure you want to hear the whole story?" asked Eddie.

"Yes, I definitely do. Let's have another cup of coffee."

"Okay, it's kind of personal, but I'll tell you my experience. Retirement seemed like a smart move at the time. It didn't turn out that way, not for me nor for most of my friends. We didn't count on the loss of identity and the boredom that comes from having nothing important to do. So we looked for other outlets. I chose writing, and it's not going well. I am discouraged, and I feel like a failure. I'm losing my self-confidence. I feel, rightly or wrongly, that when I was working, I had significance, that I was valuable. Now, not so much. That brings you up to date.

"God, you're a good listener, Phil. I didn't mean to blurt all that out. Obviously, what I've told you is confidential. I'd appreciate it if you'd keep it to yourself."

"From your lips to God's ears," said Phil.

"We'd better take these sandwiches to our wives before they send out a posse to find us," said Eddie.

"I'll see you this afternoon," said Phil.

Eddie held back at the coffee bar because he didn't want Phil to see him going down to the cheaper staterooms instead of going up to the luxury suites where all the others were staying.

———

Day Three:
The Role of Money in Retirement

1:00 p.m., the Celebrity Theater

Phil and Carol arrived just as Pat Higgins announced that everyone should join their assigned group for the day. They sat down, nodded, and smiled at the others at their table.

Pat said, "Welcome, everyone. The reporting period today will use the same format as yesterday. The assignment is, 'What did I take from our team dinner last night?' The primary focus is on the specific challenges and barriers to happiness that you and your team members are facing in retirement. Have fun and good luck."

1:15 p.m., Reporting

Alberto, the sommelier from the grand dining room, was their group leader for the day. He greeted everyone and asked them to think for two minutes, then write their answers to the question.

"Take exactly three minutes to do it," he said, smiling.

When the three minutes were up, he said, "As we hear your answers, please also introduce yourselves." Turning to the person on his left, he asked, "May we start with you?"

"Yes, I'm David Stevens from Houston, Texas, and our group had an interesting discussion last night. For me, the main idea was not to retire *from* something but to retire *to* something. I'm not retired yet. I'm the only one on our team who is still working. The others all agreed that we should be going *toward* something."

"I'm his wife, Bella, and David and I have just started to talk about that day, in the not-too-distant future, when we are going to be at home together more than we are now. My life is not going to change too much since I don't work, but his will be a lot different. What is he going to do with his time?"

"You don't work?" asked the woman next to her. "If you are a housewife, I'll bet you work plenty, right? Oh, I'm Patti Larner from Chicago. I've been cookin' meals, cleanin' house, washin' clothes, and tendin' to the kids and the house for forty years. Don't tell me that we don't work."

"I've been trying to help out more since I've retired, haven't I, honey?" said the man to her left.

"I don't see how settin' in your pajamas, drinkin' coffee, and readin' the paper until by some magic your breakfast appears is helpin' out, *honey*. Oh, this is Brad, everybody. He retired about a year ago, and now he is helpin' out around the house," she said sarcastically.

"Sounds like you two have talked about this before," said Carol.

"We have," said Patti. "And I don't think I've gotten my feelings out so that he understands yet."

"I think you got them out pretty good just now," said Phil, with a grin. "Oh, I'm Phil Butler, and this is my wife, Carol. Our team talked a lot about finding something worthwhile to do after retirement, like volunteering, as a way to replace the satisfaction we used to get from our jobs."

"I'm not getting any satisfaction from volunteering," said a grouchy-looking man sitting on Phil's right. "I go down to the food bank once a week and dole out free food to people who look like they ought to be out working and buying their own food instead of freeloading off the rest of us."

"Oh, Bill doesn't mean that," said the red-faced woman to his right. "Do you, dear?" Without waiting for him to answer, she said, "He's done a pretty good job there for the past year since he retired. He likes to talk tough, but he's actually a teddy bear. Our name is McClosky. That's Bill, and I'm Terri. We're from LA."

"How did you happen to sign up for this seminar?" asked a smiling Phil. "Won't they miss you at the food bank?"

Missing his sarcasm, Bill said in a much more subdued manner, "Terri and I knew things weren't going as smoothly as we wanted, and this topic seems to fill the bill for what we need right now."

"That's exactly why we signed up," said Patti Larner, with a lot less venom in her voice. "Brad and I haven't settled into smooth retirement living, and when we got the brochure for this cruise, it sounded like just the thing we needed."

"May I have your attention, please?" Pat Higgins's voice came over the PA system. "We're ready for a break. In fifteen minutes we're going to hear a valuable presentation on our relationship toward money in retirement. Please be back in your seats ready to go to work at two o'clock sharp."

2:00 p.m.

"Welcome back from the break, everyone. Our topic this afternoon is the role our attitudes toward money plays in retirement. Our speaker will deal with such subjects as getting comfortable with, and dealing with your finances, making the most of your money, and how to get the most satisfaction from what you have.

"Our special guest speaker is Ed McGee, CEO and founder of Edgewater Portfolio Management. For eleven years prior, Ed was the senior financial consultant at Integrity Investments in Oakland, Illinois."

Inga took out her notebook and wrote at the top of a blank page: Ed McGee, Money.

"Good afternoon, everybody. Welcome to the topic of money in retirement. It's my goal this afternoon to help you get the most bang for your buck while spending your kids' inheritance."

This comment receives a lot of nods and laughter.

"This presentation is not designed to help you manage your finances or investments. Many factors contribute to a happy and successful retirement. Let's look at our *attitudes* toward our finances to see what role money plays in a happy life."

For the next sixty minutes, Ed presented ideas they could use to improve their attitudes toward money.

———

3:00 p.m.

Pat Higgins thanked Ed and said, "Group leaders, you have thirty minutes to hear from everyone in your group on the take-home pay from Ed's talk."

Alberto said, "Let's use the same method as before. Take two minutes to think, and then write down your one best idea to share with the group." When the time was up, he looked around the group and said, "Who'd like to go first?"

"I would," said David Stevens. "When I first started out as a straight-commission salesman, I sat in a tiny room in the Central YMCA in Austin on the verge of tears. I was twenty-two years old, failing at my first real job. I was trying to sell home-study courses. My money was almost gone, and I dreaded the thought of having to move back home and prove my mother right. She said I'd fail.

"That's when I picked up a copy of *As a Man Thinketh* that Ed just talked about. The ideas in that little book are so profound that they started me on a journey that has resulted in a life of adventure, satisfaction, and rewards. I've reread it many times over the years, along with about a thousand other serious books, all directing me toward my goals. That reading deepened my understanding of what it takes for human beings to be happy and successful, by their definition. I began to understand that my thinking was the biggest barrier to my success."

"I had an Aha! moment when he talked about serving others," said Phil. "A few of us talked about the same thing at dinner last night. It's a good reminder."

Brad Larner spoke up then and said, "I had lunch with an old friend, Barry Evans. He's a successful businessman. He's at the age of retirement, but he continues to put in full days, although he doesn't need the money. I asked him, 'What advice would you give a person getting ready to retire?'

"The most important point he made was to share what you have or it will die with you. When I asked him to elaborate, he said, 'You've paid the price. Over the course of your career you've gained wisdom and knowledge. To take that with you is just not right.' After today's talk, I think Barry's right. All the people I've talked to on this cruise so far have an accumulated wisdom that others can benefit from."

"I read some place that Leonard Nimoy, you know, from *Star Trek*, said, '*The more we share, the more we have*,'" said Terri McClosky. "That ties in with what Ed said today."

"I don't know if you remember, sweetheart," said her husband in a much softer voice, "but I read that book a couple of years ago when I was first talking about retirement. What was the name of it?"

"Of course, I remember," said Terri. "It was, *You Don't Need a Million to Retire*. The guy's name was Ronald Warner, I think."

"Right," said Carol. "Wait. It was Ralph, Ralph Warner. I read it too, and I think he had a lot to say that is worthwhile for anyone thinking about the future."

"Yeah, that's it," said Terri. "I like what he said about friends and relationships. He said, 'Invest in your family, improve strained relationships.'"

Phil looked at Carol, and she returned his look with a strange expression on her face.

4:00 p.m.

Pat Higgins announced, "That's it for today, boys and girls. We've got a lot to think and talk about tonight. Remember we will be in Bermuda for the next two days, so that means we won't be meeting back here until we are at sea again. Enjoy your free time. Your evening team meetings are optional, so you can decide as a group what you'd like to do about that. Let's have one last round of applause for Ed McGee."

The group applauded appreciatively and the session broke for the day with many serious conversations and lots of plans being made for the evening and the next day.

6:00 p.m., the Porthole Piano Bar

"Let the record show we were here early," announced Arthur proudly, when the other three couples walked into the Porthole. Don immediately went to the bar and ordered a double Manhattan. The waiter took the other drink orders at the table.

"Eddie, that stuff you gave us on memory was great. Carol and I had a chance to put it into practice at the gym this morning at six."

"What? Six o'clock?" said Nicole in a mock-horrified voice. "Were they serving mimosas?"

"No," said Carol. "We went there to work out."

"More power to you," said Don. "That's a little too early for me."

"What happened with the memory stuff?" asked Inga.

"Well, we were the first ones there. We just introduced ourselves to everybody as they came in," said Carol.

"Yes," said Phil. "We made a little joke about the early hour and what warriors we were, then, as the next person came in, we were able to introduce them and practice the repetition idea Eddie gave us. We met a dozen new people and remembered all their names. It was exciting. A benefit I didn't expect was that I was more comfortable around those people and even other new people I met during the day."

Just then the waiter, a tall, good-looking Swede, brought their drinks, and Eddie said, "Thank you, Sven. Did you do any writing last night?"

Sven beamed and said, "Yes, thank you for your encouragement yesterday."

"That's great. Keep up the good work. You've got the makings of a first-rate novelist."

"Eddie, you're an inspiration to me," said Arthur. "Remembering names has always been a weakness of mine. I'm going to practice the techniques we learned yesterday during this cruise and see how many names I can remember."

"Great idea," said Eddie. "That is the best way to master any skill, and, as Phil pointed out, an extra benefit is the increased confidence that comes from doing it."

Phil jumped in. "So a guy is wandering around lost in New York City, and he asks a cab driver, 'How do I get to Carnegie Hall?'"

"Practice, practice, practice," laughed Don, Nicole, and Arthur in unison.

"Oh, I guess you heard that one before," said Phil, grinning at the group.

"Everybody's heard that one before, even me," said Inga.

"Eddie, you have a unique talent. Every retired or about-to-retire person could benefit from what you gave us yesterday. I'm glad I met you on this adventure," said Phil.

"Thank you. I'm enjoying getting to know all of you as well, and everyone likes a compliment. It's good for the ego. But you must know that, like everyone else, I've got my share of faults and weaknesses," replied a smiling Eddie, thinking of his own lifelong tendency toward laziness and lack of ambition. "You might not be so complimentary if you knew all of them. I agree with Emerson when he said, 'Every man is my superior in some way, and in that way I learn from him.' Gathered around this table is over five hundred years of collective wisdom that others could learn from, right?"

"It's even more than that if you count the experience and education of the presenters," said Don. "They bring a wealth of knowledge that we can learn from."

"Not just the presenters," chimed in Phil. "What about the small-group discussions with the other participants? They bring all their perspectives to the discussions too."

"So when you combine all those things, we're probably talking about more than five thousand years of wisdom," said Don.

"Any wisdom I have came from the stupid things I've done along the way," said Arthur.

"Stupid! I'll tell you the best example of stupidity I ever heard," said Phil. "Two guys are down digging a ditch. It's one hundred and ten degrees, and they are sweating like pigs. One of them says to the other, 'Hey, Carl, howz come we're down here making minimum wage and the boss is sitting up there in the shade drinkin' lemonade making twenty bucks an hour? That jist ain't right.'

"'I'll go ask him,' says Carl.

"So Carl goes to the boss and says, 'Me an' Frank's wunderin' how come we're doin' all the work makin' minimum wage and yer sittin' here in the shade drinkin' lemonade, makin' big money.'

"'That's easy,' says the boss. 'It's stupidity.'

"'Whaddya mean?' asks Carl.

"'I'll show you,' says the boss. He holds his hand up in front of the tree and says, 'Hit my hand.' So Carl figures this is a chance to get some revenge on the greedy, blood-sucking boss who is making them do all the work while he does nothing but benefit from their work. So he hauls back his fist and swings with all his might. Just before Carl's fist hits his hand, the boss drops it, and Carl's fist hits the tree. His hand is skinned, cut, and bruised.

"So he goes back to the ditch, where Frank asks, 'Did you find out?'"

"'Yeah,'" says Carl. 'It's stupidity.'

"'Whaddya mean?' With a smirk Carl says, 'I'll show you.' He puts his hand up in front of his face and says, 'Hit my hand.'"

The group roared with laughter at Phil's joke and his ability to deliver it with animation and action.

"That's one thing I admire about you, Phil," said Arthur. "I wish I could tell jokes like that. There are guys in my Rotary Club who can do that, and they are always a hit at our meetings."

"There's more than one side to every person, and getting to know their many facets is a key to having a rich, satisfying life," said Eddie.

"Why do you say that, Eddie?" asked Don.

"My book is on the subject of achieving fulfillment in our so-called retirement, the second half of our lives."

"That sounds like a self-help book," said Phil. Without waiting for

Eddie to comment he said, "A guy walks into a bookstore and asks the clerk where the self-help section is. The clerk said, 'If I told you, wouldn't that defeat the purpose?'"

By now everyone was ready to laugh as soon as Phil opened his mouth.

"Well, I can tell you a side of Arthur that you wouldn't suspect; the way he is always playing himself down," said Nicole. "He is an accomplished, highly respected surgeon, president of God-only-knows how many Des Moines clubs and stuff, and is the *epiphany* of the most *respectiful* man in town. But there is another side to him that you should all know. One early evening a couple of years ago, we had just watched an old movie in black and white on TV. It was a Hitchcock movie with Cary Grant and Joan Fountain called *Suspicion*. I said, 'Cary Grant is the most *sophisticationistic* man ever.' Well, Mr. I-don't-crack-a-smile-for-nobody says, 'I could be like him, you know.' I said, 'I don't think so.' He said, 'I'll meet you on the terrace for cocktails in a bit.' When I go out, there he is, wearing an old, raggedy bathrobe, one hand stuck in his pocket like it was a smoking jacket. It was one that I had thrown in the rag bin a couple of months before. He had a sweat sock wrapped around his neck. He had a bottle of champagne, not real champagne, but a bottle of California sparkling wine, in an ice bucket. It was the most ridiculous sight I've ever seen. He said, 'Hello, dahling,' with the worst English accent you could imagine. I said, 'What are you doing in that ridiculous costume?' He said, 'I'm showing you that I can be as charming as Cary Grant.' I said, 'What do you have around your neck?' He said, 'It is a cravat like Cary Grant wears with a smoking jacket.' I said, 'But it's a sock. It's a sweat sock.' We both burst out laughing, and it reminded me why I love him. He has a playful side that most people don't usually see."

The group was surprised to hear Nicole's story because their collective perception of Arthur was just the opposite. He came across as being stuffy and humorless, slow to catch jokes and certainly not good at telling them.

"That's a perfect illustration of what I mean by us all having different aspects to our personalities. Once uncovered, they help us to appreciate each other more," said Eddie.

Sonny played show tunes quietly in the background as they talked.

Melissa was in an unusually upbeat mood. Smiling, she said, "Arthur, let me tell you, the trouble with being punctual is that there's never anyone there to appreciate it."

"Oh, badda boom," said Phil. "Are you trying to take over my job of being the court jester?"

Melissa laughed and said, "You don't have a corner on all the humor."

Eddie knew by her jovial mood that she had won big at the casino the night before. "Was last night a good night at the tables, my love?" To avoid an argument, he hadn't talked to her about it all day. He knew it was safe to talk about her gambling in front of the others because she'd won.

"Yes," she said with a big smile. "I might get banned for having won so much."

"Wow, that's great," said Nicole. "I never win. What do you play?"

"Blackjack mostly, and the cards were good to me last night," answered Melissa.

"It's too fast for me, and I never know when to take a chance on asking for another card," said Nicole.

"I don't play because I think it's a waste of time," said Phil.

"I don't play because it's a waste of money," said Inga.

"Well, not when you win," said Melissa defensively.

"I'm sure there are people who win more than they lose, but they have to be the exception," said Inga. "Look at all those casinos in Las Vegas, Reno, and New Jersey. They sure didn't build those by losing."

"How many successful retired people do you know who made their money gambling? Not many, I'll bet," asked Don.

"How much would you bet?" asked Phil, laughing at his own joke.

"What do you do with all the money you win, Melissa?" asked Carol.

"She loses it back to the house the next day," said Eddie sarcastically.

"Not always," said Melissa. She was in too good a mood to be brought down by her husband's sarcasm.

"Well, what if you did, or any of us did, win a lot of money?" asked Don. "Would money make us any happier?"

"That's a question every retiree would like to have the answer to because it would influence a lot of their decisions," said Phil.

"There have been a number of recent studies and reports on that subject," said Eddie.

"You're referring to the work that Laura Vanderkam reported in her book, *All the Money in the World: What the Happiest People Know about Wealth*. Right?" said Phil.

"Right," said Eddie. "And also, Gretchen Rubin is doing a lot of work in the area of the relationship between money and happiness. Both of them are worthwhile reading for anyone getting ready to retire."

"Along with health, money is one of the most important considerations we have to deal with in retirement," said Arthur.

Phil said with a grin, "I think we're starting to agree that money can't buy happiness—but somehow it's more comfortable to cry in a Mercedes than a Kia."

Just then Sven came to the table to let them know that their table was ready in the private dining room.

7:00 p.m., the Sienna Dining Room

When they entered, Phil wanted to avoid any further upset with Carol and made a point of sitting on the opposite side of the table from Nicole, even though she looked better this evening in a pink lace dress than last night.

However, before he could sit down, Carol said, "Let's break up the seating this evening and not fall into a rut. Inga, why don't you sit next to Melissa and Don next to Arthur?" They agreed and moved toward their chairs. Nicole and Carol took two seats together, leaving Phil and Eddie to take the last two seats.

Arthur was taken off guard, and before he knew what had happened, he was seated next to the person he least wanted to sit with.

The waiters almost immediately brought jumbo shrimp cocktails, and the sommelier poured a crisp chardonnay from Sonoma County.

"You know I was being facetious when I made that remark about money not buying happiness," said Phil. "The book I mentioned earlier is one that I think retirees could benefit from. Carol and I bought copies for our three kids."

"It was written by a young woman, Laura Vanderkam," said Eddie. "She talks about issues facing young people, as I recall."

"Yes, but I think anyone could extrapolate the philosophy and apply it to themselves at any stage of their lives," said Phil. "And she also includes a chapter on retirement. Her point is, if one is aware of what brings them happiness, then they can make informed choices about how they spend their money."

"Then," said Don, "that would suggest that one heed Plato's advice that one should 'know thyself.'"

"I agree," said Arthur. "Eddie, the speaker today mentioned Abraham Maslow's *Toward a Psychology of Being*, the same psychologist that you talked about in our conversation yesterday. That certainly was Maslow's definitive work, but for a deeper look into how our motivations change as we reach retirement age, I'd recommend his posthumous work, *The Farther Reaches of Human Nature*. I found it to be an extremely interesting read."

"We've got that in common," said Don. "I was also impressed with where Maslow took his research and with his insights in that series of articles. My field included teaching philosophy, and I was especially fond of the humanist psychologists."

The waiter prepared a large Caesar salad at the table and served it with the warm, fresh baguettes that were a specialty of Imperial Cruise Lines.

Arthur turned to Don. "It sounds as though you enjoy learning and have a broad range of knowledge. I envy you for that. I never felt I had the time to expand into other areas of interest. As is the case with most doctors, our specialties are so demanding and changing so rapidly that it takes all of our time to keep up with the advances. You told us yesterday that you are doing some lecturing at the Smithsonian. In addition to philosophy, what are some of the other areas you're covering?"

"Well, of course German. I minored in that and have always had an interest in classical music, especially Wagner. I also was president of the Goethe Society while I was studying in Hamburg, so I gave lectures on Wagner and Goethe as well as philosophy. I also developed an interest in mythology. I studied it extensively and lectured on it as well."

"Mythology. Then you must be familiar with the writings of Joseph Campbell?" said Eddie.

Don stood up and bowed in exaggerated adoration. "Joseph Campbell is the guru, the master of all mythologists. His conclusions from his lifelong studies are the point of this seminar. To achieve a life worth living, we need to emulate Campbell: *follow our bliss*. I'd recommend that anyone about to retire read his book."

"I read *The Hero with a Thousand Faces*," said Eddie, "and thought it contained a lot of wisdom that could benefit anyone as they start to look at the deeper implications of life."

"I agree," said Inga. "I saw that book lying around the house and read it and was astounded at how the myths from other parts of the world were so similar to the ones I read about in Germany."

Eddie interrupted. "I call that constructive discontent. It is an inner urging that tells you there is something more for you to be and do. Some resist it, tune it out, and continue to live lives of 'quiet desperation' in Thoreau's words. As I see it, that is a real danger in retirement."

"You're right," continued Don. "The hero in us will not let us ignore the call. We wake up and draw on an inner courage that enables us to make the move out of that safe haven."

"Is that what is meant by the saying, 'If you keep doing what you've always done, you'll keep getting what you've always got'?" asked Carol.

"Yes!" said Don, delighted to have such an attentive audience. "The second phase of the journey is: we face obstacles and challenges that enable us to use strengths, creativity, and resourcefulness that we had only previously suspected we possessed. Then in the third phase, we are successful in our battle against those forces that would prevent us from victory. We would be inspired if we witnessed someone else doing the same thing."

"I know what you mean," said Arthur. "One of the docs I worked with went sky-diving on his sixty-fifth birthday. I'm in awe of him. I'd never have the courage to do something like that."

Don went on. "Exactly. The courage to face fear of any kind is one of our biggest challenges. That's why, in our everyday lives, when we share those experiences with others, we are surprised that they are inspired by what we've done. I'll bet that was true of your doctor friend, Arthur."

"Is there any practical application in Campbell's studies, especially for the retired person?" asked Melissa. "It all seems a bit too esoteric and academic."

"Absolutely," said Don. "As I said, I believe every person's journey has the potential to be heroic. We all need models to inspire and guide us, perhaps more so in retirement than at any other time. We are entering uncharted territory. Our foundation of the familiar routines of our life has been ripped out from under us. We are insecure because our historical precedents for decision-making are gone."

"But you said every person's journey has the potential to be heroic. If we are all lost in this quagmire of a new world, how do we guide one another?" asked Carol. "Isn't that the equivalent of the blind leading the blind?" She laughed.

Eddie noticed that Don had seriously curtailed his intake of alcohol. He was impressed with his knowledge, logic, and clarity of thought.

"In answer to your question," Don continued, "I refer you back to yesterday's conversation when Eddie quoted Emerson saying, 'Every person is my superior in some way, and in that way I learn from him.' Yes, as a retiree, each of us is lost in the environment of a world in which we did not grow up. A world that is changing so rapidly we hardly recognize it. Margaret Mead once said, 'No one dies in the same world in which they are born.'"

"I read that quote recently," said Phil. "Living in the heart of Silicon Valley, where new developments and innovations are happening all around us every day, I've updated her thought to this: 'No one wakes up in the morning to the same world that existed when they went to bed the night before.'"

"I think I've got your point," said Eddie. "Individually we're screwed, trying to grope our way around this new terrain, but if we pool our collective knowledge, we can find our way out, right?"

"That might be the ideal," said Arthur. "But we're a long way from that kind of advanced consciousness and ability to work together synergistically. A more reasonable conclusion to draw from Don's point is to regard each person as a potential source of valuable, useable information to help us adapt to the changing world in which we now find ourselves."

"You think you can learn something even from stupid people like me?" asked Phil. "I took an IQ test and the results were negative."

This drew a laugh from the whole table.

Just then the waiters served the main course: a baked Chilean sea bass with a red pepper sauce, rice pilaf, green beans, and a fresh basket of warm baguettes, accompanied by bottles of Laurel Hood's Oregon pinot noir. This drew the usual positive comments from everyone as they ate with gusto.

8:00 p.m., the Dinner Conversation

"Let's get back to what we were talking about," said Nicole, wanting to guide the conversation to a more familiar topic. "We were talking about money. What have we learned about money?" she asked.

"We haven't left the topic at all," said Eddie. "The ten thousand baby boomers who are retiring every day need a new set of blueprints and attitudes toward everything, including money, to be able to have rich, satisfying retirement years."

"I believe that is true," said Inga. "Donald and I have had to make adjustments in our manner of living since retiring, but we haven't had to lower our standard of living. We downsized when we sold our house in Brooklyn, which was paid for. We bought a less expensive condo in Alexandria. That was an adjustment that we were able to make by keeping informed about the changing economic environment and adapting to it on purpose."

"That's it," chimed in Melissa. "It's not the hand you're dealt; it's how you play your cards."

"Right. The people who are going to have the most difficulty adapting to this change are those who don't take it seriously and fail to recognize they are living in a different world," said Eddie. "I had an interesting experience that proves your point, Melissa. I was doing research for the book I'm writing, and I wanted to get a broader perspective of my subject, so I visited the Marshall Home for Men, a personal-care facility for elderly men of limited means. The director showed me around the building, then he gave me an hour of his time to tell me about the challenges and rewards of operating it. Then he introduced me to several of the residents. Thomas, Art, and I sat and talked for about an hour in the recreation room. It was an eye-opening interview. They both smoked nonstop. They said everyone who lived there smoked—it was one of their few pleasures. They told me that they were both retired from the military, as were a high percentage of the Marshall Home residents. They were both on medications, as was almost every other resident.

"Art was being treated for cancer and felt as though he had it licked. He was looking forward to buying a car and going to Texas to visit a couple of relatives. Thomas said that as soon as he got well enough, he wanted to go visit his daughter. They both had enough money from pensions and social security, about nine hundred dollars per month, to pay their way at the home and enough extra to do what they wanted to do, which was not much. They had limited options and limited ambitions. When I asked them about their goals, Art said, 'I don't have any more missions to accomplish. I'm seventy-nine years old, and I've accomplished everything I want to.' They both expressed a high degree of satisfaction in spite of their circumstances.

"Both Thomas and Art impressed me with their level of happiness. I came away with a feeling of respect for a couple of guys who were at peace with themselves and their circumstances. I also have a great respect for the Marshall Home and the service they are offering. The whole experience reminded me that what Benjamin Franklin said is as true today as it was in his time: 'Happiness depends more on the inward disposition of mind than on outward circumstances.'"

"Oh, that's so cool," said Carol. "I guess you don't have to have a lot of money to be happy."

"That may be so," said Phil. "but I don't have much sympathy for people like that. They've created their own circumstances, and we're paying for it with our tax dollars by supporting that kind of indolence. James Allen in his book, *As a Man Thinketh*, said, 'Circumstance does not make the man; it reveals him to himself.' They've created their own circumstances. They are where they are by choice."

"I think if you got down off your soap box, you could be a little more sympathetic and understanding, honey," said Carol icily. "After all, there but for the grace of God go you."

"Nobody ever gave me anything. I've worked for every dime I've ever made."

"Yes, but look at the opportunities you've had," said Carol. "You learned the business from your parents, and that education has proven to be invaluable."

He shot back, "You can say that because you had the advantage of a Stanford education, which I never did. A lot of your smart-ass classmates are not out taking advantage of what they learned, and our system is supporting them."

"Even though you didn't go to college, you've done well for yourself because of the opportunity of living in the United States," she said.

The conversation was getting heated and personal, so Eddie attempted to add some humor. "Yes, with our system you can always borrow money to go into business, and I recommend you borrow from pessimists; they don't expect to get it back."

"Yuk, yuk," said Arthur. "Carol has a point that we should all bear in mind when thinking about the opportunity we have as US citizens. People the world over are just as ambitious and entrepreneurial as we are in the States. They just don't have the economic system to boost them out of poverty. They work as hard or harder than anyone."

To relieve the mounting tension, Don said, "What I think we all agree on is that money and happiness are not necessarily related. Remember that Andrew Carnegie quote from Ed McGee's presentation: 'Money will not make you happy; it will merely keep you from being unhappy.' I have a friend in Portland, Oregon, who told me an inspirational story.

"Barney said, 'Many years ago, my daughter Michelle gave me a wonderful gift. It was a money clip with a quotation by Pablo Picasso: "I'd like to live like a poor man—only with lots of money." The philosophy on that money clip is one I've attempted to live by, and it has served me well. It has enabled me to live my dream. Another motto I attempt to live by is: "Happiness in life consists of savoring what you have rather than longing for what you don't have.""'

"I like that," interrupted Eddie. "That makes a lot of sense to me. I've known plenty of people leading lives of frustration and stress trying to keep up with the Joneses. They didn't realize that too many times the Joneses were trying to keep up with somebody else and were also feeling frustrated and stressed."

"Well," Don continued, "Barney said, 'I didn't want to get stressed out chasing a lot of material stuff, so I kept those mottos in mind. I wanted to be one of those people who savors what they have, live modestly, and spend less than they earn, preferring instead to invest and let my money work for me. This is the same advice given in a book I read some years before, *The Richest Man in Babylon.* So when my daughter gave me the money clip, it was a great ongoing reminder of how I wanted to live. So I never miss a chance to say thank you to Michelle for the money clip quotation by Pablo Picasso.'"

"Wow! Great story, Don. Barney's philosophy is one that is as true during our retirement years as it is in our working years," said Eddie.

By now the group had finished the main course, and the waiters cleared the table. They brought small dishes of a tasty, cool, orange sorbet. The group seemed to be in a mellow, friendly mood. Even Arthur and Don were now apparently enjoying one another's company.

"The subject of money for retirees is the most problematic issue to tackle in my upcoming book," said Eddie. "Because of the personal nature of money, it is an area that is difficult to address directly. For the most part, people do not treat money in an unemotional, analytical way. Rightly or wrongly it makes a statement about who we are, where we fit in society, and what we have accomplished or failed to accomplish. The way we use money and misinterpret its value is one of life's most fascinating studies."

"I can give you a great example of that exact point," said Phil. "I have an acquaintance who still flaunts his money by surrounding himself with conspicuous consumables, in spite of reaching retirement age. He talks about his possessions as though they are a significant extension of who he is. He makes sure everybody knows how well he's doing. He still doesn't get it. He doesn't get that the only people who care about the kind of car he drives or the house he lives in are people just like him. People who have real values are not interested and pretty much unimpressed with that kind of superficial display of affluence. I don't know about this particular acquaintance, but I do know that many people who exhibit that kind of behavior are heavily leveraged and in debt."

"Amen, honey," said Carol. "That makes me think of Peter, our English friend. When I asked him about his ostentatious lifestyle, he said, 'You have to drive a luxury car and live in a prestigious house in the UK. People judge your success by those things and won't do business with you if they don't think you are successful.' Hmm, well, maybe."

"She called me honey," Phil thought to himself. "That's got to be a good thing."

"Well, I know this about money," quipped Phil out loud. "The quickest way to double your money is to fold it over and put it back in your pocket."

"I think that none of what you've said is an argument against industry and frugality. It is an argument for prudence. I've heard that he who does not know when he has enough will never have enough," said Inga.

"My experience so far has been that those people who are the most content with their finances are the ones who use money and don't let money use them," said Melissa.

"How do you convince young people to do that?" asked Inga. "We have five grandchildren, all of whom we love very much. One of them, a grandson, is always asking for advice about business and investing, but he doesn't listen to us. I'm sure that a lot of people our ages feel the same way about their children and grandchildren. Phil, from what Carol said, you seem to have done pretty well. What advice would you give our grandson?" She looked at Phil expectantly and picked up her pen, ready to take notes.

"I guess I'd tell him my story," said Phil. "On two different occasions, I went into debt by making bad decisions, and I had to work my way out. In the process, I learned some valuable lessons about money. John D. Rockefeller said, 'I believe every young man should go as deeply into debt as possible, then work his way out.' I thought at the time he meant me. I used that philosophy to justify irresponsible behavior. I don't necessarily agree with that approach to accumulating wealth now. That's the hard way. Do it the hard way if you have to, but there is an easier way. I learned that the approach to wealth is basically simple.

"First, spend less than you earn and learn the difference between needs and wants. For years I carried a three-by-five card in my pocket with the question, 'Do I need it, or do I want it?' I referred to it before I bought anything. I did that until I broke myself of spending irresponsibly. Are you getting this, Inga?"

She smiled and said, "Shorthand, I was an office manager, remember?"

Phil laughed and continued. "Second, save and invest at least ten percent of every dollar you earn; more is better. Reinvest the earnings on your investment, and don't touch that money. Let the miracle of compound interest work in your favor. Always invest prudently; get the maximum return on your investment with the minimum risk."

"Does that apply to us if we're already retired?" asked Nicole.

"Maybe it is more important in retirement," said Arthur. "Unless we're like our friend Don here who is raking in the big bucks by lecturing at the Smithsonian, we need to husband our retirement dollars."

"Hardly raking in the big bucks," said Don. "Everyone who attends my lectures makes more money than me. Remember, unlike business people and doctors, professors don't make much money."

"Well, let me continue with my answer to Inga's question," said Phil. "Where was I?"

"You were about to give us the third approach to wealth," said Inga.

"Right," said Phil. "Third, there are four ways to *make* money:

Inga wrote them down in her notebook:

1. **I Work**—that is, work with your own hands. Develop a skill

that is in demand. Master it and get paid the highest possible wage for it.

2. **Others Work**—that is, use the work others do with their hands or brains. That is management. Get yourself promoted to the highest possible level in your organization, where you can make the most valuable contribution. Better yet, start your own business. Many successful people are independent business people.

3. **Money Works**—that is, use the same investment ideas I just mentioned. Put your earnings to work for you.

4. **Ideas Work**—that is, develop an insatiable curiosity by constantly asking yourself, 'How can this work be done faster, better, or more profitably?' Then put your conclusions into action.

"Of the four, the last one is the most powerful. All great fortunes have been the children of creative ideas implemented for the benefit of other people.

"Lastly, I would tell your grandson to remind himself that money cannot buy happiness. Money is only good for the things money is used for. Don't let it become your master. Thoreau said, 'When a man owns a piece of property, the piece of property also owns the man.' I'd say this is true of all possessions. The more things we have, the more time, effort, and money it takes to take care of them."

As during the previous evening, the waiters were hovering around the table, indicating that they would like the group to leave. They obliged, thanked the grateful waiters, and left.

9:00 p.m., in the Corridor

Carol and Nicole were still talking quietly to one another, so Phil turned to Arthur and said, "I enjoyed our chat last night in the bar, and I'd like to get better acquainted. Do you have plans for breakfast tomorrow?"

"No, other than trying to digest tonight's feast. Why do you ask?"

"Well, let's meet in the Terrace Café and have a light breakfast since the chef is probably going to put us through another culinary ordeal tomorrow night," said Phil with a laugh.

"Great," said Arthur. "Let's say seven forty-five, to beat the crowd?"

"Perfect," said Phil. "See you then." He noticed Carol had a puzzled look on her face as she watched the two of them talking.

"Excuse me for a minute," said Arthur. "I left my glasses on the table. I'll be right back."

"Hey, everybody, it's still early. What do you say we go upstairs to the Sea View and have a nightcap?" asked Don.

"Great idea," said Eddie. "They have music—a good way to wrap up the evening."

"I'm in as long as we make it the ultimate one. I'm going to work out at the fitness center in the morning," said Phil. "Carol?"

She nodded.

Melissa said, "I'll go, but not if it's going to be the ultimate drink."

Everyone looked at her quizzically. "In Spain you have your ultimate drink just before you die, so you always order the penultimate as a nightcap."

They all laughed and agreed. Nicole looked a little confused, and just then Arthur returned with his glasses. "Ready to go to bed?"

She said, "No. The gang decided we'd go upstairs and have a penalternate drink."

"A what?" he asked.

"A penalternate," she explained. "You have to do that or you die or something."

Melissa took Arthur by the arm, steered him toward the elevator, and laughingly explained. He smiled and said, "That's why I love her."

The group found a table for eight, ordered after-dinner drinks, and sat back to enjoy the music of the small jazz combo playing music from the fifties. Phil noticed again that Carol and Nicole sat together and talked.

10:30 p.m.

"It's getting late for these old bones," said Arthur when the band took a break. "I think I'll pack it in."

"I'm right behind you," said Phil. "Six o'clock comes mighty early, so I'm going to have to sleep fast."

They signed for their drinks, said good night, and took the elevators to their rooms.

————

DaY FOUR

April 10

7:30 a.m., Kings Wharf, Bermuda
Stateroom 735

Melissa woke up to the aroma of percolating coffee and saw Eddie, already dressed, bent over his computer at the desk. "Good morning," he said cheerfully, looking up from his work.

"You're up early," she said sleepily.

"I got some good ideas while I was lying in bed this morning and couldn't wait to capture them. Coffee?"

"Yes, please, I'll be right out." She went into the bathroom, splashed water on her face, and brushed her teeth. As she put on the fluffy white robe with the Imperial insignia, she felt a sensation of happiness that her husband was apparently making progress with his writing. He'd unsuccessfully tried to conceal his frustration from her, but she knew how upset he was. In their forty years of marriage, she'd become tuned to his moods.

When she came out of the bathroom, he handed her a cup of coffee with the cream and sugar already added. "Thank you, my love. Can I read what you've written?"

"No," he said, putting his hand across the computer screen. "Hemingway wouldn't allow Scott Fitzgerald to read an edited draft of *A Sun Also Rises* when they lived in Paris."

"But he wasn't sleeping with Fitzgerald, was he?"

"No, but letting anyone see your writing before it's ready is a recipe for disaster."

"Whatever," she said. "I was just trying to be supportive by showing an interest in your work. Do you mind if I turn on the TV to get the daily schedule?"

"Go right ahead. It won't bother me."

She tuned to Pat Higgins's enthusiastic morning report, and after a few minutes, Eddie joined her on the couch. Eddie found it to be a welcome diversion to keep him from the unfruitful task of trying to write something meaningful.

When Melissa saw him pouring himself another cup of coffee, preparing to settle in for a long siege of watching TV, she turned off the set. "I'll not play Zelda to your Scott and be responsible for you not working," she said.

"Are you suggesting a party?" he asked with a grin.

"No, I'm going to the pool so you can work on those good ideas you talked about earlier. I'll meet you for lunch after my massage." She put on her bathing suit, kissed him on the forehead, and left with her book in hand.

Eddie went back to the desk, turned on the computer, and read, "*Fulfillment after Fifty: How to Retire Happier.*" He liked the change in the title from happy to happier. He thought, "If I just say happy, I'm implying that my readers aren't already happy. That could be insulting. I don't want to insult people." His thinking went along those lines, and he coupled that with daydreaming about nothing in particular. His watch read just after nine. "I can't work in dead silence," he thought. "I'll go up to the top deck, where there'll be some other people and a little background noise. After all, Hemingway used to sit in a café in Paris to write. That must be the secret."

He picked up his laptop and headed to the fourteenth deck. At the Sea View, he found a table with no one around, put down his computer, and went to the buffet for a croissant and a cup of coffee.

When he got back to his table, there was a bald man with a gray goatee at the next table reading a book.

"Good morning," he said pleasantly, with an English accent.

"Good morning," replied Eddie. "I notice you're reading *A Farewell to Arms*. My wife and I were just talking about Hemingway this morning."

"Yes, I like his writing. I've read most everything he's written."

"I admire his writing style," said Eddie. "I'm trying to write a book myself and would like to be, if not the next Papa Hemingway, at least be compared to him."

"Really," said the stranger, holding out his hand. "Ron Champion."

"Eddie Townsend," he said, shaking Ron's hand.

"How's your writing going?"

"Not too well. I'm a little stuck right now. I'm wondering if it's worth it. I'm retired, and I don't need the money from book sales to live on."

Ron laughed and said, "Don't worry about having tax problems from sales of your books. It's not a way to get rich."

"You sound as though you know what you're talking about," said Eddie.

"I do. I've written three books. I sold some, but there are other reasons for writing. One of them is for the opportunities that present themselves," he said.

"What kind of opportunities?" Eddie asked.

"Let me tell you a short story," Ron said, putting down his book. "My first book was called *Build Your Own Sports Car for as Little as £250*. After it was published, I received a phone call one day from a fellow with an impeccably proper British accent. He said, 'Good morning, Mr. Champion. I'm an aide to the Duke of Edinburgh.'

"I thought to myself that it must be one of my friends having me on, but he continued. 'Mr. Champion, His Royal Highness would like to invite you to come to Buckingham Palace for a visit with him.' I asked him why the Duke of Edinburgh would want to meet me.

"The aide went on to explain, 'For the past number of years, His Royal Highness has presented the Duke of Edinburgh Award Certificate of Achievement to hundreds of deserving young boys and girls, for accomplishing a series of leadership projects. One of the projects is an elective of the applicant's choice. For the past few years, an unusually large number of those young people have built one of your cars as their project. His Highness is not familiar with your work, and he asked me to find you and invite you to come by for a visit.'

"Well, of course I would go. He went on to tell me that the visit would last for only five minutes, and there was a protocol to be observed, which he would send to me so I could be prepared. When I received it a few days later, it informed me that the meeting was to be conducted standing up. I was to stand on a predesignated spot, about one meter from the duke, with my hands behind my back. He would speak first and extend his hand, and then I could bring my hand around, shake his, and return it to behind my back, where it was to remain for the rest of the five-minute visit.

"When the day came, I arrived at Buckingham Palace early to be sure I was on time. Showing my identification, I was ushered into the palace. The aide greeted me and went over the protocol one more time, took me into the room where the meeting was to take place, and showed me the spot—there was an actual spot—where I was to stand. He reminded me to be sure to stay on my spot until the duke left. 'Don't turn your back to him. He'll indicate the meeting is over when he says goodbye and turns and walks out. After his door closes, you're free to turn around and leave. And don't worry; the duke is a nice man.'

"Right on time, the duke entered through a door on the opposite side of the room. He came toward me, smiled, reached out to shake my hand, and said, 'Good morning, Mr. Champion. I'm so glad you were able to come.'

"He explained his reason for inviting me was because of the projects the young applicants were doing. He'd received at least thirty from young people who'd read my book and built their own race cars. He said he wanted to learn more so he could talk intelligently to these recipients when presenting their awards. He said, 'I can talk about agriculture or construction projects, but I know nothing about building a race car. How do you go about it?'

"Well, I told him how my son James and I built the first car. I can't talk without using my hands, so I was gesturing and moving off my spot to illustrate and explain my points. He was genuinely interested and would periodically ask questions. 'Now, how do you do that, Mr. Champion?'

"I interrupted him. 'Please, call me Ron.'

"He said, 'Well, all right then, uh, Ron.' I noticed that he didn't invite me to call him Phil.

"By this time, we'd gone well past our five minutes. In fact, at least fifteen minutes had elapsed when he said, 'Mr. Champion, er, uh, Ron, would you like a drink?'

"I said, 'Yes, please, I'd like a lager.'

"'Well, all right then,' he said, and turning to the aide, asked, 'Do we have any lager around here?'

"'I'm sure we can find some, sir.'

"'Would you bring one for Mr. Champion? And I'll have a sherry.'

"The aide disappeared and returned about five minutes later with beer and sherry. We continued our conversation and finished our drinks.

"'Well, I must be going now,' the duke said. I began to turn when I remembered the protocol and stopped myself.

"As we shook hands, he said, 'Ron, I wonder if you might do me a favor.'

"'Certainly. What is it?'

"'I have a group of young naval officers at the navy training establishment at *Gosport* who have also been building your cars. I wonder if you would be kind enough to go down there and speak to them.'

"I said of course I'd do it. I'm an Englishman, and if the Royal Family asked me to do something, I couldn't refuse.

"'Thank you,' he said. 'I'll have my aide make the arrangements and contact you. I must be going now. Oh, one other thing. My wife is the patron of the Royal Girls School in Havant. Several of the girls there are building your cars and have been having problems with the brakes. Could you stop by there on your way back from *Gosport* and help them? It's on your way.'

"Well, yes, I allowed if the Queen of England needed me, I was available. So the arrangements were made. I went to HMS *Gosport* and was treated royally. I stayed in a suite reserved for visiting dignitaries, and I spoke to two hundred cadets and had dinner with the commanding officer. The next day, I drove to the Royal School and spoke to the girls and helped solve the brake problem.

"Eddie, my point is, *none* of this would have happened if I hadn't pushed myself to write that book. When you stretch yourself like this, all kinds of opportunities open up. From that experience, I gained the confidence to go on to write two more books."

Eddie observed that Ron's eyes were shining, and he positively exuded enthusiasm, as people do when they talk about their passion. Ron looked at his watch and said, "I must go now. I want to send a couple of emails before I meet some of the chaps from my group for lunch."

Eddie said, "Before you get away, let me ask you why you are participating in this seminar, Ron."

"Fair question. Since writing the books, I haven't found another interest that fired me up as that did. I need to set some new goals, and I'm hoping the seminar will provide the impetus for me to do so.

"There's one other thing I must tell you," he said. "The first time I visited Rome, I went to the Vatican. The highlight was the tour of the Sistine Chapel. A huge group was escorted through to the magnificent, awe-inspiring room. The guards were unsuccessful in their constant attempts to quiet everyone by reminding us all that we were in a holy place. As I looked up at the ceiling and viewed Michelangelo's frescoes, my eyes fixed on the center-most scene in which Adam is reaching up his finger to be touched by God to gain the spark of life. That scene remained vivid in my mind for years, and even though I've seen pictures of it, before and since, the actual experience of being there impacted me so dramatically as to leave a lasting emotional impression on me.

"My point is that everyone has creativity within them. My realization from all of this is that one of the most important sources of direction and guidance, at any stage of our lives, comes from that still, quiet voice that speaks to us when we are sitting and listening.

"So I don't think that it is any accident that you feel your compulsion to write. That inspiration came from someplace. Listen to it and stick with it. The most important question any writer, or for that matter, anyone can ask themselves is, 'Why am I doing this—this art, this craft, this work?' The answer to that question will propel you to do the things you need to do to achieve your goal. If one has a strong enough reason, they will succeed. In fact, I've discovered that the *why* is more important than the *what* or the *how*. Good luck."

They shook hands, and Ron left.

Eddie sat for a long time in deep thought. "There's a lot of wisdom in what Ron had to say, and I want that kind of enthusiasm. Maybe I need to ask myself his *why* question." Right there, Eddie's quest took a whole new direction. He didn't want to just sell books and make money. He wanted to make a difference in people's lives. That was his *why*. That was why he really wanted to be a writer.

"Maybe," he thought, "the lesson for everyone in retirement is to find something that fires them up the way Ron was fired up about those books."

He remembered reading a quotation by Helen Keller that seemed to fit with the experience he'd just had with Ron: "Life is either a great adventure or nothing."

He looked at his own watch and realized he had just enough time to dress and meet Melissa for lunch, so he picked up his unopened computer and hurried back to his stateroom. He felt like a changed man, a man who now had what he was looking for if, and this was a big if, he could overcome the inner demons of sloth, laziness, procrastination, and the self-doubts that always showed up anytime he contemplated doing anything big—things that had always paralyzed him in the past.

————

8:30 a.m., the Celebrity Theater

Don and Inga waited to hear the color yellow called, their signal to disembark for their shore excursion. Fifteen minutes later, they joined eighty other passengers being relieved of their identification cards by the purser at the gangway. They boarded one of the buses that took them on a four-hour tour of the southern shores, a scenic drive along beautiful pink beaches and a stop at Gibbs Hill Lighthouse for a photo op. Then it was on to the Royal Naval Dockyard, where they visited the Maritime Museum and had time to explore on their own before returning to the ship for lunch.

They ate alone in the Terrace Café and talked about the adventures of the morning, the pictures they'd taken, and how excited the children were going to be when they heard all about the trip. After lunch, they went to their cabin for a relaxing afternoon sitting on their private terrace reading, then taking naps. Just before he dozed off, Don sighed and said, "Life just doesn't get any better than this." Inga agreed and drifted into a relaxing sleep in the lounge chair looking out over the harbor.

————

7:45 a.m., the Terrace Café

Arthur was already waiting when Phil joined him at the table in the Terrace Café. "Good, I'm glad I had the time right," said Arthur. "Since I retired I've gotten a little casual about my appointments."

"I wrote it down when I got to my room last night," said Phil. "I don't know why I still do that. Just habit I guess. I have several friends who don't wear watches now that they're retired. Maybe I should try that."

They studied the menus for a short time. "What looks good to you?" asked Phil.

"Just fruit and toast for me. Nickie and I are going into town, so we'll have a salad for lunch there. I want to eat light since we're going to L'Auberge tonight."

"Sounds good to me," said Phil, closing his menu. "We're going on an island tour at nine thirty."

The waiter took their orders and asked if they wanted anything to drink. "Coffee, please," said Arthur.

"Make it two," said Phil, handing back his menu. He noticed the waiter's name tag. "Istvan. I haven't seen that name before. Is it Polish?"

"No, it's Hungarian. I suppose my name tag should say Stephen. That's the English version."

"Well, nice to meet you, Istvan," said Phil, careful to pronounce his name properly. "We'll be seeing you for the next week or so."

When the smiling Istvan left the table, Arthur said, "I'm glad you invited me. I've wanted to say something to you."

"What's that?" asked Phil, looking at him closely. He wondered if Arthur had noticed his obvious appreciation of Nicole's beauty. After all, Carol had seen it right away. But after last night, that problem was in the past, or was it?

"That thing you just did with the waiter, uh ... Istvan," said Arthur. "Talking to him, learning his name, finding out that he is Hungarian, and his name means Stephen in English. That's what I'm talking about. You and Eddie both are so at ease with people, and you put them at ease as well. I envy you both for that ability. I don't have it."

"Wow, that surprises me. From what Nicole said, you are president of a couple of organizations and head of a health clinic in Des Moines. You must be pretty good with people to get elected to those positions."

"You'd think so, but I know I'm given credit for a lot of things I don't deserve because of my family's reputation. Yes, I've been president of our local Rotary Club, the country club, and I served one term as mayor. I've always been a shy person and wouldn't have pursued those activities on my own."

Istvan brought their fruit and coffee. Phil wanted to stay away from the topic of Nicole, so he asked, "Did you always want to be a doctor?"

"No," Arthur laughed. "Far from it, but my grandfather and my father were both highly respected physicians in Des Moines. They always expected me to go to medical school and follow in their footsteps."

"What about brothers and sisters? Did they ...?"

"None," interrupted Arthur. "I was an only child. The only hope of a third generation of Dr. Gibsons in Des Moines rested on my shoulders."

"Didn't they ever ask you what you wanted to do?"

"No. It was always assumed that I'd want the same thing they wanted. When I was five years old, they even had me sign a pledge in one of their medical books that I would become a doctor. Can you imagine?"

"What would you have become if not a doctor?"

"You'll laugh," said Arthur. "I would have liked to become a musician. Not a classical musician. That would have been a little more acceptable to my family. But I loved jazz, and not just the music. The bohemian lifestyle would have been my ideal of the way to live. I went to medical school in Chicago, and I used to go to the jazz clubs when I should have been studying. I'd stay late and listen to some of the legends playing the cool sounds of the fifties."

"But you stayed the course and became a doctor?"

"A surgeon, and a pretty good one."

"How do you account for that? I mean, being a good surgeon when it was not your passion. Most of the people I've talked to who have excelled in their work were passionate about it."

"I think surgery is a lot like music, and the body is like a musical piece. When I was operating, I could see my interaction with the flow of the body like a musician playing a melodic riff. That turned the whole thing into an exciting, inspiring, and enjoyable experience. If I hadn't had that, I'd never have been able to practice for thirty years."

"Do you play an instrument?"

"Yes, but not well. I play the tenor sax. Do you know the name Charlie Parker?"

"The Bird, of course."

"Well, he was my hero. I always wanted to play with his skill, so I took lessons and practiced, but I was never able to devote the necessary time. In his book *Outliers*, Malcolm Gladwell declared that ten thousand hours was the minimum amount of time to become an expert at anything. During medical school and while I interned, I played for my own enjoyment."

"Do you still have your axe?" asked Phil, using the term musicians use for their instrument.

"I have it, but I put it away a long time ago. My grandfather called it foolishness. He felt that anything that was not related to studying or working at medicine was a waste of time."

"How does Nicole feel about you not playing?"

"She doesn't even know that I used to play. I did play when my wife was alive. She and I spent some great evenings listening to jazz and occasionally playing. She played guitar. We weren't too bad, although we never played outside the house, just for ourselves."

"I didn't know you were married before. What happened to your first wife?"

"Cancer, twenty years ago. Actually, she wasn't my first wife. She was my only wife. Nicole and I never married, although I always introduce her as my wife. Des Moines is a conservative city, and our church is old-fashioned. We've only been together for ten years."

"How did you two meet?"

"She was a flight attendant and I was flying back and forth from Des Moines to Chicago and one thing led to another and here we are."

"Do you have children?" asked Phil, his head buzzing with this latest piece of news about Nicole's marital status.

"No, my wife and I were unable to have any, and Nicole didn't want any."

"You've had an interesting and successful life, Arthur. If a young person was to come to you today and ask you for advice on living a successful life, what would you tell him or her?"

"I don't know that my life has been all that successful, but I know for sure what I'd advise them not to do."

"What's that?"

"I'd say, don't let anybody else decide your future. Find out what you love to do and do it. Even if you fail at it, you would have failed following your own path and singing your own song."

"Like you and your musical career, right?"

Arthur nodded and said, "In that sense, I don't think I've been as successful as I would have liked. I think so many other people, like you and Eddie, have led more successful lives."

"Arthur, I think we get the things we deserve in life, and I also think we don't give ourselves enough credit for the strengths we have."

"Do you think that's true for everybody?" asked Arthur.

"I don't know for sure, but I'd say yes, at least at some level. I'm always comparing myself to others and coming up short in my own estimation. As an example, I've always felt inferior to people who, like you, are better educated and in positions of power and authority. I just don't feel that I deserve to be on the same level with you."

"That's ironic. Here we are, each feeling that the other is better than we are."

"It's a little like *The Wizard of Oz*, isn't it?"

"It's not just strengths in others that we envy. It's everything. Possessions and even families. Take Nickie as an example ..."

Just then, Istvan came to the table and asked, "How is your fruit? Do you need more coffee?"

"No, I'm okay. Phil, how about you?"

"Uh, I, er, uh, guess not. No, I'm fine," stumbled Phil. His mind raced over Arthur's "take Nickie" comment. "What did he mean by that? What does he know or suspect? Is this the real reason he'd agreed so readily to meet me and the reason he's been so candid? God, the last thing I need right now is some kind of jealous husband confrontation while I'm trying to get things right with Carol."

"Well, it's getting to be time to meet Nickie to go ashore," said Arthur, when Istvan left the table. He shook Phil's hand. "This has been great. I enjoyed our chat. Have a good time on the tour. I'll see you and Carol in the bar this evening. Nicole and I will be there promptly at six."

Phil was still rattled and mumbled, "Ah, right. Six o'clock. Be there or be square."

"What?" said Arthur.

"Oh nothing. Just a dumb expression. See you then."

4:00 p.m., the Sea View
Afternoon Tea

The room was already teeming with guests as white-coated waiters scurried around carrying trays of little sandwiches and pushing carts with coffee and a wide assortment of tea. Melissa and Eddie found a small table for two by the window overlooking the harbor. They passed a large table in the center of the serving area, laden with freshly made finger sandwiches, colorful *petit fours,* and richly textured scones with a large crock of clotted cream nearby.

Four attractive Romanian women formed the string quartet that sat on the small stage in the middle of the room. They played light classical music, which added to the overall ambiance of elegance that permeated the room.

"Good afternoon," said the waiter. "May I bring you a cocktail?"

"Not for me, thank you," said Eddie. "Sweetheart, how about you?"

"No, thanks, I'm driving," she said, smiling.

"I beg your pardon?" said the waiter.

"Ignore her. We'll both have some tea."

"Right away, sir." He seemed happy to get away from the demented American woman.

"You must try to get a handle on your insanity, dahling," he said playfully.

"I can't help myself. This luxury vacation thing brings out the, oh, the *je ne sais quoi* in me."

"I know what it is. Insanity," he said with a laugh.

A different waiter, probably one who drew the short straw, brought their tea with a small plate of finger sandwiches. He asked if there was anything else he could bring them.

"No, thanks," said Eddie. "She's driving."

"Pardon?" asked the uncomprehending waiter.

"Don't pay any attention to him," she said seriously. "He's, like,"—she pointed her finger to her head and made a circular motion—"intelligence impaired."

"Oh, thank you, madam," he said, backing away from the table.

"Now you've done it. I'll never get any of these people to wait on me for the rest of the voyage," he said, laughing.

"That might not be a bad thing, given the way you are eating on this cruise," she said, smiling.

At that moment, an attractive young Scandinavian woman with a model's figure pushed her dessert cart up to their table and asked, "Would you care for anything from the dessert selection?"

"Oh, just in time," said Eddie. "I'm starving. I haven't had a decent meal since I got on this ship."

"Well, I can understand that," she said, playing along. "The food isn't so good, is it?"

"Speaking of food," said Melissa. "We'd better hold off. We only have an hour before we meet the gang."

"Right. I think we'll pass on your goodies," he said.

"Well, I'm off to speak to the chef to see if I can persuade him to do something about the quality of the food for the balance of the cruise."

They all three laughed as she left.

"Thank you dahling, for passing on her goodies. I think you made a wise decision," she said with mock sternness. "We'd better get back and change for dinner."

"You're welcome, dahling." Back in their stateroom, he said, "You know what I'd like to do tonight?"

"Oh, not tonight. I'll probably have a headache," she said, laughing.

"You're just saying that because Heidi, or whatever her name is, flirted with me and flaunted her goodies at me. But I'm glad you've got the headache thingy because I was going to suggest we go to the show in the theater after dinner. Now I won't have to worry about you wanting to get me back here right away to satisfy your insatiable appetite for a mad, passionate romp."

"Well, I don't have a headache now," she said, as she approached him with her lips puckered.

As he reached for her, she laughingly pushed him away and said, "No way, we have to be in the bar in forty-five minutes."

"You vixen! Just for that I might not take you to the show."

"Oh yes you will," she said, selecting a dress from the closet. "It's too late for you to get another date."

"You're right, and anyway, if you won't have me, I doubt anyone else will. Except maybe Heidi, and she probably has to work," he said with a mocking pout.

They both laughed and finished dressing, and at 5:50 went down to the Porthole to meet the team.

————

6:00 p.m., the Porthole Piano Bar

A smiling Phil and Carol walked in holding hands right at six o'clock. Don said, "Now we're all here and accounted for. Sven, let's have some champagne. Not the expensive stuff I drink, that's too good for this bunch." Sven looked puzzled.

"Ignore him, Sven. He knows not whereof he speaks. Bring the usual Veuve Clicquot and seven glasses, none for him," said Eddie, pointing to Don. "He doesn't deserve any."

By now, Sven could see the banter was all in good fun. He enjoyed his favorite guests. He brought two bottles of the Clicquot, seven glasses, and served everyone but Don.

"Hey, don't pay attention to him," said Don. "He's not up for living the good life like the rest of us." That brought groans from the group. "Bring me a glass right now, my good man."

Sven produced a hidden glass, and everyone laughed.

"Where are we having dinner this evening?" asked Carol. "It's hard to keep up."

"At L'Auberge, honey, and our reservation is for six thirty. They'll have some good champagne there," said her husband, winking at Don.

"I had an interesting experience today," said Arthur. "I had breakfast with Phil before we went ashore."

"That's it?" asked Don. "You have dinner with him every night. What did he tell you that he hasn't already told all of us?"

"Well, he didn't tell me anything, but I told him how much I envy his ability, and Eddie's too, to meet people and deal with them so effectively."

"What brought that up?" asked Nicole.

"I just noticed that in the time we've all been together the two of them are good with people. That name-remembering thing that Eddie did the first evening we were together is an example."

"Yes, that was great. I've been practicing those ideas ever since," said Carol, "and I've met some interesting people as a result."

"And today," Arthur continued, "the waiter at the Terrace Café was named Estefan, whose name is Stephen in English, and he is from Hungary, right?" he asked, looking at Phil.

Phil nodded and made a point of not correcting him for not getting Istvan's name exactly right. He knew that detail was not germane to the story and pointing it out would only make Arthur feel less secure. Phil observed that many people only corrected others to make themselves feel important.

"So that was the part I found so interesting. When Estefan left the table, he was smiling, and he gave us exceptional service for the rest of lunch. That is a special skill the two of them possess that I could use."

In the meantime, Inga had her notebook out and was jotting down the key ideas she was picking up from Arthur's report.

"I can't help but feel that skill has to become more important as we go into our retirement years," said Don. "We are meeting people in different milieus in a changing world."

"What's a 'mill you'?" drawled Nicole.

"An environment or a social setting," answered Carol.

"Why do you feel it is more important, Don?" asked Inga.

"Based on my experience in academia, when I was with peers in my field, we had a lot to talk about and shared a common language. But now that I'm away from that world and am meeting people who don't share that background, it is harder to have conversations with them."

Just then Inga looked at her watch and said, "Time to go to L'Auberge before they give our table away."

"How do you want us to be seated this evening, Carol?" asked Melissa.

"Pardon?" said Carol, looking confused.

"Well, last night you moved us all around and organized the seating, so I thought we should find out what you want us to do tonight," she said, grinning.

Carol realized Melissa was playing and didn't take offense. "Oh, that was a one-off. Everybody sit wherever they want. I'm going to sit next to my husband now that I've found out from Arthur what a wonderful people-person he is."

Phil laughed and pulled out her chair. Following suit, everyone sat next to their spouse. As Phil promised earlier, to everyone's delight, Marcos the sommelier brought a bottle of Veuve Clicquot to the table. They enjoyed this with the delightful morsel known as an *amuse-bouche*. As they enjoyed this predinner ceremony, they read from the menu the delicious assortment of exotic offerings:

> Duck pâté, thick bourride with aioli
> Pepper-crusted rack of lamb
> Salmon with grilled fennel and a yellow tomato coulis
> Filet mignon with batonnet potatoes
> Dessert: frozen ginger soufflé glace.

"This all sounds delicious," said Don. The others agreed and selected their entrées. The waiter took their orders, and Marcos returned to ask if they had questions about the wine list.

Don said, "If everyone agrees, I think we should leave the choice of wine to Marcos."

This was fine with the group, and Marcos went into

sommelier-speak about "hints of peaches and lavender and an after-caress on your palate." After he left the table, Melissa labeled him a "cork dork."

While the army of waiters, bus people, and other hangers-on brought and cleared dishes and exchanged cutlery, the group chatted and relished the food and the accompanying 2009 burgundy that Marcos recommended.

8:30 p.m., After-Dinner Conversation

Over coffee and brandy, the conversation returned to the subject of people.

"Don, you said in the bar that you find it harder to have conversations with people now that you're retired," said Eddie. "Is this true for any of the rest of you?"

"It's true for me," said Arthur. "Phil and I talked about that a lot this morning, and I believe it is going to be increasingly difficult for people who are retiring now."

Carol said, "Last week I read a Wells Fargo survey that reported the majority of working people do not think that they will be able to retire at sixty-five. Three-quarters of the respondents said they expected to work during retirement, and twenty-five percent of those surveyed said they expected to work until age eighty."

"Those kinds of reports usually set off a firestorm of comments, the majority of which fall into the, 'Ain't it awful what the government has done to us,' or 'I feel overwhelmed and don't know what to do' category," said Phil. "It does seem that the Gen Xers and baby boomers can benefit from the lessons learned by the generations that have gone before. Those lessons should be included in your book, Eddie."

"They will be," said Eddie. "As a result of the interviews and surveys that I've conducted over the past three years, I find that the primary goal of retirees is peace of mind, in one form or another."

"What does that mean, 'peace of mind'?" asked Don.

"I think it is what we all want," said Inga.

"Yes," said Arthur. "I know that's what I want, and I think it boils down to financial, physical, and mental health."

"If I had peace of mind, in addition to Arthur's three conditions, I would add relationship, spiritual, and emotional balance," said Melissa.

Eddie continued. "Those are the essentials. The strategies and tactics for balancing these essentials is the subject of my book."

"I've read that there are millions of baby boomers retiring every day, and they are facing a financial and emotional crisis of epic proportions," said Arthur.

"They are. The baby boomers need help in handling the threat of these challenges. If a person retiring today defines his or her life by outdated models, they are doomed for failure and unhappiness. However, there is hope in the form of updated information that I'm including in my book. Statistically, the average baby boomer has not prepared adequately for retirement. They have not prepared for the retirement of their dreams. They are left with the choice of continuing to work, if that is possible, but not all do. Many of them have had to take early retirement or have been laid off."

"You sound passionate about wanting to help them," said Carol.

"I am. I believe it is my mandate to assist them in redefining their expectations and goals and to help them develop strategies to cope with the changing world in which they find themselves. One of the ways in which I can do this is to share examples of successful retirees that I've met and tell the stories of people who are not managing retirement well."

"Where do you get the information that will help these people?" asked Arthur.

"I'm glad you asked that," said a smiling Eddie. "I follow the surveys conducted by national organizations. I also frequently talk to friends around the country who are dealing with the challenges of retirement or have friends who are attempting to deal with them.

"During a recent phone call, a friend asked me for some advice on solving his problem. Like a lot of people, he is upside down on his mortgage. I said, 'Your problem is not your mortgage.'

"'What do you mean?' he asked.

"I told him, 'Your upside-down mortgage is a symptom of the critical factor. If your mortgage problem was solved, you would still be the person who created the problem in the first place. You have to change your approach to your finances and way of life.'

"This is why people who win the lottery are typically broke in a very short time. A million dollars wouldn't do you much good if you didn't have a millionaire's mentality."

"I agree with that," said Phil. "I invest in real estate and have sold a lot of houses to low-income people. A group of us started a savings and loan to make it possible for these people to become homeowners. I've been a student of success my whole life, and the one thing I know is that this is what many people are going to have to do if they want to improve their circumstances. They will have to break out of their comfort zones, change their way of thinking, and take on a whole new way of life. One of my favorite quotes is from the diarist Anais Nin: 'There came a time when the risk to stay tight in the bud was more painful than the risk to blossom.'"

"When being broke is more uncomfortable than making the changes necessary to get on the road to prosperity, then they'll get into action, right?" said Carol.

"I don't think it's just financial circumstances. We have to change our attitudes and behaviors," said Eddie. "We need to look at everything we are thinking and doing and ask ourselves, 'Is what I'm doing right now giving me the satisfaction and happiness I want in my life?'"

"Can you give us an example of something other than money that can give us happiness?" asked Nicole.

"Sure. There are many ways to find happiness. A group of us were sitting around the bar at our country club after a round of golf. The conversation turned to retirement. Gary, who has been retired the shortest amount of time, said, 'It's been a little over two years now, and I'm getting antsy.' Mike said, 'I'm busier now than I've ever been. I don't know how I found time to get anything done when I was working.' Gary knew that Mike played golf three days a week. He said, 'I'd like to do something more than just play golf; that would make me happy.'"

Eddie continued. "I told Gary, 'I'm hearing that a lot as I'm interviewing people for my book. Some are pursuing hobbies, and others are going back to work part time, if they can find something interesting to do. Keeping busy is not the problem. There is always plenty to do. The challenge is to be busy doing the right things, not just killing time but doing something we consider worthwhile.

"'Gary, I'm putting together a program to mentor young people. We need leaders now more than ever. There are many young people who need strong role models.'

"Gary became enthusiastic about being part of my program. 'Let me know when you are ready to move ahead with it. I did some mentoring when I was with my company, and I got a lot of satisfaction from it.'"

"I believe there are many people like Gary who would like to have the satisfaction of helping to develop young people, using the lessons that life taught them. They would like to overcome the boredom that sets in after having a busy career. I believe we each have a desire to be of service to others. Satisfying that desire is one of the main ways of achieving happiness in retirement."

Inga, as usual, had been furiously taking notes and periodically asking the others to expand on their opinions.

Carol noticed the waiter approaching their table. "I think it's time to wrap it up for tonight. Let's beat them to the punch and get out of here before they say, 'You don't want any more coffee, *do you?*'"

"Melissa and I are going to catch the show tonight. Anyone like to join us?" asked Eddie.

"Carol?" asked Phil.

"Why not? Count me in," she said with a smile.

"Not for me tonight," said Don. "I'm tired."

"Another interesting evening," said Arthur. "We'll see you tomorrow; same time, same station, right?"

After a few hugs and smiles, they split up; the Gibsons and Conways to their rooms, the Townsends and Butlers to the show at the Sea View.

———

When the two couples entered the room, the jazz ensemble was playing, and people were dancing to fifties and sixties music. "There's a table for four near the front," said Carol. The rest of the group followed as she hurried to the table. A smiling Istvan greeted them as soon as he saw them come in.

"Istvan," said Eddie. "Are you working overtime tonight?"

"No, Mr. Townsend. We all work double shifts. We get a break in-between, so I am rested and ready to take your order. What would you like to drink?"

"Ladies, what is your pleasure?"

"I think you know mine, dahling," said Melissa. "It's the same as Heidi's," she leered. "Bailey's Irish Cream, isn't it?"

"Yes, it is, but what about your headache?" he said with a straight face.

"Oh, I'll be fine," she said.

"Well, all right then. Carol?"

"I'll have the same as Heidi and Melissa."

Eddie blushed when he realized that Melissa had told Carol the whole afternoon tea story at dinner.

"Well, er, Phil?"

With a big smile, Phil said, "What kind of 'goodies' do you have? Something sweet?"

Carol and Melissa burst out laughing, and Eddie said to himself, "Bloody hell, did she tell everyone at the table?"

Still blushing, he said, "Bring me a glass of ruby port please, Istvan, and a couple of Bailey's for the giggle girls."

Phil said, "Port sounds good for me too."

When Istvan left the table, a still-laughing Melissa said, "I'm sorry, honey. That story was just too precious not to share. I didn't know that Carol was going to tell Phil."

"You didn't swear me to secrecy," said Carol. "And it sounds as though the two of you had a good time at tea time."

"Well, it *was* kind of a hoot. I don't mind you knowing about it, Carol, but Melissa couldn't have known you were going to blab it all over the ship," laughed Eddie.

"I didn't blab it all over the ship!" said Carol in mock anger. "I just told one fairly discreet individual, who probably won't say anything unless he gets drunk, as is his custom. Then he'll probably use it to make some friends in the bar, but otherwise ..."

Istvan brought their drinks, and Phil said, "Here's to absent friends."

"Let's make this our 'penalternate,'" giggled Melissa.

"Chin, chin," said Carol.

"I'll have to make this an early evening," said Eddie. "I'm meeting Heidi for a nightcap."

"In your dreams," said a smiling Melissa.

"Well, maybe I'll call her and cancel," said Eddie.

Pat Higgins stepped onstage, took the mike, and announced, "Good evening, ladies and gentlemen. We are ready for our guest entertainer tonight. She is an accomplished songwriter and singer.

She has been a popular guest artist on the *Serendipity* many times before. Please give it up for Hilly Bills."

For the next hour, Hilly strummed her guitar and sang blues and country songs to the appreciative audience.

11:00 p.m.

When Hilly took a break, the group decided to say good night if they were going to get up in time to work out in the morning.

————

Executive Suite Number 1

When Phil crawled in bed tired from the long day and the extra alcohol, he'd consumed he couldn't fall asleep. He couldn't stop thinking about his conversation with Arthur at breakfast and the news that he and Nickie were not married.

Later as he came back from his workout at the gym, unlocked the door, and walked in to his suite, he was startled to see that Nickie was lying on the bed completely naked.

"Hi," she said, smiling, as though her being there was the most natural thing in the world. "I hope you don't mind. I was hot, so I used your shower and towel."

"What are you doing here? How did you get in? What about Carol?" Phil was more than a little flustered.

"A lot of questions, Phil. You know what I'm doing here, or at least I think you can figure it out by my attire or the lack thereof."

He couldn't take his eyes off of her. Her body was everything that he'd been fantasizing about for the past week and more.

"I told the room attendant we are throwing a surprise birthday party for you while I carried in a bouquet of flowers I'd pinched off the piano in the lobby. That's them on the dresser. I thought they'd add to the romantic ambiance. There's also a bottle of champagne in the ice bucket. Why don't you pour us a couple of glasses and get undressed and join me here?"

"Carol?"

"Your wife went on shore to go on an all-day sightseeing excursion, so she won't be back until after four this afternoon." She licked her lips and arched her back suggestively as she rolled over and propped herself up on one elbow.

He kept staring, now physically aroused. "You don't think this is a little bit dangerous? Where's your husband? What if a crew member walks in? What if one of the other members of our team shows up? How would we explain ourselves?"

"Again with the questions. Are you going to get undressed and climb in here with me, or do I have to get up and take another shower—a cold one this time? The whole team went on that same tour, including Arthur. So we'll be undisturbed all day. Besides, if it were a little bit dangerous, wouldn't that make it all the more exciting?"

He didn't make any kind of movement toward her, although God knows he wanted to. "I don't know if this is a good idea," he said, weakly backing away from the bed.

She pulled the sheet over her body and said angrily, "Look, you're the one who started this with your leers and witty, suggestive stories. We both know this is what we've wanted from that first dinner together when you undressed me with your eyes. Thinking about you and being with you is all I could think about, and I know it's been the same for you."

He couldn't deny that, even to himself. He had never cheated on Carol before, although he'd had plenty of opportunities. He had always been an admirer of the female form and had remembered what Jimmy Carter said in his ill-advised *Playboy* interview: "I've looked on a lot of women with lust. I've committed adultery in my heart many times."

In his reverie, a line from the old Frankie Laine song "It's a Necessary Evil" came to mind: "A man sometimes must take a sip of the grape and cast his eye on a lovely shape. If a man says he don't, then he's not a man, he's a liar."

But this was different. Nickie was the embodiment of all the qualities that any man going through a midlife crisis would want. Not only was she the hottest woman he'd ever seen, she wanted him in the worst way. He smiled to himself as he remembered the old joke about the definition of the worst way to have sex: standing up in a hammock during a windstorm.

She pulled the sheet back and pouted. "It's lonely in here, and I am really horny. Come on, please."

By this time his manhood was pulsating furiously and taking over his thinking. He went to the cabin door to hang the sign out. He laughed to himself as he read "Do Not Disturb." "Too late," he thought to himself. "I'm already disturbed."

And he was as he woke up and turned to see Carol, still sleeping beside him.

"A dream. It was only a dream," he said to himself as he got up and made his way to the bathroom.

Day Five

April 11

Eddie impatiently waited for Melissa, holding their green shore-excursion cards. They'd selected the Quintessential Bermuda & St. Georges tour. Pat Higgins announced that it was time for the green card holders to report to the fifth deck for loading into the coaches. Eddie allowed everyone to go ahead, and at the door he met Melissa on her way in. "Just in time," he said. "If you hadn't made it, there is a hot, single blond girl up ahead who was looking hopefully at me when she saw me sitting alone."

"It's a good thing I got here then," she said sarcastically. They showed their identification cards to the purser. "I saved her from having to listen to you complain about your wife taking too long to do your laundry this morning and how you had to endure the hardship of having everything taken care of for you all the time."

"Okay, okay, I'm sorry. I forgot that's what you were doing. I was so busy ordering room service for you to make sure you were properly fed, that detail slipped my mind."

"No problem. We're here now, and it is going to be a great day, now that you have clean clothes."

"Okay, okay. I get it. Truce?"

She kissed him and said, "Truce. Let's have a good time today."

The coach set off through Bermuda's parishes to St. Georges. They walked the cobblestoned streets of the quaint old town, visited some of the historic buildings, and stopped in at one of the numerous pubs along the way. Rejoining the coach, they made a brief stop to take photos of the unique pink sand beaches for which Bermuda is famous. "These will be great to show the kids when we get home," said Melissa.

"Yeah, I bet they'll be jealous." He laughed.

When the coach arrived back at the ship, they headed up to their cabin for an afternoon of reading and relaxation.

"How about if we just order room service for lunch?" asked Eddie.

"Works for me," she said. "How about a nice salad? We'll have dinner in a few hours."

"Great," he said, picking up the phone.

———

12:30 p.m., the Terrace Café

When Phil and Carol walked into the Terrace Café for lunch, Arthur and Nicole were just being seated and waved them over.

Arthur wore a stern, serious look, and Phil noticed casually that Nicole wore white short shorts, a tight-fitting hot-pink jersey top, accompanied by a large gold necklace and jewel-encrusted sandals.

The women hugged one another, which deepened Phil's mystery about Carol's friendship with Nicole. He knew that his appreciation of other women did not go unnoticed by Carol. He cursed himself for his lifelong habit of flirting with other women.

"Do you think it is ever too late to set goals?" asked Arthur. "I'm sixty-five, and I've pretty much accomplished everything that was expected of me."

"Well, I'd like to give that some thought because I have two conflicting opinions on that subject."

Arthur barely heard him. He was remembering their conversation of the day before when he'd told Phil about his tenor sax experience. He was wondering if a sixty-five-year-old retired surgeon could recapture the enthusiasm of the twenty-five-year-old intern. What would Nicole think? She'd only known him to be a straitlaced professional. "Pardon?" he said.

Carol said, "I said, I think Phil's idea is a good one."

"I'm sorry. I had a senior moment and drifted off. What was it again?"

Nicole said, "He made the suggestion that we bring up the topic at dinner and get everyone's comments."

"Oh, good. I'll go along with that. What should we have for lunch?"

"Those dinners are so heavy, I don't feel like having too much," said Nicole. "How about just a salad?"

"Or I could share a BLT with you," said Carol.

"Perfect!" she said, closing her menu.

Istvan came to the table and asked, "Is everyone ready to order?" He couldn't help staring at Nicole.

Everyone except Arthur noticed Istvan's behavior. Phil wondered if Nicole dressed that way intentionally, and Carol knew that she did.

"Oh, Istvan, these beautiful women are our wives. This is Carol, and this is ... ah, ah, Arthur, you remember this lady's name, don't you?" They all laughed, remembering Arthur and Nicole's class reunion experience.

"Yes, Esteban, this is my wife, Clarissa, er, I mean, Nicole." This brought more laughter from the others. A confused, red-faced Istvan did not notice that Arthur got his name wrong.

They talked throughout the meal about the morning and what they'd been doing and some of the people they'd met.

"It's two o'clock. Time for my afternoon nap, so I can stay awake through dinner," said Arthur.

"You're not going to the wine tasting this afternoon?" asked Carol.

"No, I want to save myself for the cocktail hour," said Arthur.

"Carol and I are going so that I can acquire a little more culture," said Phil.

"A little more culture, darling?" she said as she took his arm. "A little more would imply that there was already some in place."

"Oh right," he said, putting his knuckle up to his nose and pretending to pick it. They laughed as they said their goodbyes and reminded one another of the six o'clock cocktail get-together at the Porthole Bar.

"Be there or be square," said Arthur.

"What?" said Nicole.

"Never mind," laughed Phil. "Your husband is weird."

4:00 p.m., the Sea View, the Wine Tasting

Phil and Carol searched for Eddie and Melissa among the twenty-five people examining the sparkling variety of wine glasses on the long oak table.

"Over here!" called Melissa, peering around the shining silver buckets and small pitchers of water scattered down the table.

Jokingly, Phil pointed out, "In my old neighborhood, we drank every drop in our glass; no need for buckets for undrunk wine."

Trays of cheese and crackers were plentiful, and each person was reading a place mat with the names of the five wines to be tasted.

After a few minutes of chatting and introductions, Pat Higgins approached the head of the table and cheerfully announced, "Ladies and gentlemen, may I have your attention, please?"

"Doesn't that man ever sleep?" whispered Carol to Melissa. "He's everywhere."

"In a moment I'd like to introduce today's presenter, the wine connoisseur from *Wine Spectator* magazine. First, though, I'd like to acknowledge Imperial's sommeliers, who will be assisting him." Pat then introduced the sommeliers, all of whom had served the guests during previous dinners. "Now," he continued, "Imperial Cruise lines is proud to present to you the head of wine analysis and wine rating for *Wine Spectator* magazine, a true connoisseur, Mr. Jose Silva!"

"Good afternoon, everyone. Please join me in a toast to good wine and good food everywhere with a glass of 1999 Dom Perignon." The sommeliers moved quickly around the table, filling each person's glass.

"I guess I'd better be the note-taker since Inga's not here," said Melissa, smiling and taking her pen from her purse and preparing to make notes on her place mat.

"The first wine we'll taste is from the Loire Valley in France. It is a Sancerre by Comte Lafond de Ladoucette. You'll be able to detect pear and citrus flavors, primarily grapefruit, and a bit of smokiness. It is a well-balanced and food-friendly wine."

"What does this sell for?" asked a balding man wearing wire-rimmed glasses.

Looking at his notes, Jose answered, "That would typically retail for about eighty-three dollars. It's worth every penny, wouldn't you agree?"

"I would if I still have eighty-three dollars left after this cruise," the man joked, drawing laughter from the group.

"This next wine is one of my favorites. It is a 2010 Far Niente chardonnay from Oakville, in the Napa Valley in California."

Jose explained that they should examine the wine for "tears," the white wine equivalent of "legs" in red wines, then inhale the scent of the various fragrances.

"This wine has an alcohol content of fourteen point three percent," Jose said, and Phil wondered if it was time to take a slug to see what it tasted like. "Now take a sip and notice the taste of the oak and butter on the finish." Phil took a generous sip, polishing off his glass in one gulp.

Sophisticated Melissa was a true connoisseur of good wine. In order to keep from embarrassing her in public, her husband, Eddie, had learned over the years to follow his wife's lead and say "Mmm" when she did. Every once in a while, she'd out him by saying "Mmm" to some bad wine, and he'd get caught saying it too. That's when she'd remind him that he only recognized two kinds of wine: yum and yuck. Then they'd both laugh. He made no pretense of being at her level of sophistication.

Jose continued. "To the gentleman who is concerned about not having enough money for the Sancerre, this will be a shock. This wine retails for about one hundred twenty dollars.

"Let's turn our attention to a 2007 Costasera Masi Amorane Classico DOCG. This wine is from the Veneto region of Italy and has an alcohol content of fifteen point five percent. It should be opened at least two hours before drinking in order to breathe. This wine is much better with food, so before you taste it, have a little cheese to prepare your palate. Now, before you taste, notice the rich, dark ruby-red color."

As they swirled, sniffed, and looked for the legs, Jose instructed them to be aware of the "basket of fruit" in the flavors. "There will be plums and cherries and also the flavor of coffee and cocoa."

Eddie nodded with what he hoped was a knowledgeable look as he sipped from his glass. He threw a sidelong glance at Melissa to be sure that his response was appropriate. Phil knocked his glass back and smiled at Carol as she shook her head in disbelief at his loutish behavior.

"That wine, by the way, retails for one hundred twenty-five dollars," said Jose.

"Is that for a case?" asked the balding, so-called wine aficionado, causing Carol to be somewhat more appreciative of Phil. Jose only smiled as Baldy's friends laughed.

"Here's a wine I like, from Cakebread Cellars Vine Hill Ranch, once again, in the Napa Valley. From the quaint little town of Rutherford, it contains eighty-five percent cabernet sauvignon grapes. At one hundred fifty dollars, it is a little spendy and might be reserved for special occasions for most of us, but it is certainly worth it," he said as he pointedly looked at Baldy. "It's a 2009 vintage and should also be decanted about two hours before serving to allow it to open and breathe properly. If you order it, ask for bin number two twenty-one."

"Finally, for after dinner, from Portugal, we'll taste a vintage port, the 1991 Ruby Oporto. This wine is twenty to twenty-one percent alcohol and will set you back two hundred seventy dollars a bottle, so," he said with a laugh, "I don't recommend you bring it out when your brother-in-law comes over for dinner." This brought a laugh from everyone.

"I hope you all had a good time and enjoyed the wine." Phil signaled the sommelier closest to him to refill his and Eddie's port glasses, and they polished them off as Carol and Melissa stood to go.

————

6:00 p.m., the Porthole Piano Bar

When Phil and Carol entered the bar, Arthur and Don were standing at the piano singing along as Sammy played "Blue Moon."

"What's up with that?" asked Carol.

Nicole rolled her eyes and said, "They came down early to meet for a drink, and when Inga and I got here, they'd already had a Manhattan or two and decided to see if they could drive everybody else out so we could have the place to ourselves."

"*Ja*, and I think it's working," laughed Inga.

Just then Eddie and Melissa arrived, and he joined the other two men at the piano.

Melissa said, "I don't know about the other two, but Eddie can't carry a tune in a bushel basket. We're liable to get kicked out of here if he does more than one song."

"Nicole has already theorized that they are trying to drive the other customers out, so we'll probably have the place to ourselves before they finish the second song," said Carol.

"Eddie won't be able to do more than one song. He only knows, 'Blue moon, you saw me standing alone, without a something, something, something...' Those are his favorite lyrics." This got a laugh from the others.

Sven asked, "The usual?" And they all nodded.

"Are we that predictable?" asked Carol.

"Apparently, we are," said Phil.

"Are what?" asked Don as they came back to the table.

"Are predictable. Sven doesn't even have to ask what we want to drink," said Phil.

"Do you mean predictable as in stuffy? Is that what you are saying?" asked Arthur. He wondered if abandoning his love of jazz had made him stuffy.

"No, we already know you are not stuffy, *Cary*," laughed Carol, recalling Nicole's story about Arthur's impression of Cary Grant.

"You could count with one finger the times I did anything like that. That was a one-off and hardly qualifies as a walk on the wild side."

"Well, if any of us are stuffy, maybe we need to think of setting some new goals," said Eddie. "We are not, as we've already discussed, the same people now that we've retired, and we are not living in the same world."

"The reason I think that makes sense is because of something you taught us the first evening we were together, Eddie," said Carol.

"What's that?"

The memory thing. When you taught us how to do that and we all agreed it would be valuable, I started to practice, remembering the name of everybody I met on the ship. I've written them in this little notebook, and I keep an eye out for those people and make a point of using their names when I run into them."

"Have you remembered everyone?" asked Inga, impressed.

"No, but when I don't, I just ask them again, and they don't mind telling me."

"That's wonderful," said her husband. "It ties into the discussion we had at lunch when Arthur asked us if it was ever too late to set goals. We decided to bring it up at dinner this evening, so we could all express our opinions on the subject. If Inga is not tired of writing, maybe she could capture some of the ideas in her notebook. Okay?"

Inga nodded, and just then Carlos, the maître d' from the grand dining room, came in to tell them their table was ready.

7:00 p.m., the Grand Dining Room

"What's for dinner, Ernesto?" asked Eddie, smiling at the Sicilian waiter.

"We're going to start you with a nice chilled crab salad with the chef's special dressing, followed by clam chowder, and then grilled sea bass with a spicy tomato sauce."

Nicole, who was wearing the same tight-fitting, black Vera Wang dress that she'd worn the first evening, asked, "Is it spicy?"

"It's pretty hot, but I haven't had any complaints."

"Day-um," she said. "I wish you'd had some complaints. I'm from Creole country, and we like our sauces hot."

"You'll like this, and I can ask the chef to make yours a little hotter if you like."

"Yes, please. Anybody else want to join me and go for something hot?" Phil blushed, bit his tongue, and shook his head no. The others said no as well. They would have it as prepared.

When their food came, Eddie said, "I'd like to go back to Arthur's question about goals and age. I have an example that speaks to that issue. Melissa, do you remember the lunch we had at Splendido last year?"

"Yes, with Art and Terry Gordon?"

"Right. They are longtime friends who bought an apartment last

December in the Splendido Retirement Community. Shortly after they moved in, Melissa and I had lunch with them. It's Muncie's most upscale senior-living facility. Art, who is approaching ninety, never fails to amaze me with his energy and enthusiasm for life. He is a model of the ideal attitude one must have to live successfully and fully in the senior years, which I consider to be fifty-five and older.

"As we sat in their living room before lunch, Art could barely contain his excitement about a new business venture that he is planning. With twinkling eyes he said, 'I can't tell you about it yet, but it is going to be big.' Terry was just as excited, and Art had to keep her from 'spilling the beans,' as he put it. This is the source of Art's energy and enthusiasm. He is always looking to the future, setting goals, and making plans. It keeps them both forever young."

"That's great, but did you find out what his new business venture is?" asked Arthur.

"No, and that's not the point. I think we can follow his example and have that kind of excitement in our lives at any age, but I think it is especially important in retirement."

Phil said, "Based on your example, I'd ask these questions of any retired person: What goals and plans do you have today? What gets you up in the morning excitedly looking forward to the adventure of the day? If a person doesn't currently have an answer to those questions and doesn't have the kind of motivation Art has, it might serve him or her to look for something that gets them excited. I'd say that's where the joy of living comes from at any age."

"Exactly. I heard an exciting thought from a speaker at a meeting a couple of years ago that I'll never forget," said Carol. "'Life becomes meaningful when you become motivated, set goals and charge after them in an unstoppable manner.'"

"Was that Les Brown?" asked her husband.

"Yes, and that was an important reminder to me to continue to set goals whether I'm working or not."

"That's always been important to me," said Phil. "And I learned something else as I built my business: you can get better results by working with others."

"How do you mean?" asked Inga, who had been writing nonstop since the conversation started.

"Well, I sat over a glass of wine one evening with some friends, discussing the creation of a mastermind group that would include two or three other men. Alan, Brian, and I had been part of a Thursday morning conversation group discussing higher consciousness. In that group, we were exploring the relationship between metaphysics and quantum physics. I have to tell you that if that group ever found out about my less-than-stellar academic record, I'd have been ousted faster than the speed of a whirling electron."

"What do you mean, 'less than stellar'?" asked Nicole.

"Well, I finished in that ten percent of my high school graduating class that made the upper ninety percent possible, and I never went to college."

"You should also mention that you are as smart as a whip and you've been successful," said his wife.

"I have to admit that marrying a Stanford graduate with an MBA does qualify as a measure of success." He laughed.

Carol blushed slightly. His comment caused her to be both pleased and upset. She was pleased that the group now knew about her academic background. She would not have told them herself because she had been taught not to brag. She was upset with herself for not having had the confidence to use her degree in the corporate world to see how successful she could have been. Instead, she met Phil at the Golden Gate Athletic club in San Francisco, fell in love, and married the outgoing, confident, good-looking hunk. She could see right from the start that he was destined for success, so she went to work with him in the salvage business. Now, after twenty-five years, she was considering divorcing him.

"What about your higher consciousness friends?" asked Don.

"That Thursday group," continued Phil, "created both an

interesting and stimulating intellectual environment that I enjoyed. However, it did not have an endgame. We were never moving toward an objective of any kind. This is why I proposed the idea of a mastermind group. That is an idea with which I became acquainted as a young man when I first read Napoleon Hill's excellent book, *Think and Grow Rich*."

"What's a 'masta mine' group?" asked Nicole.

Smiling and careful to pronounce each word clearly, Phil said, "A mastermind group is one in which each of the participants has a concrete objective, purpose, or cause to which they aspire. Synergism develops from this type of alliance. There is a much more powerful connection to be made by joining with other like-minded people. The way Napoleon Hill put it was, 'Organized effort is produced through the coordination of effort of two or more people, who work toward a definite end, in a spirit of harmony.'"

"So did you put one together?" asked Arthur.

"I did. There are six of us. We meet once a week for ninety minutes, share our goals, and support one another in believing we will achieve them. I find that it is helping me set my goals for this second exciting period in my life. I recommend the mastermind approach as a highly effective means of developing the power necessary to attaining your goals."

"Would you slow down a little?" asked Inga. "My shorthand isn't as fast as it used to be."

Fortunately, at that moment, the waiters came to clear the table, so they took a break in their conversation.

———

9:00 p.m., Coffee and Dessert

Ernesto brought generous servings of key lime pie, espresso, and a little plate of assorted chocolates.

Picking up the conversation, Eddie said, "I agree with Phil that working with and through people is essential to success, and I also think that it has to begin with the individual."

"How so?" asked Inga.

"Well," Eddie continued, "this business of making our lives worth living is a creative endeavor, much like the process used by all artists in crafting their creations. An image appears, first in the mind of the artist, before he or she begins to paint or sculpt. The same is true for the musician who sits down to compose or the writer prior to creating his or her piece of literary art."

"That's true," said Don. "There is a fascinating exhibit in the Cloisters Museum in New York City that features seven large tapestries depicting a hunt for the elusive, magical unicorn. The intricately detailed masterpieces of workmanship are beautiful and complex works of art from the late Middle Ages, luxuriously woven with the finest silk and gold threads. Each square inch of the tapestries took a worker an entire day to weave. Those weavers, who crafted the magnificent tapestries in Cloisters Museum and ones like them on the walls of the great old mansions in Europe, are examples of the way in which people can craft the next chapter of their lives. The weavers imagined the finished product before they began to weave. It stands to reason that we, too, must have an image in our minds of what that finished piece of artwork will look like."

"That's interesting. Does anyone here know that as a fact from personal experience?" asked Arthur.

"I do," said Eddie. "Last week I sat down and reviewed affirmations that I had written thirty years ago last December and have looked at them nearly every day since. Those important thoughts and the corresponding images and emotions that accompany them served as a blueprint as I planned my life and went into action. A high percentage of those affirmations and the goals I set as a result of them have produced a life full of happiness and abundance that I could not have thought possible as a young boy growing up in a small town in Indiana."

"Affirmations work," said Carol. "I know because I used them all the way through school to help me get good grades and to get into graduate school. One of the best psychology classes I took dealt with the subconscious mind and how to program it. My class developed a strategy for programming our minds to excel in our studies, and it worked."

"How can we use that for our children?" asked Inga.

"My recommendation," said Eddie, "is for them to launch an action plan for the next phase of their lives. Encourage them to visualize an ideal year and an ideal five years. Then a year from now, review their progress. Ask them, 'Did your results match the image you had in mind?' If it doesn't, then ask, 'What will you need to do differently to be sure next year is better?' Be sure to include those all-important affirmations and repeat them daily."

Inga said, "That's great. I remember reading a Walt Whitman quote once that ties into what we are talking about. 'I have imagined the life of the ordinary man in ordinary circumstances, yet grand, heroic.'"

"Why wouldn't visualization and affirmations work for those of us who are already retired?" asked Arthur.

"They do," said Eddie. "There is another perspective on this whole business of imaging and affirming in the process of goal attainment. I think it is especially important as we plan and launch our voyage into the retirement phase of our lives. We tend to become set in our ways and our minds tend to become calcified if we don't take a fresh, innovative approach to planning."

"Can you give us an example of how you do that?" asked Inga.

"Yes, I live fairly near Heekin Park, so I can walk there and start my day with some silent meditation and thinking. I find this to be the most productive time of my day. I like to repeat my affirmations, visualize myself as having already achieved my goals, and think about the day ahead. Again, I'm programming my subconscious mind, if you will."

"That's the same thing Mohammad Ali did when he declared, 'I am the greatest,'" said Arthur.

"Exactly," said Eddie. "He not only said the words and visualized himself being successful, he added the element of strong emotion."

"So you all think everyone wants or needs to set goals in retirement?" asked Don. "I'm eighty years old. I don't know if I should bother."

"We just heard Eddie and Melissa's example of their ninety-year-old friend," said Phil. "It sounds to me as though we should be setting goals as long as we are breathing."

"That's consistent with the ideas I read in Stan Hinden's book, *How to Retire Happy: The 12 Most Important Decisions You Must Make Before You Retire,*" said Carol. "Hinden suggests that married couples should decide before they retire what each one wants from retirement."

"Yeah, since we're at that age," said her husband, "we should be thinking about that issue for ourselves, although I don't think I'll ever retire. I read Hinden's book too, and he has a lot of practical ideas for avoiding retirement mistakes, especially financial ones. But I think the other issues we've been discussing are as important, if not more important, than the financial aspect."

"I'll tell you why I think having goals is so important," said Eddie. "If we have goals, retirement can be the most rewarding period of our lives. It can provide us with a sense of aliveness not available to the rocking-chair-happy crowd.

"As an example, I belong to a writer's group that meets twice a month, and the level of excitement from the individuals in the group is so stimulating to be around. We are all there because we have the goal of becoming better writers. We believe that writing gives our lives meaning and that our writings are making a difference in the lives of our readers.

"Not everyone feels that way. I was playing golf recently with Rick, a seventy-five-year-old friend. During our round, we talked about this whole business of goals. My contention has been that we all need meaningful, worthwhile goals and activities in our lives to be happy. I used as an example my eighty-five-year-old uncle. He sold his company to his kids and has plenty of money. However, he keeps an office at the plant and goes in every day to 'tinker,' as he puts it. He told me about a new product he is working on, the design of a machine to produce a special product for one of their customers. He is still the best engineer in the company. The point is that he's enthusiastic and excited because he has a goal."

Eddie went on. "My friend Rick said, 'Suppose your goal in life is to have fun?' I talked to him about higher purpose or meaning, and it didn't resonate with him. He said his goal was to improve his golf game. I said any goal is better than none. Still, I would point out the difference between a regular goal and a worthwhile goal; that is, a goal that makes a difference.

"There is a level of being that is neither purposeful living nor 'dead man walking.' It seems to me that this is a form of giving up and settling for a reduced quality of life. This middle ground is a form of ennui that looks like aliveness but is merely keeping busy until the Grim Reaper shows up. I think we can do better than this. I think we deserve better than this. I think we need to guard against substituting busywork for meaningful activity. One of the most meaningful quotes on this subject comes from Simone de Beauvoir: 'Life is occupied in perpetuating itself and surpassing itself; if all it does is maintain itself then living is only not dying.'"

Eddie thought, "That sounds a lot like what I'm going through. Where is my quality of life?"

Nicole was listening attentively to the conversation, without her usual need to be the center of attention. While each person was talking, Inga was nodding, smiling, and taking notes as fast as she could.

"How do we manage all those goals?" she asked.

Phil said, "I can answer that. I've found that it's more important to manage myself now as I'm looking forward to the second half of my life than it was in the first. There seems to be less urgency to get things done now that I don't have the pressure of going to work or at least not having to meet deadlines. The truth is, however, that issues such as the care of my health are imperative and demand that I manage them.

"As an example, I walked around the track again this morning. I've been doing this fairly regularly as part of a ninety-day goal to become healthier and more physically fit. I like walking first thing in the morning. It gets my day off to a good start. I immediately tell Carol what my results were and put it on my 'I'm Glad I Did' list. I feel good about myself.

"One of the most important tools I use is a heart monitor that records how many minutes I walk and also the intensity of the walk. I've lost weight and feel more energetic. You may have a different goal, but the techniques I am using here will help you manage yourself, stay on track, and ensure you're keeping your commitment to yourself."

Carol excitedly joined in. "I have five techniques that I use for all my goals to keep me on track."

"What are they?" asked Inga, with her pen poised. "Give us some advice for our kids to use."

"Sure," said Carol. "I call them my Five Techniques for Self-Management: First, I ask myself, 'How can I measure my progress?' I'm specific. How many? How long? By when? What percentage? Et cetera. I don't try to do it all at once. I remind myself of the answer to the riddle 'How do you eat an elephant?'"

"One bite at a time," said Phil.

"I'm talking now," she said, glaring at her husband. "Next, I record my progress every day. As an example, weight loss experts tell us to weigh ourselves daily. Performance that is recorded tends to improve.

"Third, I report to someone I respect, like a boss, a friend, or a spouse, if he cares," she said, giving Phil a sarcastic look. "Performance that is reported and recorded tends to improve more. Then I remind myself how my progress relates to attaining my goal.

"Finally, I celebrate my success. I reward myself by sitting for thirty minutes before I start the day's work, relaxing with a cup of coffee and enjoying the morning. I'd heard once that if you can't measure it, you can't manage it."

"Something else we should do," said Eddie, "is find ways to avoid the time-robbing habits and activities that keep us from being able to focus on the things that are important. I used to use a good book on time management when training employees—Alex Mackenzie's *The Time Trap*. The key concepts in his book help me free up the time I need to pursue my goals. Once I've set my goals, then I just ask myself the magic question on a regular basis: "Is what I'm doing or about to do getting me closer to my goal?" It is one of the most effective time management tools available."

Ernesto and his helper were bustling around, straightening chairs, and giving the subtle hint that they were ready to get on with their after-work activities.

"Do you think there is a message there?" asked Don.

"I think so," said Arthur. He stood up, and the group followed suit.

10:15 p.m., the Lobby

"Before I forget," said Eddie, "did you all see the flyer regarding the program in the theater tomorrow afternoon?"

"Yeah, it sounds great. Carol and I are going. Are you?"

"What's it about?" asked Inga.

"A motivational speaker from Denver will be speaking about successful retirement, the stuff we've been talking about. I'll bet we can get some more good ideas. Let's all go," said Phil. "It starts at two o'clock. We can meet in the theater fifteen minutes early."

"Sounds good to me," said Don. "Inga?"

"Ja, I want to go. Maybe I won't have to take so many notes. My hand is tired from today."

Arthur said, "I'm in. Nicole?" She nodded and then, surprisingly, said, "I learned a whole bunch from what y'all were talkin' about this evenin'. Y'all gave me a lot to think about. That talk tomarah should be fun. Ah'm tard. Ah'm *goin'* to bed now. G'nite, y'all."

"Me too," said Inga, "What a session today."

"We did cover a great deal of ground this evening," said Arthur. "I got a number of ideas that I can use. Tomorrow should be great."

Eddie said, "I'll just say good night to everybody and see you in the Celebrity tomorrow. Are you coming along, my love?"

"No, I think I'll just go claim some of the money I loaned Imperial, as an advance on the money I'm going to win from them. Do you mind?"

He couldn't say yes with the others standing there, so he said, "No, my love. Go have a good time. I'll see you later."

Everyone went their separate ways. Eddie was fuming inside at Melissa's clever trick of asking him that question in front of the others, knowing he wouldn't be able to say no. "I'll have a nightcap," he said to himself. Why did he have this yo-yo relationship with her? "She just doesn't get me, or she'd be more considerate."

10:30 p.m., the Porthole Bar

Sonny was playing a blues song, entertaining two small groups seated around cocktail tables and one couple seated at the bar. Eddie sat at the bar too and ordered a glass of port. The music seemed to speak to Eddie's mood. He thought about his failure at writing, his loss of belief in himself, and his inability to aggressively confront Melissa about her gambling. He ordered another port just as Sonny segued into "One for My Baby." Eddie tapped his fingers on the bar and hummed along with the music. "We've lost it," thought Eddie of the openness that he and Melissa used to have. As he sat there listening to Sonny and feeling sorry for himself, he lost track of time and how many ports he drank before he stumbled off his barstool, feeling sick and needing some fresh air.

Craig Burke watched as Eddie, unsteadily, got off his barstool and staggered to the door and walked out into the night on the eleventh deck.

He followed him quietly to make sure he made it back to his cabin safely. Eddie was one of the thirty-two participants he had profiled from his application as a potential psychological risk. The indications of potential stress buildup and overload showed up on the answers to their questions, so Craig had made a habit of hanging around the bars every night, watching his thirty-two at-risk people. So far, one week into the cruise, there had been no incidents. However, unlike his Pollyanna CEO, Mac Katz, Craig wasn't convinced that everybody could withstand the pressure that the heavy subject matter, coupled with their own preexisting stress issues, would place on them. He watched as Eddie leaned over the rail, puked, wiped his mouth on the sleeve of his jacket, and stared at the water below.

He thought how easy it would be to end it all—to have all his problems disappear. No more money worries, no more of the self-loathing he was feeling for being such a fraud and a failure. *This is it. Melissa will be sorry she ever criticized me and sorry that she didn't take the time to be interested in me—sorry she didn't know how hard I tried.* He made a decision. He lifted his weight up on the railing, when he heard a deep resonant voice behind him.

"Good evening, Eddie," said Craig. "It's a beautiful night. I was just going to take a turn around the deck, and I could use some company. Will you join me?"

Eddie was taken by surprise. He'd only talked to Craig that one other time and didn't expect to see him or anyone else up here this time of night. He could only nod and turn to walk beside Craig. His legs were wobbly, and he hardly noticed when Craig linked his arm into his and steadied him. "How are you enjoying the seminar so far?" he asked.

Eddie cleared his head and gave what he imagined was a sober sounding answer: "Good food for thought."

"Food for thought?" asked Craig.

"Yesh," slurred Eddie.

"How do you mean? What kind of thought?"

"I'm juss thinkin' wus thu use?"

"What's the use?"

"Yesh, wus the use of tryin'? The whole thing is not worth it. I can't make dany progess."

"Progress on what?'

"On my riding."

"Riding?"

"Yesh, am a rider."

"Like a horse rider?"

"No, Ah'm a wannabe book rider."

"Oh, a writer. How's it going?"

"Like crap. Ah'm no good. Ah've never been good at anything. Ah've been a fraud my whole life. And my damn wife is no help. She doesn't think Ah'm worth a damn. Soo, oh, oh, Ah'm gonna be sick agin." With that, he leaned over the railing and puked.

They walked around the track several more times before Craig said, "It's getting late. Let's pack it in for the night."

Eddie agreed, having forgotten about his suicide plan. When they reached his cabin door, he turned and spontaneously hugged Craig and said good night. When he opened the door, Melissa was still not back from the casino. He undressed, dropped his clothes on the floor, and fell into bed.

———

10:15 p.m., the Lobby

"Are you ready to head upstairs?" Phil asked his wife.

"No, not yet. There's no meeting tomorrow, so why don't we find a quiet bar and have a *penalternate*?" she said, laughing.

"Fine with me as long as we don't have the alternate."

"How about the Crow's Nest on the top deck?" he asked. "It's quiet there."

She smiled and pressed the up button of the elevator.

————

DAY SIX

Eddie Townsend rolled over in his empty bed with the worst hangover he'd had in years. His head ached, and he felt nauseated as he looked at the clock on the nightstand. He hurriedly got up and made his way to the bathroom, his head pounding. "What did I do?" he asked himself. "I shouldn't have had that last port."

He poured himself a glass of water and found a note on the table beside a cold pot of coffee, two Alka-Seltzer tablets, and a box of aspirin.

"Good morning, my love. You were already sleeping when I came in last night and also this morning. I didn't want to disturb you. I know you'll probably want to write up another storm when you get up. I'm going to the pool. I'll be on the side next to the Waves. Love, M."

"A dip in the pool will feel good," he thought, putting on his swimming trunks and the robe supplied by Imperial Cruise Lines. Stepping off the elevator near the pool bar, he saw Phil and Arthur on stools, each nursing a Bloody Mary.

"Wow, look what the cat dragged in," said Phil. "Did you just get up? We saw Melissa, and she said you were dead asleep."

"Yeah, I feel like crap."

"You don't look *that* good," said Arthur.

"Yeah," Phil said. "You look like you've been rode hard and put away wet."

Alphonso, the bartender, greeted Eddie. "Good morning, Mr. Townsend. How are you this morning? Oooh, you look in worse shape than these two. Same medicine?"

Eddie nodded and said, "I drifted astray last night."

"Let me guess, with these two?"

"No, they must have done their own damage, but bring them a couple more too."

"What's going on with you?" asked Arthur.

"If you want the truth, I'm struggling with feelings of incompetence."

"You? You don't have an incompetent bone in your body," said Phil.

"Remember all that stuff I said about you yesterday?" asked Arthur.

"That doesn't help when I'm trying to write and can't spit out anything decent."

"You must be able to take the same ideas you've been sharing with us at dinner and put those into your book," said Arthur.

"You'd think," said Eddie. "And because Melissa is so much smarter than me, it doesn't help me feel any more capable."

"How do you mean?" asked Phil.

"She'll be reading a book and insist on reading stuff to me."

"Stuff, what kind of stuff?" asked Arthur.

"Elegant stuff that makes my stuff sound like rubbish. She insists on reading me flowery, flowing, fluid phrases from some classic she's reading," he said, gesturing like a sixteenth-century European dandy.

"What kind of flowery stuff?" asked Phil.

"Well, like, she'll read, 'The fragrance of the countess's perfume wafted across the room and into his nostrils like gardenias in the springtime, with the early-morning dew poised on the petals of a rose still waiting like an expectant lover parting pulsing lips waiting to be devoured by her lover,' or something like that. Then I'll look down at what I've written and scratch it out. It's usually something like, '"Damn, she sure looks hot," said Bubba, wiping the spittle from his mouth.'"

Phil and Arthur burst out laughing.

"I don't know, Eddie. That sounds like pretty good writing to me," said Phil, trying to keep a straight face.

He and Arthur were still laughing when Melissa and Carol walked up to the bar. "Are you going to be able to make the meeting in an hour?" asked Melissa.

"In an hour! Good Lord," said Arthur. "I was supposed to get Nicole for lunch a half hour ago."

"No need to worry," said a smiling Nicole, who walked up behind them just as the other two women arrived. "Ah knew after last night where y'all would be."

"Let's all just grab something quick at the Waves and get to the meeting," said Phil. They hurried over to the snack bar.

"Order me a burger, my love, while I take a quick wake-up dip in the pool."

"Okay, my love. Oh, by the way, how did the writing go this morning?" she asked innocently.

Picking up on the sarcasm dripping from her voice, he didn't answer.

1:00 p.m., the Celebrity Theater
Pat Higgins's Announcements

Eddie and Melissa accepted programs from Istvan, the breakfast waiter from the Terrace Café, as they entered the room. A different crew member ushered them to their assigned table, where they met their team for the day.

"Hi, I'm Richard Morgan," said a short man wearing horn-rimmed glasses, "and this is my wife, Karen," indicating the frumpy, over-weight woman to his right.

"A pleasure. I'm Melissa, and this is Eddie, my husband."

Eddie reached across Melissa, shook Richard's hand, and nodded to Karen. In sharp contrast was the stylishly dressed woman wearing a pearl necklace and matching earrings, who smiled warmly and said, with a decided southern accent, "We're the Conleys. I'm Hillary, and this here is Dean. We're from Biloxi, Mississippi. It's good to meet y'all. These folks are a couple of Yankees, but nice ones, Frank and Marilyn Jefferson, from New York."

Eddie and Melissa made a point of remembering their names.

1:15 p.m., Reporting

Pat Higgins welcomed everyone and announced the reporting period assignment: "What did I take from our team dinner discussion last night?"

Carlos, the maître d' from the grand dining room, was their group leader for the day. He asked everyone to think about Pat's question for two minutes, then take three minutes to write their answer to the question.

"Whose birthday is closest to today?" he asked. Dean Conley's was last week, so Carlos said, "Tell us what you have written, Dean."

"The big idea I got from our discussion last night is I've got to start thinking differently than I have been."

"What do you mean?" asked Carlos.

"Well, up until now all my goals have been about work and money. I'm not fully retired yet, but I'm getting close, so I've got to start thinking about what I want to do when I don't have my job to fall back on."

"Yes," added Frank. "Marilyn and I discovered, and we talked about this at our team dinner last night, that when I retired last year, I upset her routine."

"That's right," said Marilyn. "I had my schedule, a certain time to do my work, and now all of a sudden, he's disrupting everything."

"Give us an example," said Carlos.

"Tuesday's my washing day, and he'll up and say, 'Let's go to a movie today.' Well, I can't just let the clothes sit there dirty, but he didn't understand that."

"That was my big lesson, and it's takin' me some time, but I'm startin' to think of her before I upset things."

"It's gettin' better," said Marilyn.

Carlos said, "Richard, what was your benefit from your dinner discussion last night?"

"Some indigestion from that sauce." He laughed.

Dean laughed and nodded in agreement.

"But the other thing I got was how busy I am. I thought I was all alone, but the other people in our group all agreed. We don't know how we had time to do our jobs before we retired."

Karen said, "We also talked about how we had more time to pay attention to each other."

"Yeah, that's another thing that's keeping me busy," laughed Richard.

———

1:45 p.m.

"May I have your attention?" announced Pat Higgins. "Our program will begin in fifteen minutes."

2:00 p.m.

"The topic for the day is healthy living.

"Our speaker will be talking to us about what the latest findings in the field have revealed about living a healthier life during our retirement years. He draws from his studies and work at the Mimosa Health Spa. Please join me in welcoming Dr. Ernest Neidelmeyer."

The doctor spoke for the next sixty minutes about aging and the quality of life. Melissa took notes on the back of her program.

3:00 p.m.

When Dr. Neidelmeyer finished his presentation, Pat Higgins asked everyone to regroup and, using the reporting period format, answer the question, 'What one idea did I take from today's talk?'

After the think and write exercise, Carlos asked, "Who'd like to go first?"

"I would," said Dean. "I thought it was an interesting talk. Aging brings balance, wisdom, and as a result less stress. It all depends on how we look at things. My uncle, despite being quite old, is always learning new things. He is even taking piano lessons. I believe aging helps people feel happier, more relaxed, and younger."

"The big message I got was to never stop working to make your life happy and meaningful," said Marilyn.

"I think the whole issue of aging boils down to our attitudes and how we think," said Eddie.

Richard said, "I deal in municipal bonds and have done so since I turned twenty-two. Our group manages a large portfolio of bonds, so I have the opportunity to meet our clients regularly. A majority of our clients have a high net worth and are self-made. They have spent their lives working and are now enjoying the fruits of their labor.

"I am impressed by this group. They have no debt and never did; even when they were starting out. They never spent more than they had, and cash is king with them. They are savers and tend to live their lives accordingly. They will look for deals and check local gas prices to save a few pennies. It is these skills that have allowed them to amass millions of dollars and enjoy life in retirement. When they invest, it is for safety and income. They use tax-free bonds to squeeze out every cent from their investment. When they buy equities, it is for the dividend, not the appreciation.

"There are exceptions of course, but a sampling of several hundred clients also reveals a consistent characteristic; they are healthy. My top ten clients are well into their eighties and are doing great. They play golf, take vacations, host family gatherings, and are intellectually sound of mind.

"They approach their health the same way they invest, consistent and cautious. They are conservative and treat everything with moderation. They are careful to not overeat or drink to excess, and rarely do I see any of them smoke.

"The takeaway here is, we need to invest in our health. My wife commented earlier this week that we need to invest in our health now for a big pay-off in the future."

"That's consistent with the findings of Thomas Stanley in *The Millionaire Next Door*," said Eddie. "It's a good read for our kids as well as the rest of us."

"Well," Karen said, "it's just common sense; life gets better every day."

———

3:30 p.m.

"Attention, please!" Pat Higgins's voice quieted the buzz of conversation in the room. "That's it for today. I hope you had a productive discussion and can continue it tomorrow."

The room began to empty. Eddie and Melissa passed Arthur and Nicole on the way out.

"See you in the bar at six," said Eddie.

"Be there or be square," said Arthur, smiling.

"What's that?" said Melissa.

"I learned that from Phil. I'm not sure what it means other than, ah, just be there."

They waved goodbye and headed for their rooms.

"I like Arthur," said Eddie, as he filled the Jacuzzi and slipped out of his clothes.

"He takes a little time to open up," said Melissa, "but you're right. The more I get to know him, the more I like him."

"I think most of us are that way. Are you going to climb in here with me?"

"What did you have in mind?" laughed Melissa.

"Get in and you'll see," he laughed.

She put the Do Not Disturb sign on the door, threw her shorts and blouse on the bed, and climbed in beside him.

———

5:50 p.m., the Porthole Piano Bar

"Everybody's early," said Don, as he and Inga arrived and saw the others already seated with their drinks.

"I know," said Phil. "When Carol and I got here five minutes ago, these lushes were already knocking back their cocktails. Pretty soon we're going to have to come straight from lunch so we don't fall behind."

"What an interesting meeting on healthy living today," said Inga.

"I got a lot of good ideas. Did you take a lot of notes?" asked Melissa.

"Two pages. I think all the material we're getting here will be beneficial to our kids."

"Well, I hope you'll share what you've been writing with all of us before we leave," said Phil.

"I'm not sure I can allow that," said a laughing Don, as he picked up his glass of sparkling soda water. "That is copyrighted material, and, as her agent, I'll have to collect a slight fee from all of you in exchange for her work."

"You'd have your wife do all the work, and you'd take the money?" asked Phil. "We have a name for guys like you in San Francisco. They usually drive pink Cadillacs."

"I'm going to give her some of the money," Don said, continuing the joke.

"Well, if it doesn't violate any of your copyrights, Inga, would you tell us the most important idea you heard in the talk today?" asked Carol.

"Why don't we save it until we get to the dinner table and get some food in us?" said Arthur. "I didn't have any lunch today, and I'm afraid I won't be able to absorb all your gems of wisdom on an empty stomach."

"Here are some munchies," said Don, pushing the bowl of pretzels and nuts toward Arthur. "This should hold you until dinner."

"I'm hungrier than that. Maybe we should order an appetizer."

"You'll spoil your appetite, dahlin'. It's almost time to go in anyway," said Nicole.

Arthur pushed the bowl of snacks away and leaned back in his seat and sulked.

"Phil, what kind of West Coast hip-hop stuff have you been teaching Arthur?" asked Eddie with a grin.

"What do you mean? What hip-hop stuff?"

"On our way out of the meeting today, he said some odd phrase that he got from you. What was it Arthur?"

Arthur, enjoying the bantering and forgetting his snit, said, "I just told them, 'See you later, alligator.'"

"No, that wasn't it," said Nicole. "It was your other one."

"Oh, yes. It was, 'Be there or be square.'" He laughed.

"No," laughed Phil. "You don't use that saying with someone like Eddie. He's already so square, no amount of advice is going to make him un-square."

"Typical West Coast snobbishness," laughed Eddie.

Before they could continue the bantering, Francisco came into the bar and said, "Your table is ready, Dr. Gibson. The captain would like you to control your rowdy friends this evening and not let them get too boisterous." He winked at Arthur.

Everybody laughed as they followed Francisco to their table.

————

7:00 p.m., the Grand Dining Room

As the group was seated, Ernesto greeted them all by name, which impressed everyone.

"Bravo! How did you do that, Ernesto?" asked Don.

"*Señor* Eddie," he said. "He taught me to make pictures during my break yesterday."

"That's impressive. *Felicidades*," said Carol.

"*Gracias.* I'm trying to do that with everybody. They like it too."

"Too bad you are not working for tips," said Phil. "You'd make a lot of money."

"I want to get a job at a high-end restaurant in the States when my contract is finished."

"Where do you want to go?" asked Nicole.

"I have a cousin in San Francisco. He says it is a grand city. I think I'd like to go there."

"Be sure to get in touch with me," said Phil. "We live there, and I know some people in the restaurant business. I can introduce you, and I'll provide you with a good reference."

"*Muchas gracias*, Señor Butler."

"*De nada.* What's special this evening?"

"We have a special dinner for you this evening." From memory, he rattled off the delicious menu.

"The *amuse-bouche* is a jicama and cilantro salad with avocado oil and tequila. The jicama is thinly sliced for this small dish. It's delicious. You'll all love it, especially you, Mrs. Gibson. It is *muy picante*," he said, smiling at Nicole.

"We're also serving an appetizer, a Mexican barley casserole with fresh cactus.

"Then for the main course, you have a choice of either pan-fried filet of fresh grouper or slow-roasted rack of lamb with an herb crust. Both are accompanied by vegetable fajitas. Chef leaves the skin on the grouper, and it makes it crunchy and delicious. We've selected a couple of different wines that complement the appetizers and either of the entrees—a California chardonnay and an Oregon pinot noir.

"For dessert, we offer mango mousse with passion-fruit crème and lime and basil sorbet. The serving dish includes both desserts, and we all especially liked the sorbet."

"Wow, let's eat," said Don, with more than his usual enthusiasm. "I'll have the lamb."

The *amuse-bouche* arrived almost instantly, and they enjoyed it with a bottle of Napa Valley chardonnay.

After the Mexican barley casserole appetizer was devoured, Nicole said, "Mm, mm, mm, that's jist lahk home cookin'."

Everyone agreed, and while they waited for the main course, Phil said, "Let's go back to the discussion of your notes, Inga. I believe Carol's question was, 'What one idea stood out for you today?'"

Carol noticed that Inga's manner of dressing had become progressively more colorful since they started meeting. This evening, while she still wore a black dress, she accessorized it with a bright yellow scarf and a large gold pin in the shape of a tortoise.

"One idea I got today is the importance of society showing respect for its elders. We were taught this at a young age in Germany. And we learned lots of things from our elders. As a society, we should be sure that we care for them and treat them as a valuable resource."

"This is certainly true in many cultures," said Eddie. "In Japan, as an example, age is equated with wisdom. Young people honor their elders and listen to them."

"I sure wish that were true of some of the young people in our country, especially my kids," joked Don.

Eddie said, "Chronological age is associated with time left in life. Goals change across our life span. When we are children, our minds are simple because we don't know about society; we have no realization of rights, obligations, responsibilities, and so on. We don't worry about anything because we believe our parents will solve our problems for us. So during that time, we are happy.

"As we grow up, we gradually enter society and learn more and more about it. We pursue our rights. We shoulder obligations and responsibilities. During the process of looking for the meaning of an individual's life, worry, sadness, loss, and other negative emotions will appear. We are full of energy, so we choose higher goals. Once we succeed, we feel happiness. When we fail, we feel a sense of loss and sorrow."

"You sound like a Buddhist," said Phil.

"I've studied Eastern philosophy and religion for many years and practice tai chi every morning. I have a real interest in the wisdom of the East."

"That's interesting," said Phil. "I also practice tai chi and am a student of Zen. We'll have to get together and talk about that."

Eddie nodded, bowed, and said, "Namaste."

Ernesto and a couple of servers brought their entrees to the table, and as everyone began to eat, Nicole chorused again, "Yum, yum, yum," joined this time by Carol.

"Speaking from experience," said Don, "senior citizens have experienced the most brilliant and gloomy times of life. This gives perspective and meaning to our lives. We have a new understanding of life and choose to put more time and energy into our families and friends and to savor life."

"Harvey Penick, the golf teacher, in his *Little Red Book,* preferred to call us seasoned citizens," said Arthur. "I like that better."

"As we age, I think we become more childlike," said Inga. "Children and older people are happier than middle-aged people. They look at things with simpler eyes and hearts. This is the reason there are some similar behaviors between older people and children."

As Melissa listened to Inga, she regarded her with a new attitude of respect. She thought back to her conversation with Eddie earlier about Arthur and said to herself, "It's true you can't appreciate another person until you get to know them."

Phil chimed in. "It always irks me when I hear that people are living longer and there are more old people per capita. Actually, this is not true. Measures of life expectancy include newborn survival numbers, and since these numbers are so much better, it appears to some that we are living longer. Older people have always been there. However, as baby boomers are now becoming the older people, there will be more, but as a group they are not living longer."

Then Carol said, "I don't think it is because one grows older that people become happier, but rather as you get older you have a steadier and more constant life. Insecurities like unemployment, money problems, and choosing a career are common in younger generations. Of course, one can be insecure at any age, but it is clearly more prevalent in youth. Generally, people are happier when they are secure. I believe most people would agree that security is a big part of happiness."

"I agree with what Eddie said earlier," said Nicole, who had been silent. "There's a reason we call our senior years the golden years. I'd bet that it has less to do with age and more to do with perspective. They go together. As I've gotten older, I've become more comfortable with my ability to deal with the changes in my life. I've learned not to fret over things I can't change. I've learned not to be overly anxious about the future or overly concerned with the past but rather just be in the present moment. That's the only place where true happiness can be found."

Phil looked at her as though he couldn't believe those words came from her mouth. That depth of thinking was not what he expected to hear from the Nicole he knew or the Nicole he thought he knew. "There I go, making judgments without all the facts again," he said to himself.

"The one idea that stuck home with me," said Arthur, "is what Dr. Neidelmeyer said about maintaining a healthy weight as we get older."

"You don't look as though that's an issue for you," said Don, patting his huge belly.

"Well not anymore, but ten years ago, I would have made you look like Adonis. I weighed fifty pounds more than I do now, but I was able to take it off, and I've kept it off ever since."

"How did you do it?" asked Don, leaning forward.

"Well, the how was pretty simple. It's all common sense. We've all read the research. Cut down on calories and increase our physical activity."

"That's hard for me to do," said Don. "You may have noticed I like to eat, plus I think it's too late for me at my age."

"Nonsense. I've had patients well into their nineties who have successfully dieted. Check with your doctor first, then they can give you a common-sense diet. I can give you a very effective one that will safely take the weight off, but you'd need to provide the most important factor in weight loss."

"What's that?"

"A strong enough reason. For some people, it's a health scare. For others, it's pure ego; they just get tired of looking at themselves in the mirror."

"There it is again," thought Eddie. "The *why*."

"What was and is your reason, Arthur?" asked Don.

Arthur smiled and pointed to Nickie. "When I met her, I said I'm the luckiest guy in the world. I also said, if I expect to hang on to her, I better shape up. No way would a hottie like that want to be with some old fat guy."

Nickie spoke up and said, "I didn't fall in love with you for your body."

"I know. It's my razor-sharp wit and sense of humor, right?"

She leaned over and kissed him. "Absolutely, but I like your body too."

"I don't know if I have the will power and self-discipline of Phil, getting up and going to the health club every morning no matter how much wine we pour into him every night."

"Hey, since you dragged me into this health lecture, Dr. Gibson," said Phil, I've got an addition to what you said on the subject. I agree that you have to have a reason or a motive, if you will. Mine is that I live in a very competitive environment with younger, sharper people coming along every day. I heard a long time ago that it takes a lean hound to run a long race, so I go to the club whether I feel like it or not."

"So you've got an answer to *why* you do it," said Eddie in an excited voice.

"Yes, but there is another essential in controlling your weight and maintaining your health. It's keeping records."

"What do you mean?" asked Melissa, who had been listening with interest because of her own poor eating habits.

"I keep a chart posted where I see it every day with a record of my exercise. It's there to remind me and to hold myself accountable for staying on track. I think that is at least as important as motivation."

"That's true," said Eddie. "When we trained managers at Amalgamated, we told them that performance that is recorded tends to improve and performance that is recorded and reported tends to improve more."

"Well, that's it then, isn't it?" said Don. "If I want to get myself healthy and in athletic trim like Phil, all I need to do is identify a strong enough reason, keep track of my progress, and report it to somebody. Right?"

"Yes," said Phil, "but you better do it gradually, or you'll run the risk of driving Inga into a frenzied fit of passion with your new physique."

"I don't think I could take him being any sexier than he already is," laughed Inga.

At that, everybody, including Don, laughed.

8:30 p.m.

"Ah, here's dessert," said Don, as Ernesto and his crew once again rolled up the serving cart. They all enjoyed the crème and sorbet with cups of fresh, hot coffee.

When they finished dessert, the consensus was that it had been a long day, so they would call it a night.

————

9:00 p.m., in the Lobby

"Good night, everyone. See you at the lecture tomorrow," said Nicole as she and Arthur stepped into the elevator to their suite.

Amid a chorus of good nights, they ended another stimulating day.

"I'm feeling lucky," said Melissa. "I think I'll go take some more of Imperial's money. Do you mind, honey?" she said to Eddie.

"No, go ahead. I think I'll go into the lounge and see if Sammy needs any vocal help with his piano playing. I'm only going to have one because I'm going to get up early in the morning and get right to my writing." He leaned over and kissed her on the cheek, and they went their separate ways.

When he arrived in the Porthole Piano Bar, Sonny was playing soft melancholy songs to a mostly empty bar. Eddie ordered a Dewar's and water and began to think about his plight, then he ordered another and another.

2:30 a.m., Stateroom 735

Melissa opened the door quietly so she didn't disturb her husband. She was surprised to find he wasn't there. She crawled into bed and tried to sleep. When he came in thirty minutes later, also trying to be quiet, she pretended to be sleeping. She could smell the strong odor of alcohol when he climbed in bed beside her. "This is so not like him," she thought, and then she lay awake for some time before sleep overtook her.

————

Day Seven

April 13

Eddie woke up with a hangover that was worse than the day before, and when he rolled over, he saw Melissa sitting on the couch staring at him. "Good morning," he said sheepishly.

"Good morning," she said coldly. "What's going on with you?"

"What do you mean?"

The anger in her voice rose as she said, "You know damn well what I mean. You were three sheets to the wind when you came to bed. It was the middle of the night. You stunk of alcohol and snored so loud I couldn't sleep."

"I was surprised you were here," he said sarcastically. "I thought you'd still be having fun at the tables."

"What I do at the tables doesn't have anything to do with you," she said defensively. "I play with my own money."

At that, he picked up the book lying on the nightstand and threw it across the room, hitting the closet door. "Damn it! Don't talk to me about money. We could be in one of the suites with everyone else if you didn't try to get rich quick, living in the fantasyland of a system for winning that is absolutely bogus."

Controlling her temper, she said quietly, "I do make my own money, and what I do with it is my business."

"Yeah, you make your own money, but I pay all the bills."

"Don't change the subject. Why have you been drinking like you have?"

"I don't know," he said, holding his aching head between his hands.

She sat on the bed beside him. "I worry about you. You know I love you, and if you have a problem, it's my problem too," she said softly.

"I'm sorry," he said. "We don't have any problems that I can't handle. I'm going to the pool and take a dip to get the cobwebs out of my head." He walked into the bathroom, and when he came out dressed in his bathing suit, she was gone.

———

9:00 a.m., the Pool Deck

As soon as Eddie arrived at the pool, he threw his robe on a vacant lounge, dove into the cool water, and swam three laps. When he climbed out, there was a smiling Phil standing by the edge of the pool, holding out a towel.

"I missed you at tai chi this morning," he said. "I assume you got up early and started writing. Am I right?"

Toweling himself off, Eddie said, "You couldn't be more wrong."

"What do you mean?" asked Phil as they sat down on adjacent lounges.

"I told you at lunch the other day that I'm a wannabe writer. I've been sitting at that damn computer every chance I get and have nothing to show for it. I feel like a total fraud, and Melissa has run out of patience with me. I got drunk again last night, and she lit into me this morning about it. We had a major fight. That's not like us."

"So you think the answer is in a bottle, right?" Without waiting for a response, he went on. "I'm no writer, but I know that writing has got to be like any other new skill you want to acquire; it takes work. I recently read an interesting quote by Tom Clancy, the author of *The Hunt for Red October*. He said, 'When advising beginning writers, I tell them "You learn to write the same way you learn to play golf. You do it and keep doing it until you get it right. A lot of people think something mystical happens to you, that maybe the muse kisses you on the ear. But writing isn't divinely inspired—it's hard work."'

"I'd bet that you didn't get ahead at your job by waiting around to be inspired. I bet you put in a lot of hours of study and worked at it until you were good at it. Am I right?"

Eddie looked at him blankly and nodded.

Phil went on. "You didn't ask me, but if you did, I'd just say, 'Get off your butt and write something, even if it's crap.' It's better than feeling sorry for yourself, drowning your sorrows in booze, and screwing things up with Melissa, who, by the way, is one terrific gal."

Eddie got up and moved toward Phil, who stood up at the same time.

"Maybe I shouldn't have said that, and you can go ahead and punch me if you want to."

Instead Eddie reached out with tears in his eyes put his arms around Phil. He said, "Thank you. I guess I needed to hear that. I've been a sucky baby, wishing it were easier instead of wishing I were better and doing what I need to do to get better."

Phil, a little embarrassed about Eddie's outpouring of emotion, punched Eddie on the shoulder and said, "Hey, what are friends for?"

Eddie did the guy thing and punched him back. He said, "I think I'll go back to my room and write some crap."

They both laughed. Eddie left, and Phil sat back down on his lounge and picked up his book.

———

10:30 a.m.

Phil looked up from his book to see Nicole standing at the foot of his lounge, staring at him. She was wearing a red bikini with a see-through cover-up.

"Phil, may I talk to you privately?" she asked.

"Privately," he thought. "What could this be about?" His mind raced. "If she is going to try to set something up with me, how am I going to handle it? I probably shouldn't have given off those vibes. Damn, I know I didn't mean anything by it, but she's pretty naïve. Oh yeah, the emphasis should be on the pretty. She's downright hot. Back in my single days, I'd have cured her of her innocence ..."

"Phil?" she said, interrupting his fantasy. "Can we do it?"

"Ah, do it?"

"Yes, talk privately?"

"Oh yeah, sure, of course; your place or mine?" he blurted.

She laughed in the cute way he'd seen at the bar and at the dinner table. "No, silly, up at Barista's. It's quiet there."

"Oh, you mean now? Yeah, sure." His mouth was dry as his usual cockiness and self-assurance deserted him. "Damn," he thought. "Why does she do this to me?"

He picked up his things and followed Nicole up the stairs to the coffee shop. Phil noticed that the three or four men who were there gave Nicole admiring looks. They ordered espressos and sat in the corner, away from the few others having their morning coffee.

As she leaned toward him, he inhaled her lavender-scented perfume, and she said, in a low voice, "Thanks for seeing me. This is kinda personal."

———

10:45 a.m., the Pool Deck

"I wonder where Phil went," said Carol to herself. "This is his usual lounge." She'd just come from having a relaxing massage at the spa. "I'll just return these books to the library and come back and wait for him."

Climbing the stairs to the library, she passed the open doorway to Barista and saw Phil and Nicole sitting close together at a corner table. Nicole was smiling as she was talking. "Should I go in and see what that's all about?" she wondered. "No, it's probably nothing. I'll let it go." She kept walking, but she didn't let it go.

————

11:30 a.m., Stateroom 735

Eddie didn't want to face Melissa just yet, so he went to the Sea View with his computer and sat down to write some crap, as Phil had encouraged him to do. After a while, he went back to the room and found Melissa sitting on the couch, reading. He said, "I'm here to beg your forgiveness for the millionth time in the last forty years."

She put her book down, pulled him down beside her, and kissed him. "Apology accepted, and to set the record straight, it should have been the two millionth time, but I overlooked the other times."

He smiled and said to himself, "I'm one lucky guy to have a wife like this." He kissed her and drew her closer to him.

She pushed him away, saying, "I haven't forgiven you enough to entertain the idea of makeup sex. Besides, we're meeting Don and Inga for lunch in twenty minutes, so get yourself ready."

He pouted as he stood up and said, "You'd rather eat than enjoy the delights I have to offer?"

"No, not really," she said in mock sincerity, "but I gave my word that we'd meet them, and I'm afraid that once I fall into bed with you, I won't be able to tear myself away in time."

"Sarcasm?" he asked.

"You think?" she said, laughing.

He took a quick shower and hurriedly dressed. He felt an enormous sense of relief that things were back on an even keel.

————

1:00 p.m., the Celebrity Theater

After lunch, Don and Inga went to the theater with Eddie and Melissa. They received their programs for the day and were ushered to their separate tables. When Don and Inga arrived at their table, only one other couple was there, a heavyset gray-haired man with a receding hairline and a well-dressed woman to his left. She had a pleasant smile and neatly coifed hair that suggested she had recently been to the salon.

"Hello," said Don with his usual broad smile. "I'm Don Conway; this is Inga, my bride of fifty-two years."

"Hi, we're the Bensons, Lou and Maryann, from Duluth."

After shaking Lou's hand and smiling at Maryann, Don continued. "We're from the Washington, DC, area now, not actually in Washington. We're over in Virginia—Alexandria, to be exact. We've only lived there for three years. I retired from New York University, where I was a history, German, and music professor. I was born in Brooklyn, and we lived there for forty years. Inga is from Germany. We have three children, and—can you believe it?—five grandchildren."

"How do you do?" asked Inga, before her husband told them more of their life story.

Two more couples were ushered to their table. "Brad Hargrove," said a tall Abe Vigoda look-alike with big ears and pronounced, bushy eyebrows. He extended his hand to the two men.

Don and Lou each shook his hand, introduced their wives, and looked expectantly at the woman with Brad. He didn't offer her name, and there was an embarrassing silence until she meekly spoke up and said, "I'm Lynn Hargrove. I'm Brad's wife."

"Good to meet everybody," said the other new arrival in a loud voice. He had a crew cut that looked unchanged from his army cut forty years ago. "We're the Wilsons from Sioux Falls. I'm Dexter, but you can call me Doc, and this is Becky."

They shook hands all around, and Gustav, one of the head waiters, thought to himself, "This will be interesting—Doc and Don trying to outdo one another."

"Welcome, everybody! I'm Gustav, and I'll be the discussion leader today."

————

1:15 p.m., Reporting

Pat Higgins stood and welcomed everyone and announced the reporting period assignment. "What did I take from our team dinner discussion last night?"

Gustav asked everyone to think about Pat's question for two minutes, take three minutes to write their answer to the question, and then share their answers with the rest of the group. "This think-write-share format is apparently a standard method that all the group leaders use," mused Don.

"Which of you has been married the longest?" asked Gustav.

They immediately looked at Don, who had already volunteered that he and Inga had been married for fifty-two years.

"It looks as though you and Inga are it, Don. Ladies first; what have you written, Inga?"

"I think we need to appreciate what a valuable resource we are to society," she said. "I mentioned to our group that, in Germany where I grew up, we were taught to respect our elders."

"I was reminded that we have a lot to offer the generations following us," said Don. "We've gained perspective from our successes and our failures. That perspective puts us in a position to be able save our juniors a lot of the pain and suffering that we've endured."

"I'll go next," said Lou Benson. "We have a realization, sometime after age sixty for most of us, that time is running short and we need to make our remaining time on earth count for something."

"You're right," boomed Dexter "Doc" Wilson. He never did explain why he wanted to be called Doc. "A speaker at our Rotary Club asked a provocative question and then told us an interesting story. I'll tell it as best I remember it because it fits in with the whole purpose of this seminar.

"He started his talk with the question, 'What do you think about when your feet hit the floor in the morning?' There are probably as many answers to that question as there are people in this room and, for that matter, in the whole state of South Dakota. Well, it might not be the first thing, but I would hope that when you get up in the morning, retired or not, you have a reason for getting up beyond the necessity of feeding yourself and making it through another day. That is mere survival! It does not promote the kind of aliveness and enthusiasm that contributes to successful living.

"'When our daughters were small, they talked my wife and I into buying them a pet rabbit. He was a beautiful white rabbit like the one Alice chased down the rabbit hole. The girls promised to feed him and take care of him. Those of you who have bought a pet for your children know what's coming. I ended up feeding Fluffy. He didn't move around much in his wire cage. I actually think his name should have been Poopy. Because of his inactive lifestyle, all Fluffy did was eat and poop. That was Fluffy's life. Now here's the part that has to do with you and me.

"'To the degree our lives mirror Fluffy's, that is, just getting by, just marking time, we miss the whole adventure of living. So let's be sure we have a vision for today and tomorrow.'

"That talk stuck in my mind as I've been thinking about retirement."

"That reminds me of a quotation by Henry David Thoreau," said Brad Hargrove.

This surprised Don because he thought the Abe Vigoda look-alike did not seem like the kind of guy who would sit around in his smoking jacket in front of the fireplace reading Thoreau, or anything heavier than the daily comics.

"I don't remember it exactly, but he said something like, 'Most men lead lives of quiet desperation and thereby go to their graves with their songs unsung.'"

"If that's not the exact quote, it's close enough," said Lynn Hargrove. "We've been talking about not wanting to waste our retirement years."

"I have another point of view on the whole issue of longevity," said Maryann Benson. "I watched a TED talk by Gregory Petsko, and in his message, there is a little less to be happy about. He said, 'The average life span has more than doubled since 1840, and it's currently increasing at the rate of about five hours every day.' And this is why that's not entirely a good thing: because over the age of sixty-five, your risk of getting Alzheimer's or Parkinson's disease will increase exponentially. By 2050, there'll be about thirty-two million people in the United States over the age of eighty, and unless we do something about it, half of them will have Alzheimer's disease and three million more will have Parkinson's disease. Right now, those and other neurologic diseases—for which we have no cure or prevention—cost about a third of a trillion dollars a year. It will be well over a trillion dollars by 2050. I found those statistics to be disturbing."

"I would hope we take some positive action to deal with those diseases," said Becky.

Inga thought, "At last that woman spoke up. I'll bet she doesn't get much of a chance to express herself. That's something I have to be grateful for in our marriage. Don is a talker, for sure, but he does make me feel as though I have something to contribute and encourages me to express my opinions." Smiling to herself, she thought, "I should probably tell him that sometime."

Her reverie was broken by the sound of Pat Higgins's voice. "May I have your attention?" announced Pat. "Take a break, and we'll be ready to start our program in fifteen minutes."

2:00 p.m.

Pat picked up the mike once again and said, "Welcome back, everyone. We're in for a real treat today. The topic for the day is titled, 'Making the Most of Life.' We're all looking for increased quality of life, and our speaker is an expert on helping organizations and individuals achieve quality-plus living.

"Addison Clancy is our speaker today. Her message and enthusiasm will inspire and engage us. She has an upbeat message that is timely and universally relevant. The feedback we've received from other organizations where she has spoken describes her as super-engaging, a dynamic speaker, inspirational, intelligent, humorous, and outstanding in her field.

"Please join me in welcoming Addison Clancy."

Addison Clancy spoke for the next sixty minutes about positive living.

3:00 p.m.

When Addison finished her talk, Pat Higgins asked everyone to regroup and, using the reporting format, answer the question, What was the one best idea I took from today's presentation?

After the think and write exercise, Gustav asked, "Who'd like to go first?"

"I would," said Lou Benson, with typical Minnesotan brevity. "That was a thought-provoking talk."

When he did not continue, Gustav prompted him. "In what way was it thought-provoking, Lou?"

"Well, since I retired, I don't think she," he said, indicating his wife sitting next to him, "listens to me as much as she used to. We don't have the conversations at the end of the day we used to have." Maryann nodded without speaking.

Inga couldn't restrain herself. "How about you, Lou? Do you do as good a job of listening to Maryann as you used to, or did you ever listen to her?"

"Let's cut the guy a little slack," said Doc Wilson, afraid that the same criticism could be leveled at him.

"Well, let's hear from some of the others," said Gustav, in an effort to defuse the potentially tense atmosphere.

"No, no. I'd like to answer her," Lou said. Looking at Inga, he said, "Hilda, I—"

"It's Inga," she corrected him.

"I'm sorry. I've never been good with names. I think you have a point. The girl who talked, er, Madison—"

"Addison," interrupted Inga again, with an uncharacteristic note of hostility. "Addison Clancy. She talked to us for an hour just ten minutes ago."

"Well, yeah, she made me think I don't do a good job of listening in general, so it's got me to wondering."

"May I say something?" asked Becky Wilson, who had issues of her own with a husband who didn't listen to her. She was emboldened by Inga's assertive behavior.

"Of course," said Gustav.

"I mean to you, Mr. Benson?"

"Well, yes, go ahead; and call me Lou," he said, a little surprised that Becky spoke up since she had said little during the reporting period.

"I don't know you except for sitting with you at a big table for lunch with a large group three days ago. You didn't remember me. From what I've seen today, I think you don't listen to people because you are not interested in them. That's why you don't remember people's names."

"I would have to agree with that," chimed in Don. "We are two peas in a pod, Lou. I'm just like you, and I'll bet there are a lot of others like us who have to learn some new skills in retirement. I think being interested in other people and listening to them are a couple of those skills."

"Thank you," said a surprisingly receptive Lou. "I came to this seminar to learn, and this has been a helpful and instructive conversation."

3:30 p.m.

"Attention, please," Pat Higgins said over the PA system. "That's it for today, everyone. I hope you had another worthwhile discussion and will continue it with your teams at dinner this evening. Have a great rest of the day, and I'll see you tomorrow."

When the room began to empty, Inga made a point of talking to Lou to be sure he wasn't offended by her assertiveness. He assured her that he was fine and repeated his appreciation of her honesty. Then he did something that was uncharacteristic for men of his age from Minnesota. He leaned over and hugged her. For her part, Inga did something even more uncharacteristic for women of her age raised in Germany. She allowed him to. Don gave her a strange look as they started for their suite.

————————

5:55 p.m., the Porthole Piano Bar

"Good afternoon, Mrs. Conway, Dr. Conway," said Sven, smiling just warmly enough to keep from leering. "You are the first ones here. Shall I bring your usual drinks?" he asked.

"Hold it. Don't bring the cheap stuff he drinks," said Melissa, coming up behind Sven. "Bring us a couple of bottles of Veuve Clicquot. I'm celebrating."

"Did I hear celebrating?" asked Phil as he and Carol arrived with Don and Inga. "What's the occasion?"

"It's a good-news, bad-news deal," said Eddie. "The good news is Miss Lucky just took the casino for a pile of money at the craps table, so she can afford to buy. The bad news is Imperial Cruise Lines can no longer afford to put those chocolates on our pillows at night due to the trouncing they took at the tables."

"*Quel dommage*," said Nicole. "Ah look fowahd to those chawklets evree naht. Ah'll jest have to dhruwn ma disaponment in Malissa's free champagne."

"Ah do declah," said Carol. "You sound more like Blanche Dubois every day."

"And frankly, my dear, you've got the worst southern accent of anyone I've ever heard," said Phil, smirking at his wife.

"Well, it's not fair. Blanche there has had years of practice, and Ah'm still a-learnin'.'"

"You take that back. Ah havunt had *that* many years of practice," said Nicole.

"No offence, dahlin'," said Carol.

"None taken," said Nicole in her Blanche accent.

"Speaking of the devil, here he is," said Don, as Sven brought the cold champagne in ice buckets and eight chilled glasses.

"To absent friends," they all chorused, laughed, and drank.

"Good meeting today," said Don. "I have a lot to think about."

Eddie noticed that Don had stopped drinking Manhattans before dinner a few days ago.

Phil noticed that Eddie only took a sip of his champagne, then pushed his glass aside.

"What's one of the things you're thinking about, Don?" he asked.

"One of the guys in our discussion group came up with a story about making our lives meaningful. He told the story of a young girl's pet rabbit that just ate and pooped. The point was, there was no point to the rabbit's life. It had no purpose. I'm thinking I'd like to know what I'm going to do that matters with my remaining years. I don't want to be like Fluffy."

"One of the men in our group told an interesting story that made me think," said Phil. "He said, 'I learned a lot from a guy I met when I was just a young man; Bob Peterson was his name. We took a Greyhound bus from Detroit to Miami because he got us fired after he got drunk and didn't show up for work. Bob was about ten years older than me, resourceful, with a great personality, and he was a good salesman—when he was sober. When we got to Miami, he got a job selling magazines on the phone and a room for us to share while we were getting settled. Bob almost immediately started dating the girl whose job it was to call his reported sales to verify their legitimacy.

Bob's sales always got approved, even though he frequently did not understand when people said no. When management found out they were cheating, both he and the girl were fired. I learned some valuable things from Bob about selling and the downside to dishonesty.'

"It made me think; our thoughts are a collection of memories and are influenced by past experiences, and we have selective memories. We tend to block out those unpleasant memories and many times do positive revisions of our history, which is why we should have a healthy suspicion of most autobiographies.

"However, there is tremendous value to be gained by looking back on those past experiences to examine what we've learned from them and how they've shaped us into becoming the people we are. We can redefine ourselves, based on a new, more mature perspective of ourselves."

"That tracks with an observation of mine," said Melissa. "The more I read the writings of Joseph Campbell, the more I grow to appreciate that each of us is on our own hero's journey, as we discussed the other day. Your life and mine can be great sources of inspiration and learning for ourselves and others."

"I think that is exactly what Plato meant when he said, 'The unexamined life is not worth living,'" said Inga.

Sven came to the table to tell them that Maurice, the maître d' in Red Ginger, called to let them know their table was ready. Melissa signed the check. They thanked her and Sven and took the elevator to the Asian restaurant.

7:00 p.m., the Red Ginger Room

Maurice greeted them by name as they entered. Eddie wondered how the staff knew the guests when they hadn't seen them before. Just one more example of the superior service Imperial provided.

Looking around, they commented on the restaurant and its décor. Red Ginger made an immediate and powerful statement with its decorative centerpiece: three fabulous, multi-colored Buddha heads, each carved from a single piece of glass and brightly lit from within. The décor simply radiated with modern Asian artwork.

Nigel, their waiter, seated them while his assistant brought water, tea, and menus. As they studied the menus, they noticed Red Ginger's chefs had created striking, mouth-watering choices, with contemporary interpretations of Asian classics. They all ordered the roast duck and salad with watermelon, cashews, mint, and Thai basil. Next, they chose a savory, nutty braised beef Malay curry with coconut rice and paratha roti. The entrée was Asian-spiced rack of lamb with kohlrabi, creamed spinach, and truffle oil.

As they ate and enjoyed the delicious food, they picked up the conversation from the bar.

"You know, Addison was talking today about being happy," said Carol. "That is the goal of many of us when we retire, to be happy. I guess we could say that if we achieve that happiness, we are a success."

"Well," said Eddie, "I think we are already successful and may not fully appreciate it. I read that the British comedian Ricky Gervais said in a recent interview, 'If you get up in the morning and go to bed at night and have done exactly what you wanted to do in between, you are a success.' I want this year to be an outstanding success. I want to go to bed at night having done exactly what I wanted to do each day this year."

"How's that working out for you, my love?" asked Melissa sarcastically, her tongue loosened by the champagne.

"Do I sense a little bit of cynicism about your husband's lofty goals?" asked Phil with a grin.

"Not just a little—a lot, and it is justified," jumped in Eddie before Melissa could answer. "You might as well know this about me. I've told you that I'm writing a book on successful retirement. What I didn't tell you is that I've been writing it for five years. The reason for Melissa's cynicism, as you so indelicately put it, Mr. Butler, is that I am bone lazy, and I don't stick to a disciplined writing schedule. Isn't that right, my love?"

Inga noticed that whenever Eddie and Melissa used "my love" to one another, it was not always a term of endearment. Many times, it was used as a weapon in their marital sparring.

"Based on our conversations around the dinner table, I'd say you've got a lot of good material that you can use in your book," said Don.

"Oh," said Melissa, "he's got plenty of good stuff. He's got good stuff up the ying-yang, but he has to stop talking about it and do it. Isn't that right, my love?"

"Okay, then," said Eddie. "This might fall into the category of 'do as I say, not as I do.' To make sure you do go to bed each night with that sense of accomplishment, create a vision of the ideal way you'd like your life to look at the end of the year. We think in pictures, so that vision or mental image of what happiness and success look like to you will ensure its attainment."

Phil said, "I would add the additional element of purpose to what you are saying, Eddie. It is our way of ensuring that this year, more than ever, our living will have mattered. I think, to make our lives matter, we need to be guided by a purpose."

"I'd agree with that," said Don. "Those two essential building blocks, vision and purpose, will serve us in designing our lives for this next year. I think that my having a vision and a purpose for my daily life enables me to achieve the maximum amount of happiness and satisfaction."

"That's just like a man," said Melissa. "You talk about building blocks as though designing a satisfying retirement plan is like a construction project. Yes, we need vision and purpose in our planning, but those are insufficient components to providing us with a rich, full, and satisfying life. Go back to Don's rabbit story. The critical aspect of the rabbit's life plan that is clearly missing is any emotional outcome to doing something other than eating and pooping."

"Melissa's right," said Carol. "Remember when Simone de Beauvoir said that thing about life consisting of not only sustaining oneself but also in surpassing oneself? If it doesn't, then living is only *not* dying, and life becomes an absurd vegetation. I don't believe we can attain that level of enriched living without a deep emotional commitment to our lives and the plan for our lives."

"I've identified my purpose," said Eddie. "It is to assist the maximum number of people in achieving a full, rich, satisfying retirement by using all of their potential, and to contribute to the world. That *purpose* gives my life meaning. It is the reason I am here on this earth for this short time. I think there are as many different purposes as there are people on earth. Each person is unique and perfect, as is their purpose. Everybody has a purpose, and I'd be willing to bet that they are already being true to it. Whatever one is doing to make their home, neighborhood, city, state, country, and the world a better place for themselves and others is that person, in action, fulfilling their purpose in life. That is the reason God put them here. They might not fully recognize that what they are doing is what they should be doing. It might be recycling or saying a kind word to another person who needs it. It might be serving on a neighborhood or church committee. It might be demonstrating when their voice needs to be heard. The point is we are all perfect in who and what we are. We're even perfect when we are searching for our purpose."

"Well, *ah* swear, that was quite a speech, Revrund," said Nicole. "I've got a little different slant on this whole thang. Ah think the whole purpose of life is to be happy, period. If y'all do that, y'all will make the people around you happy."

"Easy to say," said Carol. "How do you do that?"

"Ah've got a real simple method that Ah use. Once a year Ah set down an' go back over my activities for the last year, an' I make a list of those things that Ah'm glad I did. The things Ah feel good about. Then Ah make a list of those things I wisht Ah had'n dun or wisht Ah'd dun more of, less of, or not atall. Then Ah jist do more of the good stuff and less of the bad stuff."

"Hold it," said Inga, taking out her notebook. "That sounds pretty good; let me write it down. You said make lists of the things you are glad you did and things you wish you had not done in the previous year, then change your actions for the next year. Right?"

"Egzacklee," said Nicole, smiling.

"You wouldn't have to wait a whole year. You could do that monthly, weekly, or even every day," said Carol. "That would keep you on the right track for successful living. Thank you for sharin' that, Blanche."

"Yer welcome, dahlin'."

"Didn't Doug mention well-being in the orientation session as a desired outcome for this seminar?" asked Melissa.

"Yes, he did, and going back to what we were saying about vision-ing, I like that thing we talked about before that Walt Whitman said about visualizing. 'I have imagined the life of the ordinary man in ordinary circumstances, yet grand, heroic.'"

"Well, she gave us a lot to think about today," said Inga.

"Yes, I got some good notes," said Carol.

"Great. Would you read them to us as a review?" asked Nicole.

"Yes, and would you share them with me?" asked Inga. "I'll print them all before we separate in Barcelona and be sure everyone has a copy."

"Sure. Here they are," said Carol.

Tools to Make Us Happier

- Create an environment of energy, enthusiasm, and fun for people
- Show your appreciation to someone every day
- Help others reach their goals
- For your own well-being, get outdoors as much as possible
- Travel with your friends at every opportunity
- Remember the value of face-to-face communication
- Share your talents by being a mentor

- Make time for important people in your life
- Smile often to improve your "face" value
- Appreciate every precious day of your life

8:30 p.m.

Nigel brought dessert. It consisted of green tea banana cake with toffee and hazelnut sauce, served with coconut ice cream. It was a perfect ending to a perfect meal.

When everyone finished, they made a point of thanking Nigel and Maurice on the way out.

9:00 p.m., the Lobby

"Who's up for some dancing?" asked Carol.

"Ooh, me," said Nicole.

"Yeah, I'm in," said Eddie. "Melissa?"

"No, I think I'll go see if they brought a fresh supply of money to the casino, so I can take them apart again."

"That's the trouble with gambling," said Eddie. "They'll let you win in the short run because they know you don't know when to quit. Isn't that right, my love?"

"When you're good and know how to bet, you don't always lose, my love."

Don and Inga turned toward the elevator, and Arthur said, "Wait for me. I don't feel like dancing. Will you two gentlemen see to it that Nickie gets a twirl or two around the dance floor?"

"Sure," said Eddie enthusiastically.

"Have him home by daybreak," said Melissa to Nicole. "He has to bring me breakfast in bed."

"I can't promise anything. He's awfully cute." She linked her arm with his and started toward the elevator with Phil and Carol close behind.

———

DaY eIGHT

April 14

When Eddie opened his eyes, Melissa was already up, sitting on the couch reading the paper and drinking coffee. She'd been asleep when he came in from his dancing and drinking adventure with the Butlers and Nicole.

When he came out of the bathroom, she spoke. "Good morning, sleepyhead. How did it go last night? Coffee?"

"Yes, please. Last night was great," he said. "Phil and Carol are good dancers, and Nicole has enough energy for two people. I couldn't keep up with the three of them."

"Did you learn anything new about any of them?" she asked. Her legal training and law degree always kicked in after he'd been with other people or at a meeting. She always had more questions than a normal person, so he was prepared.

"I did," he answered. "I think there is trouble in paradise with the Butlers. While they danced well together, she seemed a bit icy when they came back to the table. It wasn't overt, but I sensed something. Have you had any indication of that?"

"Oh yeah, big time. Nothing that you'd pick up on in a casual meeting, but we've been with them for a week, and there are plenty of signs. I've seen the same symptoms in my practice with couples going through a divorce. Mostly from Carol; Phil seems oblivious."

"That's too bad. I've become a fan of Phil's. He seems like a sharp guy with a ton of personality. Should I talk to him?"

"It couldn't hoit," she said. "What about Nickie?"

"Ah, Nickie. She's an attractive woman."

"I've *seen* her," she said sharply. "I mean did you learn anything new about her?"

"Yeah, I did. She is a whole lot sharper than she lets on. She held her own when Phil and I got into a conversation about Eastern philosophy. She's read more and has done more serious thinking than one would suspect."

"Did you dance with her?" she asked, with a hint of jealousy.

"Oh yeah," he laughed. "She clung to me like I was the hottest thing she'd ever seen."

"In your dreams. Phil seems more like her type. Did he dance with her?"

"No. She asked him several times, but he said no and was actually even downright cold and, I thought, a little rude. I'm not as intuitive as you, but I don't think she would have any interest in Phil or anybody else. The way she talks about Arthur tells me that in spite of her va-va-voom persona, she is crazy about him and is devoted to him."

"I don't know if he gets that," she said. "He seems a bit obtuse when it comes to their relationship. She is quite a bit worldlier than he is."

"I don't think of her as being sophisticated at all," he said.

Melissa answered, "I didn't say sophisticated. The subtle difference is, what she lacks in education she makes up in *worldly* experiences, if you get my drift."

"I'd like to know more about that. Maybe you'll have a chance to dig into it a little further."

"You want to know if she'd leave Arthur and run off with you, right?" She laughed.

"I have no doubt that she would do that in a New York minute," he said. "If she wants to, can I have the money to finance the adventure?" he asked laughingly.

"We don't have enough money for you to support her in the fashion to which she has become accustomed. Plus, you know our long-standing deal: you can go, but you have to take the kids with you."

They both laughed, and she leaned over and kissed him. "What do you want to do?" she asked.

"I'm going to take a shower, and in spite of your lack of belief in me as a soon-to-be-published *New York Times* bestselling author, I'm going to sit down in front of this computer and tap out some brilliant prose."

"I believe in you. I know you are going to produce great work. I can't wait to read it. I just wonder if it will happen in my lifetime." She laughed.

"Get out of here," he said. "Do you think Hemingway's wife would have been as cynical about his writing?"

"Which one?" she asked. "He never kept one around as long as you've kept me.

"None of them were as sweet as you. Now get out. I've got great literature to produce."

Laughing, she opened the door. "I'll meet you for lunch. Say eleven thirty at the Terrace Café?"

"Perfect." He kissed her on the cheek and said, "Now go, woman. I've got a classic to write."

11:30 a.m., the Terrace Café

"Guess who's here?" said Melissa as Eddie walked into the restaurant. "Phil and Carol," she said, without waiting for him to answer. "They are in line at the buffet. I told them you were coming and I'd hold the table until they got here."

"What would you like? I'll get it for you," he said.

"How about a Caesar salad and a dinner roll?"

"You got it; be back in a minute."

He passed the Butlers on the way to the salad bar and told them he'd be right with them. When they were seated, Melissa said, "I understand you all had a great time last night."

"You mean, y'all with Blanche?" asked Phil.

"Did she try to steal my husband?"

"No," said Carol. "I don't think she wants to steal anybody's husband, even one as handsome as yours."

"What makes you say that?" asked Melissa. "That's a different story than the one I got from Eddie this morning."

"What?" said Phil and Carol at the same time.

"Yes, I think he said something like, 'When we danced together, she was clinging to me and looking into my eyes like I was George Clooney.'"

Everyone laughed except Eddie, who blushed and took a drink of his iced tea.

"You're safe," said Carol. "I had a couple of opportunities to talk to her last night when the guys went to get us a drink, and she is happy with Arthur, Des Moines, and her life."

"So she has a happy marriage, then, like Eddie and me. I think that's super important for enjoying life in retirement or this so-called second chapter of life, don't you agree?" she asked, looking directly at Carol.

"God, she's good," thought Eddie to himself. "It didn't take her long to get that question out there."

"Oh, I absolutely do," said Phil. "You know we are celebrating our twenty-fifth wedding anniversary on this cruise, and I have never been happier in my life."

Melissa didn't take her eyes off Carol while Phil was speaking and noticed that there was no change in her expression. "That speaks volumes," she thought. "Eddie was right, it is not going well with them, and he is clueless."

"Well, it's twelve thirty," said Carol, looking at her watch. "I want to freshen up before the meeting."

"I'll go up with you," said Melissa. "I'll meet you downstairs at the meeting, my love."

They walked out together, and the guys finished their coffee.

"Everything all right, Carol?" asked Melissa as they got on the elevator.

"Yes. Uh, what do you mean?" she asked.

"At the table when we were talking about a happy marriage, I noticed you didn't say anything. I was just wondering if you agreed with our opinions."

Carol didn't answer; she just looked at the floor indicator lights.

"Phil said you were celebrating your twenty-fifth, and that can be a tough one for a lot of couples. I'm a divorce attorney, and I'm always amazed when people who seem to have every reason to be happy decide to end it. I've developed an intuitive sense when there are unspoken feelings in the room."

"Here's my room," said Carol, taking out her key.

"I don't mean to intrude, but I've grown to like you during this week we've had together," said Melissa. "If you ever want to talk, I'm available."

Carol looked at her seriously. "Thank you. I'll see you downstairs," she said, and went into her room.

1:00 p.m., the Celebrity Theater

Don and Inga walked into the meeting room ten minutes early and were each given a handout on perspective.

1:15 p.m., Reporting

"Welcome, everyone," Pat Higgins enthusiastically greeted the group.

"We have another exciting day ahead of us. Here's your reporting period assignment: 'What has happened for me as a result of our team dinner discussions so far?'"

Carlos, the maître d' in the grand dining room, was their group leader for the day. He asked everyone to think for two minutes about their answer to Pat's question and then write it down using no more than three minutes.

When the time was up, he said, "The person who has taken the most cruises will go first. If there is a tie, I'll arbitrarily break it because," he said jokingly, "I'm in charge here."

"That is probably us," said an overweight, balding man sitting next to Carlos. "This is our fifteenth cruise. Can anyone top that?"

They all laughed and shook their heads.

"It's you then. Tell everybody who you are and what you've written."

"My name is Martin Kennedy. I've had some amazing insights on personal growth as it relates to happiness. At seventy-eight, I had pretty much decided that my growing days were over, but there is an eighty-five-year-old man on our team who, a few nights ago, said something that was eye-opening. He said, 'We know from our own experience, or that of our children, that physical growth is visible and apparent. We outgrow our clothes. We stand on the scales to see how much we've gained or lost. We make a mark on the doorway as our offspring stands dutifully waiting to see how much he has grown since his last birthday. These are the ways in which we monitor our physical progress.'

"Then he said, 'More important is our mental, emotional, and spiritual growth.' That is the part that got me to thinking."

"My name is Gladys Kennedy," said a matronly woman to his right. "I'm Martin's wife, and we've been married fifty-five years. We've never talked about nonmaterial things much, but this seminar got us both thinking."

"That's the whole point of this cruise and this seminar, isn't it?" said a pasty-faced beanpole of a man to Carlos's left. "To get us to do what we mostly don't do? At least most of the guys back in Port

Clinton, Ohio, don't think or talk about mental, emotional, or spiritual growth. Oh, I'm Marshall Palmer, by the way."

"That might be a function of our ages," said Don. "Most of us around this table are products of the Depression era, and our parents were more concerned with putting food on the table and paying the mortgage than any esoteric stuff."

"And you are?" asked Carlos.

"Oh, I'm sorry. Dr. Donald Conway, and this is my wife, Inga," he said, pointing to her. "We're from New York. We don't live there now, we moved to Washington three years ago."

"Not to interrupt," interrupted Carlos, "but we do want to hear from everyone before our time is up. We'll come back to you a bit later, Don. Inga, how about you? What have you written?"

"We've been talking all week about the importance of continuing to grow and set goals as we are in this next chapter of our lives, and that has impressed me so much."

"I'm Beatrice Palmer," said the beanpole's wife, sitting on his left, "And I have a question for everybody, I guess. How do we go about measuring those intangibles? I mean like the mental, emotional, and spiritual growth?"

Before anyone could answer, Pat Higgins announced the break. "Be back in your seats at two o'clock sharp," he said. "Doug Carson is back with us today for another thought-provoking talk on attitudes of success."

————

2:00 p.m.

"Welcome back, everyone," said Pat. "Let's hear about the attitudes of success from the man who invented the words. Get your feet flat on the floor and once again give a great big Imperial welcome to Mr. Enthusiasm himself, R. Douglas Carson."

A noisy round of applause greeted him as he took the mike and stepped up on the stage.

"Hello, Imperialistics," boomed Doug Carson into the mike. "Is everybody happy?"

"*Yes!*" Everybody yelled back at "Mr. Enthusiasm himself."

"Did you all read the handout you received when you entered the room?"

When everybody yelled yes again, Doug went on. "Can you hear me in the back? I'm always nervous when I ask that question. Once I was giving a talk in Las Vegas, and about halfway through, I asked if everybody could hear me. A guy in the back row yelled no. A guy in the front row stood up, turned around, and yelled, 'Would you trade places with me? I can still hear him.'"

This brought a round of laughter from the group.

"That's why I asked you before I got too far into my presentation. I told you the last time we met about buying a new Cadillac on my fiftieth birthday. Well, now I'll tell you the rest of the story, as Paul Harvey used to say. As much as I wanted that car, I was reluctant to spend the amount of money it cost.

"Steve 'Pepper' Anderson, the car salesman at Anderson Motors, is a friend and a good salesman. While we were talking, a funeral procession went by on the street outside the dealership. He stopped talking, looked out the window, and sighed.

"'A friend of yours?' I asked.

"'No. I was thinking, whatever amount of money he had, he left it *all* behind. You know,' he said, pointing to the hearse, 'Someday you *will* ride in a Cadillac.'

"Well, that did it for me. He gave me perspective, and that's why I went ahead and bought the car. This whole seminar is about perspective rather than a series of tips on what you should do. There are plenty of good books on the nuts and bolts of retirement, and many of you have read many of them, so we don't have to go over that ground. This seminar is about perspective; how we look at and think about things and, more importantly, what we do about what we think about.

"So let's look at the way we think; the way in which we use our minds. Much of this is review for you, but that won't hurt. Herbert Spenser, the great English philosopher and educator, said, 'We all need to be reminded rather than taught.' Visioning is a first step to personal growth and achieving one's goals. That, of course, is a necessary but insufficient step to promoting and monitoring our growth in those vital nonphysical areas of our lives.

"To be a fully functioning, productive human being, we need to access and use all our talents and potential. That includes the genius that resides in all of us, if we would avail ourselves of it. Part of the visualizing process is to allow our minds to create a set of attitudes and conditions that answers the question, 'What would my life look like if everything were ideal?'"

Inga had her notebook out and was scribbling like mad.

Doug continued. "The answers to that question will give us the necessary behaviors and measurements we need to achieve growth in those less physical areas. Once we've identified the vision of our ideal selves, we can set goals with measurements attached to them.

"Examples of that would be the books we've read and the seminars we've attended to promote our mental and spiritual growth. We can also use feedback from others on behaviors that indicate progress in those areas.

"I'm a member of a discussion group that meets every Thursday morning to discuss the relationship between consciousness and the insights being supplied by the quantum physicists. Of course, I am always listening for the pragmatic application of any of the conclusions drawn by the group in these conversations. In our discussion recently, the subject of intuition came up. The *American Heritage Dictionary* defines intuition as 'the art or faculty of sensing or knowing without the use of rational processes.'

"We are all intuitive, aren't we? Who has not had the experience of knowing who was calling even before the phone rang, only to have that person on the line? Before the days of caller ID, it was pretty impressive to pick up the phone and say, 'Hello, Bill.' Now, not so much.

"I think each of us possesses an inner genius. How can you and I use this phenomenon to enrich our retirement? I see a close inner relationship between intuition, inspiration, and intelligence. Those are the components of that inner genius that is the mother of our creativity and the father of achievement. Our ability to produce meaningful results in the world depends on our ability to use this vast, mostly underutilized resource. It is there for us to use, for as Carl Jung said, 'Intuition is perception via the unconscious.'"

Inga made a note of that statement and underlined it several times.

Doug wrapped up his presentation by saying, "If we're to maximize our remaining time in life, I suggest we tap into our inner genius and our intuition and produce meaningful results for our fellow man. Thank you."

The audience applauded enthusiastically as Doug left the stage.

———

3:00 p.m.

Pat Higgins took the mike and said, "Thank you for another outstanding presentation, Doug. Let's give him another round of applause.

"We're ready for a fifteen-minute break, everyone. Please be back in your seats right on time for our discussion."

When everyone returned and was seated, Carlos said, "Please take two minutes to think, then write your answer to the question, 'What were the three most important ideas you got from today's presentation?'"

When the time was up, he said, "Martin, you were writing pretty fast and furious. What have you written? Just your number-one item?"

"Doug did not say it directly, but what I inferred from his talk was that we need to reevaluate and set some new goals for ourselves. I think we need to do that to achieve fulfillment and overcome the ennui that tends to accompany maturity and fulfilled goals."

Marshal Palmer spoke up. "I no longer get the jolt I used to get when I was building my business. That's how I know it's time for me to retire and set some new goals."

"There is a reason for that," said Don. "When the frontal cortex of the brain stops producing serotonin, the organic compound formed in the brain from tryptophan, the needed stimulation to go into action is missing. No serotonin, no stimulation, and thus no jolt. Consequently, no drive to take on new challenges and set new goals."

"Having goals and getting into action is important to me," said Gladys Kennedy. "That is, if they are the right kinds of goals and actions."

Inga said, "That question Doug asked us," reading from her notes, "'What would my life look like if everything were ideal?' struck home with me. That is an important question for anyone to answer at any age."

Then Beatrice Palmer said, "I still have the same question as before: How do we go about measuring mental, emotional, and spiritual growth?"

———

3:45 p.m.

"That's time, everybody." Pat Higgins's voice interrupted the hubbub. Once again, Beatrice's question went unanswered. "Please continue your conversations at your team meeting this evening, and I'll see you all back here tomorrow."

The room emptied quickly.

Don and Inga walked out with the Palmers, and in an uncharacteristic display of brevity, Don said, "Beatrice, to answer your question, we must use different metrics in measuring those ethereal qualities such as emotions and spiritual and mental growth progress. We measure those things experientially rather than with hard data. In other words, do we feel better, are we more spiritually centered today than yesterday, do we perceive ourselves as being more mentally astute today than yesterday?"

She smiled, thanked him, and said that he had been helpful. However, he could see her shaking her head as she walked away.

6:00 p.m., the Piano Bar

Coincidentally, the group all walked into the bar at the same time. They greeted one another with smiles. The women hugged each other in turn, and everybody talked about their morning while Sven brought their drinks.

"What did you think of today's session?" Phil asked Eddie. "Seems like stuff that is right up your alley, right?"

"Doug started to get close to some things I know something about, motivation and goals. The thing missing for me is not enough emphasis on knowing what our *purpose* in life is. The successful people I've known and worked with are mission- or purpose-driven people. I think there must be some application of that attribute in retirement planning."

"We talked about the need for stimulation in our group discussion," said Don. "That mission or purpose is the ingredient that supplies the stimulation to produce and to achieve."

"We need to have that stimulation in order to create discomfort," said Eddie. "We seem to need it to keep moving forward. We also need it to set new and higher goals in every phase of our lives."

"I've heard you refer to 'constructive discontent,'" chimed in Arthur. "I think that plays an important role in our setting personal growth goals and accessing that inner genius Doug talked about today."

"You always told me you didn't think you were that motivated during your career," said Nicole to Arthur.

"Well, I didn't think I was, but so much of my life was scripted that the goals seemed to be preset for me."

"What would you have done differently if those goals hadn't been preset?" asked Inga.

"I've always had an interest in music but didn't follow that passion the way Don followed his."

Don was pleased to receive that acknowledgement from Arthur since he felt somewhat inferior to his accomplishments.

"Why don't you do something about that now?" asked Carol. "It's not too late. George Sands said, 'It is never too late to become all that you can.'"

"Yes," Don said. "You mentioned our inner genius, and I heard once that 'genius creates the conditions which assure its success.' You can still do that. I think you and all of us should tap into our inner genius at every stage of our lives, especially now in retirement."

"I agree," said Inga. "I liked the ending of Doug's presentation today when he said"—she referred to her notebook—"'to maximize our remaining time in life, I suggest we tap into our inner genius and our intuition and produce meaningful results for our fellow man.'"

Sven brought their tab and said Carlos had just called from the main dining room to let him know their table was ready. Inga signed the bill, and they left for dinner.

———

7:00 p.m., the Grand Dining Room

Carlos greeted them in the dining room foyer. Don noticed that he was more formal than he had been when he was leading the group discussion in the afternoon.

Don asked, "Has anyone else noticed how the crew's personalities change as their duties change? It must be the way they are trained to carry out the variety of assignments they are called on to perform."

"We had an interesting discussion in our small group today," said Eddie. "I've found the variety of people I've met on this cruise to be fascinating. We had a banker, a retired school administrator, and a painting contractor in our group."

"A painting contractor! A painting contractor!" said Phil. "You've got to watch that bunch. You want to know why?"

"Why?" asked Eddie.

"Well," Phil went on, "I heard of a dishonest house painter who cheated his customers by adding paint thinner to his paint in order to increase his profits. No longer able to abide by it, God called down from heaven, 'Make amends for your evil ways. Repaint and thin no more.'"

Groans from around the table.

"I thought you'd been cured of your vice of telling bad jokes," said Arthur.

"You know what Quentin Crisp said?" Phil rejoined. "'Vice is its own reward.'"

"What's on the menu?" asked Nicole. "Ah'm hongry."

Melissa said, "Your favorite, my love, filet mignon and *pommes frites*."

"Say what?" asked Nicole.

"*Pommes frites*. You know, french fries."

"We just called them taters at home," she said in her Blanche Dubois accent.

This drew a laugh from everyone, and Phil once again marveled at how she could so easily and comfortably take over the stage.

When Armando came to their table, they ordered. The guys all ordered steak, and the women all ordered sea bass. As they ate their salads and fresh, warm baguettes, they continued their conversation.

"I think the whole point of this seminar is to be proactive in our retirement years," said Inga. "There is no reason why we shouldn't be using the same success tools we used during our careers and our working years now that we're in this next, more mature stage of our lives."

"I like what Doug had to say about visualizing today," said Phil. "I've been using the technique of thinking and picturing my goals all my adult life. Those important thoughts and the corresponding images and emotions that accompanied them served as a blueprint as I planned my life and went into action. I'd review them and update them on an annual basis. A high percentage of those affirmations and the goals I set as a result have produced a life full of happiness and abundance that I would not have thought possible when I was growing up."

"Then," said Don, looking thoughtful and speaking slowly, "your recommendation as we prepare to launch the action plan for the next phase of our lives is to spend some time visualizing what an ideal year and ideal next five years will look like. Then, a year from now, go back and review our progress, right?"

"That makes sense to me," said Carol. "I don't know about the rest of you, but I've gotten lax in the past few years. We've achieved most of our goals, and I find myself kind of coasting."

"We talked about creating our lives as if we were artists," said Phil. "During the review process, I ask myself, 'Did my artistic creation match the image I had in mind?' If it doesn't, then I ask, 'What will I need to do differently to be sure that the next year is better?'"

Don said, "Remember that quotation by Walt Whitman that we talked about before? It ties in perfectly with this visualizing process. How did it go? 'I have imagined the life of the ordinary man in ordinary circumstances, yet grand, heroic.' I like that a lot."

"Another quotation that fits here," said Eddie, "is one by Cicero. He said, 'The most valuable of the arts is the art of living.' I like the idea of thinking of myself as an artist designing my retirement years."

"Yeah," said Phil, "And you can't count on anybody else doing it for you. I walked into a barbershop one day and asked the barber, 'Can you make me look young, distinguished, and handsome?' She looked me over and said, 'Well, I can do young.'"

"Oh, Phil, can't you ever get any new material?" asked Carol.

"Don't need to," he said. "It's easier to get a new audience than it is to get new stuff."

"Well, there is some value in using the old stuff," said Eddie. "We can draw from our past experiences or the experiences of others to update our goals and affirmations now. In doing this, we assure ourselves that our second chapter lives are as rich or richer than they were in the first chapter."

Armando and his assistants cleared the salad plates, served the entrees, and filled their wine glasses.

"*Ah* know somebody that did something with the picturin' thing," said Nicole. "They had a nice house in my hometown in Louisiana that they wanted to sell. The market was tight then. Houses weren't selling and theirs was a real expensive one. The realator they used is a friend of mine, and he's also an architect, so he did something interesting. He did a rendering of what their one-story house would look like if a potential buyer were to add a second story. It captured the imagination and aroused the emotions of the people who bought the house and contributed to their decision to buy it. The reason is that the drawing made it possible for the family to see themselves livin' in and enjoyin' the modified home, which would have been too small for them as a one-story. That's kinda the way we could be picturin' our lives, isn't it?"

"Yes, we can do that for sure, what your *realtor* friend did," said Phil, emphasizing the correct pronunciation. "It was a creative, artistic, and pragmatic solution to a business challenge. Here's how we can use the same approach for achieving fulfillment of after-fifty goals. Turn our goals into pictures that capture our imaginations and enable us to see what our lives will look like when those pictures become reality. Look at it every day. Visualize ourselves as having already attained those things and conditions. By doing this we experience the emotions that accompany that new reality. By adding affirmations and repeating them as we go, we'll see positive lives unfold."

"Tell them about your treasure map, honey," said Carol.

Phil looked surprised at her use of the term of endearment. She hadn't been that loving toward him the whole trip.

"Well, yes then. I know people want to know if that approach will work. Yes, definitely! How do I know that? It works for me. I have a poster board a few feet away from my desk that depicts my vision. This approach has been called by different names. I call mine a treasure map.

"It is a collage made up of pictures I cut from magazines, some photographs of my wife and daughters, a bag of shredded thousand-dollar bills totaling a million dollars, and other items that illustrate my heart's desires. Looking at my treasure map every day keeps me focused, mentally and emotionally, on the things that are important to me.

"The result of this technique and doing the work necessary to bring those images into reality has paid off big time for me over a period of years. I believe it will for anybody."

Carol said proudly, "I know it works for him. I've watched him practice this for twenty-five years. I've seen him start from nothing and build a successful business."

Phil noticed that Carol was smiling and looking at him with pride.

Armando and his crew had been listening and waiting for Phil to finish speaking. Now they stepped in and cleared the dishes and served dessert.

"What's this?" asked Inga.

"It is called Bananas Foster, and if you do not care for it, I can bring you something else, Mrs. Conway, and I'll eat that." He smiled.

"No." She smiled back at him. "I'll keep it."

Don said, "What this conversation brings up for me is that this is the time, after age fifty or perhaps a little later, for us to determine what it is we value or honor. We've had enough time to sort it out. Enough time to find out what gives us pleasure and what gives us pain. We can then cultivate the former and weed out the latter. For me, this is sometimes a painful process and is taking longer than I'd like."

———

9:30 p.m.
Armando and his team cleared the table for the final time, signaling that it was time for them to move.

"What this conversation brings up for me is a headache," said Nicole. "Y'all have gotten into some deep stuff here. Is anybody else up for some music and dancing?"

"I am," said Melissa. "How about you, my love? You game?"

"Yeah, I can probably last for an hour or so. Anybody else?"

"Color me in," said Phil. "Carol?"

"Would I ever pass up a dance with you?"

He couldn't tell if she was being sarcastic, but he often missed subtle signals from her, so he pulled out her chair, and they left with the others for the dance floor.

———

Day Nine

April 15

Eddie and Melissa stepped out on the track in the cool morning breeze and joined a couple dozen other passengers for their morning aerobic walk. They saw Phil and Carol and waited for them to catch up.

"Hey, you guys," said Carol. "Good to see you out here." She wore shorts and a bright red tank top, and Melissa noticed that both she and Phil were trim and physically fit. They were an attractive couple, she thought, and, reflecting back on her conversation with Carol after lunch yesterday, she wondered what could be so wrong with them. They obviously had serious money and were both articulate and intelligent. As they made their way around the track at an aerobic pace, they talked about the ship and the amenities it offered.

When they finished two miles' worth of laps, Phil said, "I'm going up to hit some golf balls into the net and practice my putting. I don't want to get too rusty while I'm away. Do you want to join me, Eddie?"

"Absolutely. Do you mind, my love?"

"No, not at all. I'm in the mood for a latte at Barista."

Carol said, "Do you mind if I join you?"

"No, not at all. I'd love it," she said. The guys headed up to do their guy thing, and Melissa and Carol walked up to the espresso bar next to the library. They ordered lattes and scones and took them outside to sit on lounge chairs.

"What a beautiful day," said Melissa.

"I'm thinking about divorcing Phil," said Carol softly.

Melissa didn't comment. She knew Carol would keep talking.

"I feel awful. He is the sweetest guy in the whole world. I was all set to tell him before this cruise and seminar thing came up. I couldn't do it because of the way he sprung it on me."

Melissa, smiled, nodded, and took a sip of her coffee.

"We've been married twenty-five years. Oh, you know that and ..." Her voice trailed off.

"Do you love him?" Melissa asked.

"Do I love him?" she asked, more to herself than to Melissa. It was almost as though she hadn't thought about it until now.

"We met at the Golden Gate Athletic Club. He was different from the guys I knew at Stanford. That's where I went to school. He was so real, so down to earth. He wasn't trying to impress anybody. We played tennis, and I thought he was the hottest thing I'd ever seen."

She looked embarrassed for having been so forthright, but Melissa gave her an approving look and a smile.

"Why am I telling you all this stuff?" She went on. "I threw all kinds of hints at him, but he never asked me out. I wasn't short of suitors. Plenty of guys wanted to date me. I wasn't the homeliest old thing in town. One of the guys at Stanford from a wealthy family would have done anything to marry me. Honestly, after all these years, I still think Phil is the most obtuse person I've ever met. I finally had to ask him out."

She paused, so Melissa said, "You said you are *thinking* about divorcing him. Does that mean you are not sure?"

"I was before we left home, but since we've been together nonstop for almost two weeks, I'm having second thoughts."

"Second thoughts?" asked Melissa.

"Yes, listening to Phil talk to others in the seminar has reminded me of how special he is. I wish my mother were still alive to appreciate that about him."

"She didn't appreciate him?"

"No, she didn't approve of him or our marriage, and she and Dad died before Phil became successful."

"Let me interrupt, Carol. If you're telling me all this because you're thinking that I could represent you in obtaining a divorce, I have to tell you I am not licensed in the state of California. I could recommend an attorney there through our network to be sure your financial interests are properly handled."

"Oh no, no. I'm talking to you because I feel a need to talk to somebody and you offered yesterday. I don't have anyone else to talk to."

"No one? What about a close friend?"

"That's the problem. I had friends all through college; my roommate and I were close. But Phil comes from a different background than mine, and that is why my parents didn't approve of him. He was in the scrap business with his father, and then when his parents died, he took over and ran the business. My father was a successful businessman. He owned an investment company and was ashamed of Phil. Phil was a high school dropout, and I graduated magna cum laude with a degree in marketing from Stanford. So we came from opposite ends of the spectrum. Mom and Dad were disappointed in me for not putting my degree to work after they spent so much to finance my education. Instead of going to work for a major company, I went to work with Phil."

"But he was—how did you put it? 'The hottest thing you'd ever seen.'"

"It wasn't just that. We'd talk between sets, and I could see that he was intelligent and ambitious. He was going to go places, and all I knew was, college or no college, I wanted to be with him. But that was then, and this is now. Now it's all gone; the sharing, the communication, and the closeness."

"The closeness?"

"Yes, we started out with barely more than the clothes on our backs. We both lost our parents when we were in our twenties; his were killed in an automobile accident, and mine died when I was twenty-two. We knew we wanted more from life than survival, so we paid the price and worked together. We did whatever it took. Nobody else believed in us, but we didn't care. We knew we could do it, and we did."

"You made it in what way, if I may ask without being too personal?"

Carol looked at her for a moment and said, "We made it big. The company is worth millions. Phil and a couple of his rich friends started Global Savings and Loan, lending money to low-income families, making it possible for them to be homeowners. Phil and I did a series of money management seminars, at no cost to them, and they never betrayed us. The number of defaults has been low. We both know what it's like to be broke and to have to scrape to get by. We have a lot of compassion for people in that situation. A few years ago, Phil was interviewed for a book about millionaires."

"What was the name of it?" asked Melissa.

"*The Millionaire Mind.* Have you ever heard of it?"

"Dr. Thomas Stanley, right?"

"Yes, a nice man. We spent quite a bit of time with him and his associates answering questions."

"Wow, that's something. So you wouldn't be hurting for money if you do divorce Phil?"

"No, not at all. I've got a good handle on our net worth, and money hasn't been an issue for us for a long time now."

"Well, I still don't understand. You're married to a hunk of a man with whom you were in lust." Melissa giggled. "Who is successful, with a great personality, and you've got more money than most people, especially at your age, about thirty-five, right?"

"Thank you," said Carol, laughing at Melissa's joke. "Forty-eight."

"Well, what then? Why leave?"

"Phil's moved on without me. He doesn't need me anymore. He has all kinds of employees and an assistant, so we don't talk anymore the way we did. We're just not close anymore. He's always buying me things, but that's not what I want."

"What do you think I can do for you, Carol?" asked Melissa.

"You've already done it by listening to me," she answered.

They talked a little longer, and Melissa said, "I'd better get up to the room, or Eddie will think I got lost."

They hugged and walked together to the elevator. Before the elevator arrived, Melissa said, "I do want to offer two thoughts. I've talked to a lot of clients who wanted and got a divorce, then found afterward that it was the biggest mistake of their lives. That isn't true for everyone; some found that getting divorced was the best thing for them. It is especially traumatic when people are entering the retirement years. Just something to think about. It is a big step. One other thing—every marriage has its rocky times. When Eddie and I had been married about the same amount of time, I was contemplating divorcing him, but I didn't."

"What changed your mind?"

"Two things. Unlike California, Indiana is not a community property state, so the financial consequences would have been devastating. It is called cutting the baby in half. It would have ruined us both financially, and it would have been too late to start over. The most important reason though: I asked myself the same question I asked you earlier, 'Do I love him?'

"When I realized the answer was yes, that changed everything. That's when I came to the conclusion that no one is perfect until you fall in love with them."

They hugged again, and Carol got on the elevator going up to her luxury suite. Melissa took the stairs down to her stateroom.

———

10:30 a.m., the Computer Room

Carol went to the computer room to check her email. The cruise line supplied her suite with a laptop, but after her revealing conversation with Melissa, she was feeling too raw to interact with Phil.

She opened her email and found a message from Sylvia Blount, her former roommate, Sigma Chi sorority sister, and best friend from college.

> "I haven't heard from you in ages. I'll be in San Fran next month. I just got a marketing job with Google, and I want to have lunch and bring you up to date on all the changes that have taken place. I got a message on your answer machine saying you were out of town. Call me when you get back. I remember all the fun we had at Stanford when we worked on that project together. XXXXXToo bad we can't work together again. ☺ We were so good together. Love, Sylvia. PS. Google could use you too. Interested?"

"Sylvia," she thought. "I haven't heard from her since she got married and moved to Boston with Brad Nichols after I broke up with him. Why is she using her maiden name?" she wondered. "Why is she going to work? What happened to the kids I read about on Facebook?" She mulled these questions over in her mind.

"Can I help you with anything, ma'am?" asked the manager, a helpful techie from Latvia, whose name was Vadim.

One of the cruise company staff, he was eager to help older, inept, technologically impaired passengers who couldn't remember their email passwords from one day to the next. Like all computer nerds, he was always ready to dig into any problem and find a solution. He was a warm, likable, self-described geek.

"Yes and no," said Carol, smiling. "You can stop calling me ma'am; it makes me feel old. I was just looking at your computers and see that they are a lot more advanced than the ones I used when I was in school."

"How is Sylvia going to keep up with the kids at Google with her out-of-date skills, and what did she mean, Google could use me?" she asked herself. "I better answer her right away."

"Sylvia! What a pleasant surprise. I'm on a cruise ship to Barcelona. Will be back in the city next week. Love to get together and get caught up. Google? What's that all about? Don't they want people born after the nineteenth century? Lol. Got a million questions. Call me after next Saturday.

Love, Carol
PS. What happened to Nichols?"

————

10:30 a.m., Stateroom 735

"Where have you been?" Eddie asked as she came in the door. "I was starting to worry about you. I thought you were just going to have a cup of coffee."

"I had coffee," she said with a little grin.

"And ...?"

"And what?" she asked, innocently.

"Something's going on. I can tell by that look on your face."

"Well, okay. I do have the tiniest bit of dirt, but you've got to promise not to breathe a word of it to anybody."

"I promise, I promise. Now, dish."

"Well, we went to Barista and ordered lattes, and at first we couldn't decide between the little cookies and the scones ..."

"Skip that. Get to the dirt," he interrupted impatiently. He knew she was teasing him, but after an hour with Phil, he was eager to know what was going on.

"Carol's thinking about asking Phil for a divorce," she announced dramatically.

"Yeah, I know that. I just had a long talk with Phil."

"B-b-but, Carol hasn't told him," she sputtered.

"Yeah, I know, but Phil is more intuitive; not as dense as he appears. He told me that he knew she was unhappy, and that is one of the reasons he booked this trip. He wanted to see if there wasn't some way he could save the marriage. He is crazy in love with her," he said with a smirk. "Now, did you say you have some dirt?"

"I suppose you know about the money, too, then," she said.

"Money. What money?"

"Oh, I guess you didn't dig enough to ask the big questions."

"Stop it. Tell me everything you've got, or I'll punish you by withholding sexual favors."

"Oh, I wouldn't want that to happen, my love," she said in mock horror.

"Sarcasm?"

"You think?" she asked. "Okay, when we talked about divorce, I assumed that, like all my clients, she was concerned about money. That is not an issue. They are an interesting couple. They were both twenty-two when they lost their parents, his first and hers five years later. His were killed in a car accident, and hers died. She didn't elaborate on that, and I didn't want to press her."

"Wow, I didn't know about that. Phil did tell me that his father's salvage business was on the verge of bankruptcy when they were in the accident. So when he met Carol, he was struggling. He didn't talk about their present financial situation. Did she?"

"Did she ever. They started out poor as church mice and apparently had complementary strengths, hers in marketing and administrative skills and his in knowing how to buy and sell and turn scrap of all kinds into money. They lived frugally and invested, primarily in real estate, and now they are wealthy."

"How wealthy?" he asked. He knew that his tenacious wife had probed for all the information.

"Wealthy," she said. "He was one of the millionaires Thomas

Stanley interviewed for his book, *The Millionaire Mind*. They bought up run-down real estate, refurbished and sold it to low-income buyers, and financed the purchases. He is the founder of Global Savings and Loan. Oh, one other thing. They have three children. With both of them being only children, they agreed that having a family was an important value of theirs."

"You know how to dig out information. No wonder you are such a good lawyer."

"Remember your promise. Carol did not swear me to confidentiality, but a lot of the stuff she told me was personal."

Eddie made a zipping motion across his mouth and threw away the imaginary key.

"Let's go have a bite of lunch before the afternoon session," he said. "I'ze gots the hungries."

———

1:00 p.m., the Celebrity Theater

Arthur and Nicole found their seats with their assigned group and sat down just in time to hear Pat Higgins's welcome and the announcement of the thirty-minute discussion topic for the day: 'What part of the cruise, other than the seminar, have you enjoyed so far and why?'

Rosanna Della Sandra, their group leader for the day, asked them to use the think-write-share formula. When they finished writing, she said, "We need introductions. Let's start with the person whose name is closest to the beginning of the alphabet."

They looked around at one another. "I'm *C*," said Clark Everett.

"I'm *B*," said Bill McClosky.

"I guess it's me," said Arthur. "I'm Arthur Gibson from Des Moines, and the part of the cruise I'm enjoying most is the complete change of pace from my usual routine at home."

"Ah'm his wife, Nicole, and Ah'm lovin' the music and the dancing. Ah'm havin' more fun than Ah've had in a long time."

"Bill, why don't you go next?" said Rosanna.

"Hi, I'm Bill McClosky from LA. The big thing that has happened for me since the start of this cruise is, I've changed my attitude. I don't know if the seminar or the cruise is responsible. I think even if we hadn't had the seminar activities, I would have experienced the attitude change. There's just no stress here."

"I'd like to second that," said Terri. "I'm Terri McClosky, and I've seen a real change in Bill in the last nine days."

"How about you though, Terri?" asked Rosanna. "What part of the cruise have you enjoyed most?"

"The same," she said. "Because Bill is more relaxed, I'm less stressed. I think a cruise is the best therapy any couple can take."

"I'm Roger Morris. I'm not going to lie; it's the food. I haven't eaten this well ever. No offense, Dixie," he said, looking at his wife.

"Well, I'm Dixie Morris," said his rotund wife. "I want to say it is the food too, but for a different reason. I haven't had to cook three meals a day for an unappreciative husband who doesn't know good cooking from Denny's."

Everyone but Roger laughed at her joke.

"I'm Maryanne Benson. I've enjoyed lying around the pool reading every morning. I just don't get an opportunity to do that at home."

"How about you?" asked Rosanna, looking at Lou. "What did you write?"

"I'm Lou Benson. "I had food and relaxation too, but although this might sound a little strange, the time to think and meditate has been great for me."

1:45 p.m.

"That's time, everybody," boomed Pat's voice. "Be back in your seats ready for a discussion to be led by our own Doug Carson on the subject of working, or not, in retirement. Fifteen-minute break beginning now. Ready, go."

2:00 p.m.

To Work or Not
Doug Carson

"Welcome back, everyone," announced Pat Higgins. "As promised, we're in for another interesting discussion led by our own Doug Carson."

Applause

"How's everyone today?"

"Why do people ask questions that are impossible to answer?" asked Bill McClosky cynically. "I couldn't possibly answer the question, 'How's everyone today?' without talking to each person individually and finding out how they are doing."

Doug went on. "As you know, we are going to start a conversation on the subject of postretirement activity and employment. Group leaders, use the think-write-share format to get everybody's best answer to the question, 'Are you working or planning to work or engage in some other type of activity after retiring? If so, why or why not?'"

Rosanna asked, "Is the assignment clear?" Hearing no questions, she said, "Fine. Please think for two minutes, then write your answers to the question."

When the time was up, Rosanna turned to Bill McClosky on her right and said, "What have you written, Bill?"

"I retired at the end of last year," he said angrily, "and I am not planning on working ever again. Why? Because I put in thirty-five years in a mind-numbing, boring job for a company that cut my benefits to increase their profits and never once said, 'Good job.' So I've paid my dues. I'm done with work of any kind."

"Why don't you tell us how you feel, Bill?" laughed Lou Benson.

"Lou, what have you written?" asked Rosanna.

"I'm just the opposite of Bill. I'm still working, and I love my job. It seems pretty secure. I don't see any signs that they are going to let me go, and I'll stay as long as they'll have me. I'm still young enough, and I've got the kind of job that stimulates me. I'm learning new things every day; my company is a big believer in ongoing training and development."

"Yes, and that's fine with me," said Maryanne Benson. "I've got my routine at home, and we do things together on the weekends. So in that sense, I'm still working and will continue to work until something changes with Lou."

"I've got a lot of sympathy for what Bill said," said Clark Everett. "I've got two more years before I'm eligible for my pension, and I'm not going to wait another day after that to retire. My company hasn't been that bad, but I'm burned out. I've got a workshop at home, and making furniture is my passion. I love it. I'm going to spend more time doing that and selling some of my pieces. People seem to like them. I think I can supplement my pension doing work I love."

"I think that is so important," said Dixie Morris. "Having something worthwhile to do is one of the most important contributors to mental and physical health."

Terri McClosky spoke up. "I've been telling Bill that you can't just retire *from* something, you've got to retire *to* something. Otherwise you're going to wilt away."

"Well, maybe I want to wilt," said a still-angry Bill. "It's my life, and I'll live it the way I want."

Rosanna jumped in and said, "Obviously there is room for different interpretations of what constitutes a successful retirement."

"I'm not going to wilt," said Arthur. "I'm plenty busy with club activities, committees, local politics, and involvement with our local health clinic, but I'm not sure they are the right activities for me."

Turning to Roger Benson, she said, "Roger, we haven't heard from you yet. What have you written?"

I'm already retired, have been for five years now. I didn't do much of anything the first couple of years except fish. After that grew old, I started volunteering at the food bank. I love that work. They need people who care about helping others, and I get a lot of satisfaction from that. I'd say, if anybody asked me, find a cause that you feel strongly about and support it."

"BS," said the ever-positive Bill McClosky. "Terri got me to do that food bank thing, and I hated it. A bunch of freeloaders coming in for a handout instead of finding honest work."

"Bill, you've got me thinking," said Nicole. "Ah'm retahd, and Ah thought my job was to be Arthur's wife and support him with all his different activities. Ah still think Ah should be doin' that, but Ah also think Ah should be lookin' for ways to be helpin' out in the community. It would be good for me, so Ah don't grow old and bittah. Thank you."

Bill looked confused, but before he could reply, Doug's voice was heard calling the room back to order.

3:00 p.m.

"That's time, everybody. I hope you had a good discussion and will continue it this evening with your team. We'll look forward to hearing your reports tomorrow morning. Have a good evening."

As Arthur and Nicole walked out, they spotted Don and Inga. "What did you think?" asked Arthur.

"This whole seminar, today in particular, has given me a lot to think about," said Don. "I think since I retired I've been too casual about what I do and why I do it. I'm going to rethink the way I'm spending my time."

"That's great," said Nicole. "What's the first thing you're going to do?"

"He's probably going to take a nap," laughed Inga.

"That's right," said Don with a straight face. "That's where the creative process begins."

"You've inspired me," said a laughing Arthur. "I'm going to participate in that creative process myself. I'll see you in the bar at six o'clock, rested and refreshed."

At the elevators, Phil asked, "You going back to the room?"

"No, not just yet," said Carol. "I want to be by myself to think about today's presentation." She gave him a smile and a peck on the cheek and left.

"Strange," he thought, and took the elevator to their suite.

3:15 p.m.
Computer Room

Carol opened her email and read the expected reply from Sylvia.

> "Hi, I'm glad you got back to me so promptly. I've got a million answers. Something for you to think about until we get together next week. Google needs some major maturity in marketing. They have a lot of sharp young people, MBAs even. They want to bring in some seasoned people, as they so tactfully phrase it, to communicate with the baby boomers (like us). You'd be terrific in that role. I'll call you on Saturday. Love, Sylvia.
>
> PS. I'm no longer Mrs. Nichols. You can have him back. ☺"

Carol's mind buzzed. Brad divorced. They'd had a two-year platonic relationship during her undergraduate studies, and he had even asked her to marry him. She might have, but by then she'd met Phil. "Google hiring 'seasoned people,'" she said to herself, laughing. "That certainly describes me. The past twenty-five years had been hard work and long hours. They were rich, but was it worth it? Google has a reputation of being a good company to work for. I wonder. Google. Brad ..."

As hard as she tried, she couldn't erase the image of her husband and Nicole talking about God-only-knows what. Phil hadn't told her about his coffee date with Nicole, so she didn't know what he was hiding. She logged out and went back to the suite.

6:00 p.m., the Porthole Piano Bar
Eddie and Melissa found the others already seated with drinks in front of them. Eddie signaled Sven and held up two fingers. Sven smiled and nodded.

"What a day today," said Don.

"Yes, the last time I saw you, you were off to be inspired," said Nicole, winking at him. "How did that go?"

"Great! I'm a new man—rested, refreshed, and inspired by the conversation today. We had a good group."

"What happened?" asked Melissa.

"I had a kind of Aha! moment when we discussed the questions regarding postretirement activity. It took me to the deeper question of the meaning of life. I know that wasn't the assignment as such, but I believe it essentially addressed that question. There is an underlying question we all must answer: 'What is the purpose of my life, and what am I here to do?' Obviously, each of us has to find our own unique and personal answer to these questions. Since I have a teaching background, especially with a doctorate in philosophy, I'm often asked, 'How can I find my purpose? I don't feel connected to a purpose.'"

Phil said, "I've done a lot of thinking about that subject. I like to think of our purpose in life as being unique to each one of us. It doesn't have to do with our accomplishments or our résumé. It's something deeper that connects us to our passion. When we find it, it adds meaning to whatever we do and helps us feel truly successful."

"Maybe that will be a more worthwhile conversation over dinner this evening than the 'work or not work' topic," said Eddie.

"What?" asked Nicole, feeling a little lost.

"Our life's purpose, retired or not, right, Eddie?" said Phil.

"I think it's a conversation every person should have with themselves," said Eddie.

Right on cue, Sven brought their check and said their table was ready in the Firenze Italian restaurant.

7:00 p.m., the Firenze Trattoria

"*Buena sera*, Ernesto," said Phil as they were escorted to their table.

"*Buena sera*, Mr. and Mrs. Butler, Dr. and Mrs. Conway, Mr. and Mrs. Townsend, and Dr. and Mrs. Gibson," He allowed his eyes to linger an extra moment on Nicole, who was wearing a tight-fitting Versace dress with a pearl necklace. Arthur, as usual, was unaware of Ernesto's subtle flirting. Phil, on the other hand, was inexplicably jealous, even though he knew Ernesto was just appreciating a beautiful woman.

"Ah'm goin' to the ladies' room, dahlin'," said Nicole to her husband. "Y'all go ahead."

"*Buena sera, signori.* My name is Luigi," said the good-looking young waiter. "I'll be serving you this evening. We have some specials this evening, but before I tell you about them, would you like an appetizer?"

"*Prego*," said Phil. That just about exhausted his Italian vocabulary designed to impress Luigi.

"May I suggest the calamari?" said Luigi. "It is fresh."

No one asked the obvious question: How do you get fresh anything three thousand miles out to sea?

"I love calamari," said Melissa. "I'll have it."

"Me too," said Carol.

"Is one order enough for all of us to share?" asked Eddie.

"No, I think you'll need two."

"Everybody in?" asked Phil, who seemed to have appointed himself as the one in charge.

"Yes, let's do it," said Don.

"Shall I start you with a bottle of Prosecco?" asked Bruno, the sommelier.

"By all means," said Don. "All right, everyone?" he asked as an afterthought.

Everybody nodded politely except Phil who said, "Is the Pope a Catholic? Get it? We're in an Italian restaurant—Italy, Catholic, Pope?" He was alone in laughing at his joke.

Melissa noticed, again, that Phil had that little rough edge that suggested a lack of proper education and a tendency to be inappropriate.

When Nicole returned to the table, the men stood to greet her. She said, "Y'all have got to see the frescos in the ladies' room."

Melissa said, "Okay, while you're all standing, I'll excuse myself and go see them."

"We ordered calamari and Prosecco, Nickie," said Arthur. "Is that all right with you?"

"You know me and bubbly," she said. "And I do like calamari, so yes, fine, bring it on. Has the waiter told us the specials yet?"

"No," Inga said. "But I spoke to a couple in our discussion group today who were here last night, and they said that everything is delicious. They had the sea bass and loved it."

Just then Melissa returned to the table. Eddie could see that her face was flushed, and she appeared nervous. "Is everything all right, my love?" he asked.

The Prosecco had already been served, and at that moment, Luigi brought the calamari. Everyone looked at Melissa.

"To absent friends," said Don, lifting his glass.

"To absent friends," they said in unison.

When Luigi left the table, Carol asked again, "Melissa, are you all right?"

Melissa leaned forward and lowered her voice, "Ernesto just hit on me." She was flustered and felt both flattered and embarrassed.

"How do you mean, he hit on you?" asked Eddie.

Melissa, blushing, looked around to be sure no one else could hear. She said softly, "When I came back into the room, he took my hand and said, 'You are so beautiful.'"

"Oh yas, y'all, he said the same thing to me," said Nicole.

"What?" said Melissa, shocked. "What did you say?"

"Ah said, 'Why, thank you.'"

Everyone burst out laughing.

"I guess I'm not as hot as I thought," said Melissa.

Luigi appeared behind Melissa. "We have some special dishes to tell you about this evening. First, one of Chef's specialties is lasagna. He adds a touch of brandy to give it a unique flavor. We also have sea bass drizzled with a light marinara sauce and served over a bed of angel hair pasta. Both dishes are served with broccolini."

"Those both sound delicious," said Carol. "I'm ready to order. Is everyone else?"

"Give us another minute, would you?" said Phil, reading the menu.

"Why?" said Carol. "You're going to order the lasagna anyway. You always do. Let's order. I'm hungry."

"Fine," said Phil, closing his menu. "Lasagna sounds good."

The others made their selections and agreed with Luigi on house salads with vinegar and oil dressing.

Bruno came to the table a few minutes later and said, "Based on your dinner selections, I recommend a Chianti with the lasagna and the chicken and a Soave with the sea bass."

"That sounds wonderful," said Phil. "Everyone concur?" Without waiting for an answer, he said, "Good recommendations, Bruno."

"Where were we in our conversation?" asked Don.

"You told us about your Aha! in the meeting today, leading you to a deeper question beyond how we should spend our time," said Eddie.

Melissa spoke up and said, "I think I speak for all the wives of men who have just retired or are about to retire when I say we would want them to be happy and that they should have some kind of meaningful activity."

Bruno brought the wine to the table. Phil went through an elaborate and pretentious approval process; swishing the wine around in the glass. He held it up to the light, examining the glass for either legs or tears. He sniffed it, took a generous swig, and swirled it around in his mouth. "That's excellent, Bruno," he said, after doing his act with the taste of Chianti. "What do you get from this one?"

Bruno said, "I taste ripe cherries and plum with a little pepper," or something like that.

"Yes, exactly," said Phil. "These will do fine."

Melissa wondered about the underlying insecurity that caused him to feel it was necessary to put on such a show.

"I know the meaningful activity aspect has been true for Don," said Inga. "While he was giving lectures at the Smithsonian, he was more enthusiastic and alive than during the two or three years after he stopped teaching at the university. Right, Schatze?"

"Yes, that is definitely true," he said. "I even got more satisfaction from those lectures than I did during the last years of teaching. The people who came to the Smithsonian lectures were interested in the subjects and gave me great feedback."

Luigi brought the salads and a basket of warm bread, and they all dug in. Their predinner drinks gave them a robust appetite.

As they enjoyed their salads, Phil said, "I learned of a great example of enthusiasm and the lack of it from a couple of guys I met a few months ago. I was in Tucson, Arizona, on a business trip, and I attended a Rotary Club meeting at the hotel for a make-up. I sat at a table with a half dozen men and women, and the conversation turned to retirement. One of the men, Grant, had relocated there about six months earlier. He'd moved to the warmer weather from Maryland. He enthusiastically told the group about a wall-building project he was doing at his house. Ernie, one of the other guys, said,

'I did some home-improvement projects when I first moved here, but after they were finished, I found that there was nothing else I was interested in doing. I wish I could find something. I tried volunteering but didn't enjoy it. I play golf once in a while, but it's not that much fun anymore.

"'Mr. Positive,' Ernie went on to say, 'when you finish that wall, you'll see that there are not a lot of interesting things to do here.'

"'What are you going to do when you finish the wall?' I asked Grant.

"That's when he lit up. 'I've got a terrific idea for a business here. I'd like to get a dune buggy and take people out in the desert for tours to see the real Arizona, things they wouldn't normally get to see when they just stay in town.' He expanded on his idea, which may or may not be a viable business, but that wasn't the point. He was on fire with excitement about his idea. Of course, Ernie immediately came up with reasons why the business wouldn't work."

Don said, "That's a perfect example of the difference between aliveness, fulfillment, and enjoyment and the ennui of marking time and finding nothing interesting to do.

Melissa said, "That reminds me of a couplet from my childhood, 'Two men looked out from behind prison bars, one saw the mud, the other the stars.' Both Grant and Ernie were living in the same beautiful place, but they each saw it differently."

"Isn't that what this whole seminar has been saying?" said Carol. "That it's all a matter of attitude?"

"It is," said Don. "The best idea I've heard on the value of purpose came from Martin Seligman. He is a psychologist at the University of Pennsylvania and does research on happiness. He said, 'Human beings want to have meaning. They want to not wake up in the morning with a gnawing realization that they are fidgeting until they die.' I just love that."

"Well, if Ah were askin'," said Nicole, "Ah'd be askin', Do I wanna be a Grant, or do I wanna be an Ernie?"

Inga smiled and copied that amusing observation in her notebook, which she'd been keeping open on the table beside her during every meal. She pushed it aside and said, "Well, my question would be along those same lines. I'd ask myself, 'Am I motivated by the positive possibilities before me, or do I make a practice of thinking of all the reasons why they won't work? Do I have something worthwhile to get me up in the morning?'"

"Let's hold on a minute," said Don. "By insisting that everyone find meaningful activity that makes a difference in the world as the royal road to happiness, we leave the impression that the *only* activity that is moral or socially acceptable is to be engaged in some mission that will potentially save the world. I don't think that is the case at all. There are seasons in growth, development, and progress. I also make a distinction between being contented and indolent. I know I've said this before, but as Herbert Spencer said, 'We all need to be reminded more than we need to be taught.' I believe contentment is a worthy ideal, one to which we should all aspire. Satisfaction is only temporary. For example, we get comfortable in one position in bed for a short time, and then we must turn over to find a more comfortable position. The attempt to find happiness and satisfaction by acquisition of material goods is the cause of a lot of unhappiness and dissatisfaction in life. Henry David Thoreau said it best: 'Many men go fishing all of their lives without knowing that it is not fish they are after.' For me, I think it is best to know what it is that I'm after in my retirement years."

"Wow," said Eddie to himself, "Don is like Yoda, full of wisdom."

Luigi and his assistant cleared the table and served the entrées. Carol was impressed with the meticulous and professional way in which they did this job. They always took the tiny crumber from their pocket and brushed the crumbs onto a little silver plate. She thought how much more elegant it was than brushing them onto the floor, as Phil did at home.

Everyone thoroughly enjoyed the wonderful Italian cuisine, commenting once again how delicious the food had been on the cruise.

"You know," said Eddie, "this seminar is causing me to realize that retirement can be an exciting time of my life and, I suspect, for yours too. It can mean a clean slate, a *tabula rasa,* if we erase the irrelevant memories of the past and plot the direction of our future. Here's a great analogy about goal setting. If you were planning a ski trip and hadn't unpacked your suitcase from your last trip to Hawaii, you'd have to sort through your mask, fins, bathing suit, shorts, and maybe some dirty underwear before you'd get to the things you need for skiing. It is the same for us when we plan our journey into retirement. We must discard the baggage from the past that no longer serves us in order to move forward. That's just plain good sense to me."

At this point, everyone was ready for dessert, so Luigi and his assistant cleared their dishes. "Tiramisu, everyone?" asked Luigi.

"Yes, please, if it's all right with everyone else," said Phil, looking around the table for agreement. "And coffee please, Luigi."

"Espresso?" he asked.

"Cappuccino for me," said Eddie.

The others placed their coffee orders, and they continued the conversation.

Don said, "I think that in order to achieve the highest and most satisfying experiences at any age, we must listen to Eddie's inner gnawing feeling of constructive discontent. The sensation that tells us the next most satisfying thing to pursue. I call it intuition. At some point, we all find ourselves feeling that there is more to life than what we are currently experiencing. When that happens, we will automatically pursue the next step. Wherever we are, in whatever season, it's good to remind ourselves that it is the perfect time and place for us. A major barrier to advancement and progress is calcified thinking. At this point in our lives, it might be valuable to draw on the wisdom of others to be sure we are on the right track toward living our dream. I think we should take every opportunity we can to learn from others. We all know people who have made up their minds thirty years ago and are not receptive to hearing any new ideas. What a shame!"

Luigi brought the tiramisu and coffee, and once again Carol noticed the tiny crumb scraper, even though they hadn't eaten anything since he did it last. "Must be a habitual thing," she thought to herself. "Maybe we're all like that. Maybe I'm like that, and maybe Phil's like that. Maybe we need to break some old habits."

Startled, she heard her name through her reverie. "Pardon me?" she asked.

"I asked if you would like sugar for your espresso?" said her husband.

"Oh, thank you, honey," she said. She realized what a thoughtful person he always is. She remembered what Melissa said to her earlier in the day. 'No one is perfect until you fall in love with them.' She smiled at him and squeezed his hand. As usual, she thought he had no clue.

Inga, reading from her notes, said, "Wherever we are, in whatever season, it is the perfect time and place for us. To me, that sums up this whole conversation."

"I couldn't agree more," said Carol. "And I think we're getting the stink-eye from Ernesto. I think he wants us to pay up and get out."

"Ah think he's just disappointed that Melissa didn't give him any encouragement, and that's the reason he wants us out of here," laughed Nicole.

"Too bad. He doesn't know what he's missing," laughed Eddie.

"Why, thank ya, dahlin'," said Melissa, doing her best Nicole impression.

———

9:50 p.m.

"Are you all signed up for the whisky tasting event tomorrow afternoon?" asked Don.

"We wouldn't miss it," said Eddie. "It should be educational."

"Right. Like you're going for the education," laughed Arthur. "But don't worry; I'll be there to keep an eye on you."

"We're going for sure," said Phil.

"That makes it unanimous," said Don. "The entire BCGT number-one team will be there, getting more than our share of Irish whisky."

"Anybody up for the show or some dancing tonight?" asked Phil.

"Not me," said Melissa. "I'm going to bed. I have an appointment at the spa for a massage and a facial in the morning."

"I'll go with you, my love," said Eddie, pleased that she had stopped going to the casino every night.

"I think I'll pass too," said Arthur. "It's been a long day."

The others agreed and went their separate ways.

Day Ten

April 16

12:45 p.m., the Celebrity Theater

When Eddie and Melissa arrived, the room was already crowded and buzzing with excitement in anticipation of the day's program. As they took their seats, they read the program:

The Challenge of Change
- Overcoming the discomfort of living in a changing world
- Identifying positive and negative mental attitudes
- Overcoming counterproductive mental attitudes
- Find the things that contribute to joy in your life
- Discover who you are in your new environment

Special Guest Speaker: Dr. Craig Burke

After the usual reporting period, Pat Higgins reassembled the group and introduced the day's program.

2:00 p.m.

Pat Higgins picked up the mike and said, "Welcome back, everybody. We're in for a real treat today. Our topic is The Challenge of

Change. We're all looking for increased quality of life, and our speaker is an expert on helping people to achieve quality-plus living. Please welcome psychologist and best-selling author of *You and Your Brain,* Dr. Craig Burke."

The seminar participants gave Dr. Burke a warm round of applause.

"Good afternoon, everyone," said the tall, distinguished-looking, high-energy goateed man in his early sixties. "Our goal today is to learn what actions to take to achieve fun in living. For the past two weeks, you've been talking and thinking about retirement. Should I work or not? Should I volunteer or not? Should I play golf, fish, garden, or sit around a lot? Or should I just watch more reruns of *Gilligan's Island?*"

The group smiled and laughed along with the down-to-earth, friendly speaker.

"What? That's not on anymore? It's been a while since I've watched TV.

"Whichever way we spend our time, when we connect to our heart's calling, everything begins to have meaning. So thanks to Agapi Stassinopolos, author of *Unbinding the Heart,* I'll ask you his five questions. But first, Stassinopolos had a question of his own that led him to ask the five questions. It was, 'How can I find my purpose?' He added, 'I am frequently asked this question by successful people, unemployed people, happily married people, single people, etc. "I don't feel connected to a purpose," they say.'

"I like to think of purpose as our individual calling. It does not have to do with accomplishments or our résumé; it is something deeper that connects us to our heart's pulse. When we find it, it adds meaning to whatever we do and helps us feel the true sense of success.

"Either way, when we connect to our heart's calling, everything starts to have meaning. So here are Stassinopolos's five questions that, as you answer, can bring your calling closer to you.

"What am I here to learn?

"What am I here to teach?

"What am I here to overcome?

"What am I here to complete?

"What am I here to express?

"If you take a moment to answer these questions from an authentic, truthful place, the answers may be different from what you previously thought. These questions are meant to break down self-imposed standards we have bound ourselves with. The answers to these questions are ongoing and evolving. At different stages in our lives, we are here to teach and learn different things. Nothing is set in stone. As you answer these questions, you may find that a blueprint emerges that can guide you to what calls you, and as you follow that thread, you start to experience more of an inner fulfillment.

"Knowing that we are all teachers, we are all students, and we all have something to contribute alleviates the sense of separation we often feel. That knowing can bring solace and comfort to the basic question, Why am I here? It helps us create a bigger arena where we can explore the dimensions of our lives. It adds tremendous creativity to our existence and helps us welcome the unknown instead of fearing it. It also puts us in the driver's seat so we become the creator of our lives. Everything that happens in our lives, the good, the bad, and the ugly, becomes part of life's tapestry. Our life's experiences are the alchemy that helps us transform and awaken to who we are. My mother used to say, 'We are all born an original, and it is a challenge to remain an original in a world that tries to mold us to fit in.'

"I personally started my life thinking that I was here to be a father and to be responsible for others. The answers to these five questions can bring your calling closer to you. These questions all refer to your life as a whole.

"Please use the think-write-share format you've been using and answer these one at a time.

"The first question is, 'What am I here to learn?'"

After the group took two minutes to think and another three

minutes to write, Gustav said, "Let's start with the best-looking man here. Who would that be?" Everyone laughed.

"Since no one else volunteered, I guess it's me," said Fred Hargrove.

Inga said to herself, "That wouldn't have been my choice."

For the next forty-five minutes, the room was humming with excitement. The different groups shared their answers to Craig's provocative questions.

————

3:00 p.m.

Craig returned to the front of the room and said, "Here's the most important part of today's meeting. Please select the one best idea that you believe you can use to enrich your life and write it down. When you've done that, pair off with another person other than your spouse or partner and make a commitment to them to follow through on your idea."

After everyone completed the assignment, Craig said, "Congratulations! Now go make the rest of your day a good one."

Everyone except the BCGT number-one team went back to their staterooms and suites or to the pool. With Don leading the way, the group headed to the whisky tasting.

————

4:30 p.m., Whisky Tasting in the Sea View

When the others arrived, Don and Inga were already seated at the long rectangular table with a dozen small glasses in front of them. Ten other people were already seated, and another couple came in right at four thirty. Pitchers of water were spaced around the table at every other chair and water glasses at every place. In the middle of the table were baskets of little pieces of bread and small plates of assorted cheeses.

Just as they took their seats, Pat Higgins stood up at the head of the table and said, "Good afternoon, everyone. Welcome to Imperial Cruise Lines special whisky tasting seminar. You'll notice on your program that whisky is spelled without an *e*. According to today's featured expert, this is the correct way to spell it. I'll let him explain that to you. He has had a forty-year love affair with whisky. It has been his hobby and his passion ever since he first went to work in a distillery in his native country of Scotland, as a wee lad of twenty-two. He learned to make whisky from experienced distillers and has developed the ability to discern the differences in all the different whiskies in Scotland. Ladies and gentlemen, I present, from Dunkeld, Scotland, Duncan—his friends call him Dunc—Menzies."

Inga opened her notebook and wrote "Dunk Menzies, Whisky, Day 10" at the top of a clean page.

"Gud afta nune," said Dunc, with a strong and lilting Scottish accent. "So ye wanta know about whisky, and ye might even wanta taste a wee dram or two, is that right?"

"That's why we're here," said Don. "Let's get started."

"Okay then," said Dunc. "Here is the first one. Ye might think that there canna be that much difference in whiskies, since they all come from the same country, and the distillin' process is the same in every distillery. But the whiskies are all different, even when the distilleries are on neighboring lands, because of the water."

For the next sixty minutes, he delighted his audience with the history and stories of whisky in Scotland while the sommeliers who were assisting him poured a never-ending number of glasses of delicious samples. He explained the subtle nuances of each type and label.

At the end, they walked out with varying degrees of unsteadiness and giggles. The sommeliers had provided small silver buckets to pour out any whisky they chose not to drink, but, other than Inga, no one seemed willing to participate in what Phil called "alcohol abuse."

"We'll have to hurry to get to the cocktail hour on time," joked Melissa.

"Yeah, I wounna wanna be late for that," slurred Nicole.

"See you in thirty minutes," said Phil, looking at his watch. "I gotta get changed for dinner."

———

6:30-ish p.m., the Porthole Bar

When Don and Nicole walked in, Phil, Eddie, and Arthur were leaning on Sammy's piano singing, "Shine on, Shine on Harvest Moon,'" off key. Sammy, as always, was smiling and trying to play around their uneven performance.

Sven brought their usual drinks to the table, and they all sat down and toasted absent friends.

"That whisky tasting was quite an experience, wasn't it?" said Eddie.

"Interesting," said Arthur. "I hope you got some good notes, Inga. I'll never remember all those different whiskies and where they came from."

"None of us could be expected to remember them, especially after the fifth or sixth one we tasted," said Phil.

"I took good notes," said Inga. "In fact, I got Dunc's notes. By the way, he spells his name with a *c*, not a *k*."

"What?" said Nicole. "Dunk would be spelled with a *D*, right?"

"No, Dunc is short for Duncan, so it is D-u-n-c."

"Well, that wasn't the only interesting meeting today, was it?" said Carol.

"No. I don't know about anyone else, but those questions that Craig asked us today were eye-opening," said Melissa.

"Ja, I thought so too," said Inga.

"The answers from the members of our discussion group seemed a little too brief, even shallow," said Don.

"Yeah, I thought that was true in our group too," said Eddie. "I think there wasn't enough time for people to expand on their answers."

"I wish I could have heard your answers," said Arthur.

"We could do that now, couldn't we?" asked Melissa.

"How do you mean?" asked Carol.

"Answer the same questions here," she said.

"Okay. Our answers will be better than those in the meeting because we get to drink," laughed Don.

Inga thought to herself, "Why does everything have to be about drinking with him?" It bothered her a lot, but she had always been subservient to him and never had the courage to speak up to him about it.

———————

"All right," said Melissa. "Remember, the questions refer to our lives as a whole. Who is first with the first question? What was it again, Inga?"

Inga opened her notebook and read, "'What are you here to learn?' I'll go first. I'm here to love. I think I've been insecure most of my life and haven't allowed myself to open up to people and let them know how I feel."

Sitting next to her, Don said, "I think I'm here to get know myself. I mean my real authentic self. So much of my life has been about having to play the role of professor and authority figure. I think somewhere along the way I lost the real me."

"Patience," said Melissa. "I've always wanted to get on with it and for everybody else to get to the point. I'd like to be more patient with myself and others."

Eddie said, "I'd like to know my real purpose in life. Since I've retired, I seem to be drifting. This so-called book I'm supposed to be writing is an example. It seems to be forced and mechanical and not tied to anything real."

"Well, Ah'd like to know what it is that God wants me to do. Then Ah could git on with doin' it," said Nicole.

Phil said, "I'd like to grow up. I still have a lot of juvenile thoughts that I should have outgrown by now."

Melissa didn't miss Carol's quizzical look as she glanced at her husband.

Carol said, "I want to learn to trust; to trust myself and to truly trust others."

Phil reached over and squeezed Carol's hand. She didn't pull away.

Arthur said, "I guess that leaves me. I need to stop making the mistakes of my youth. I think I'm still doing some of the same dumb stuff I did forty years ago."

"That was great," said Melissa. "What's the next question, Inga?"

Inga read from her notebook again. "'What am I here to teach?'"

"I'd like to go first," said Arthur. "In line with what I said I'm here to learn, I'd like to be able to master my demons, so that I could help some young people avoid the same mistakes."

"Well, if that's the way it works," said Carol, smiling at Arthur, "I must be here to eventually teach people to be warmer, more open, and even more loving as they learn to trust more."

Smiling at his wife, Phil said, "Staying with that theme, I'm not sure I know how to grow up yet, although we're getting a lot of ideas in this seminar that should help us all to mature. If I could teach others to do that, it would be a real boon to them and a source of great satisfaction to me."

"You've got me excited," said Eddie to the group. "Finding purpose will be the theme of my book, and I'll teach it there. I've been wallowing in self-pity over my inability to make any significant progress with my writing," he said, winking at Phil.

"Hah, 'significant progress,'" said Melissa, "*Any* progress, to be more accurate."

"Patience, my love," he said. "When I finish this book, it is going to be so good you'll be sorry you weren't kinder to me all these years."

"When you finish that book, I'll be too old to feel anything, much less sorry."

"I'll bet the ex-Mrs. Hemingway regretted not being kinder to Papa after *The Old Man and the Sea* was published," he shot back.

"So far you haven't learned to write like Hemingway. All you've done is learn to drink like him."

"You know," he said, "you're going to feel differently when this becomes a *New York Times* best seller."

"Wow, when the student is ready, the teacher will appear. I just had a blinding flash of the obvious from this conversation, my love. If patience is what I need, what better place to learn it than with your soon-to-be *New York Times* best-selling book project? If I can patiently see you through this, I'll be able to teach a graduate-level course in patience at Stanford."

"Do they teach patience in college?" asked Nicole.

"No, but they should," said Carol. "It would help people learn to deal with life's vicissitudes."

"Life's what?" asked Nicole.

"Life's ups and downs," answered Carol.

"Well," laughed Nicole, "when Ah find out what it is that God wants me to do, maybe I can use that to help you heathens git on the straight and narra."

"After being with this group for the past couple of weeks, I don't see that happening anytime soon," said Phil with a grin.

"Have faith," laughed Arthur. "Everybody's soul is redeemable."

"Well, maybe I'll just become a minister then," said Nicole.

"If I could teach people in my lectures to internalize the material and relate it to their lives, it would elevate my communication to its highest level," said Don.

"I'd love to be able to teach love by example," said Inga. "That must be what I'm here to teach."

"'What are we here to overcome?'" asked Inga, reading again from her notebook.

"Wait," said Carol. "Here's Carlos to escort us to dinner."

They signed for their drinks and followed him to the dining room.

———————

7:00 p.m., the Dining Room

When Carlos seated them and described the special dishes of the evening, they were so eager to return to the discussion that they all said, "Fine, bring us Caesar salads, sirloin steaks, steak fries, and some burgundy wine."

"Let's continue with Inga's last question," said Eddie. "'What are we here to overcome?' For me it is worry, worry about being good enough, worry about not being good at my next endeavor."

Don said, "I'm not sure why, but I overdo—eating, drinking, socializing, you name it."

"I think I know why," said Inga, speaking up in an uncharacteristic show of assertiveness. "I think you have all those behaviors to avoid looking at yourself. You've never talked about it to me or anyone else, but since Donnie died, you've never let anyone know how you feel."

"Who's Donnie?" asked Phil.

"He is our son, and he died five years ago last week," said Inga.

"Let's tell the truth," slurred Don. "He killed himself on my birthday."

"What?" gasped Carol.

"He shot himself in the head," he said, making a gun with his hand. Holding his finger to his head, he pulled the trigger, said "Bang," then started to cry deep, painful sobs.

Carol burst out crying. Phil put his arms around her and pulled her close to him. Arthur went around the table to Don, pulled up a chair and put his arm around his shoulder. He said softly, "Let it out, buddy. I know the kind of pain you are feeling. My wife died ten years ago, and I still hurt."

Nicole looked at Arthur with disbelief. In the time they had been together, she had never seen him so loving and open with anyone.

Eddie went to Don, put his hand on his shoulder, and stood next to him.

Melissa handed Don a tissue from her purse, poured a glass of water, and passed it across the table to him.

Inga looked sad and somehow older as she watched Arthur comforting her husband and the show of affection from the others. She felt a wave of gratitude sweep over her as she realized how close the group had become in the short time they'd been together. The breakdown of Don's protective facade spoke volumes about the value of having in-depth, personal relationships rather than the superficial ones they'd developed the past three years in Virginia. She thought to herself, "I'd rather have just a few close friends like these than a thousand others who don't allow you to get to know them."

Don blew his nose and said, "I'm sorry. I get carried away sometimes."

Carol wiped the tears from her eyes. She put her arms around Don and started crying again.

"What is it?" he asked. She didn't answer but continued to weep.

Phil said, "Your son's death stirred a painful memory in Carol. Her father ..." He let his voice die away.

No one had touched their food.

"Well, this has become way too lugubrious," said Don. "Let's have a drink and forget the whole thing."

"No," said Inga. "I don't think we should have another drink, and I don't think we should forget the whole thing. I think we should talk about the things that are bothering us, so we can put them behind us. We're talking about what it is we're here to overcome. I'm here to overcome my timidity, about speaking up when things aren't right.

I don't think it's right to not deal with Donnie's death, so let's deal with it once and for all, right now."

"Okay," said Don. "You want to talk about it, we'll talk about it. If I hadn't been so wrapped up in myself, I would have seen it coming. I'd have been able to be there for him. That's why I can't forgive myself."

"You were a good father, Schatze. You did everything you could for that boy."

"Let me say something," said Eddie. "You can go on for as long as you live, blaming yourself for something that someone else did. Obviously I don't know all the details about your relationship with your son, but at some point in our lives, the only thing any of us can be responsible for is ourselves. We have an opportunity to take responsibility for our attitude. I'd like to think that we've become friends, and I don't want my friend to suffer. From what I've seen of you, I think you are a pretty terrific guy."

"Amen to that," said Phil. "And if there is anything I can do for you to ease the pain, I'm available."

"That goes for all us," spoke up Arthur.

"Thank you, all of you," said Don. "That means a lot to me. I don't know what I touched off in you, Carol, but I'm sorry."

"No, don't be," she said. "I don't mind talking about it now that you've been so honest with us. I was just twenty-six when it happened." She looked at Phil. He smiled and nodded encouragingly.

"My father was a successful investment broker, but he got into some serious financial trouble and he, he ..." She started to cry again.

Phil took her hand and said, "Let's let it go for another time, honey."

She sniffed, buried her head in his neck, and nodded.

To give Carol time to recover, Inga asked, "What are you here to overcome, Melissa?"

"Gambling," she said, without hesitation.

"What?" said Nicole. "I knew you went to the casino, but I didn't think it was something to overcome or anything."

"I didn't fully realize it until this seminar. I've been aware for some time that what had started as an innocent diversion has become an addiction. I wasn't too concerned about it because I didn't let it dominate my life. But Eddie has never approved, and I see it as threatening the most important thing in my life, my relationship with him. Perhaps by admitting this in a safe, trusting environment, I can put it behind me."

Eddie looked at her with a warm, loving smile and then spoke up. "I guess this is honesty time. I'm here to overcome something more than worry. I'm disgusted with myself and embarrassed by my laziness and excuse-making about this damn writing business. I've been lying to myself and everybody else, especially Melissa, about the progress I've made on my so-called book. I've had all the support any person could ask for and encouragement from a lot of different quarters, yet I'm still dragging my feet. I'm done with that. I'm going to commit to working at my writing or quit all together."

Nicole burst into impromptu, enthusiastic applause, "I'm looking forward to reading it, Eddie. Since I'm talking and we are all being so downright honest, I'll tell you what I'd love to overcome: vanity an' bein' a flirt. Ah'm always tryin' to look sexy lahk Ah wuz still sixteen or somethin'." Her voice dropped to a whisper. She said, "Ah think Ah'm doin' it becawz Ah'm afraid of gettin' old." Arthur put his arm around her and pulled her close. Everyone could see the genuine love in his eyes as he comforted her.

Phil took a deep breath and said, "This is hard for me to say, but I've got to say it. Nicole, my reaction to beautiful women is to fantasize that they would be attracted to me. I know why I feel that way. I'm not educated, and I've always felt inadequate. I thought if I at least looked good, I'd be interesting to beautiful women. Not that I ever wanted to act on these feelings, and I never have." Looking at Carol, he said, "And I never would. But it's always there in the back of my mind. I'd like to overcome that one." He looked at his wife, hoping for some understanding, but she returned his look with no expression.

There was a quiet pause, and then Carol spoke. "Now I'd like to talk this out. Don, the reason I had such a strong reaction to hearing about your son's suicide is because my father not only committed suicide but he killed my mother before he did it."

Nicole gasped.

"He did more than get into financial trouble. He was running a Ponzi scheme much like Bernie Madoff's, and he took a lot of people, good people who trusted him, down with him. It was the most painful experience I could imagine.

"I'm ashamed at how much I disappointed him and my mother by not taking full advantage of the education they gave me." Looking at Phil, she said, "They never gave Phil a chance. They thought he was the reason I threw away all those years of school and that I married beneath myself. I feel guilty that they never got to see what an honest, loving, and talented man he truly is."

Phil looked at her with tenderness and mouthed the words, "Thank you."

After a long silence, Arthur said, "I worry about what other people will think if I make an abrupt change in my life. I don't want to be involved in all those phony social and charity events, just burning up the little time I have left. I don't want to spend the rest of my life doing things other people expect me to do because my father and grandfather did them."

"You've all given me the courage to speak my mind," said Inga. "I've been a doormat all my married life, following him around," she said, pointing to Don. "Never speaking up when I should have. I'm tired of it. I need to overcome it, not just for me, but for Don too."

Carlos appeared to ask if they would like dessert.

"Not for me," said Don. "I've had enough for this evening. I'd like to go off by myself and think about our discussion. It's been a lot to take in."

"I agree with that," said Eddie. "Everyone else?"

They all nodded agreement and left the table.

———

They stood in an awkward group around the elevator doors, embarrassed by the raw honesty they'd shared with one another. They didn't quite know how to complete the evening. They stood in silence, watching the lighted numbers as the elevators slowly made their way to the dining room floor.

When the first one arrived, Phil and Carol and Arthur and Nicole got on, pressed the button for the eleventh floor, and stared fixedly at the lighted numbers as people tend to do. At their floor, before turning to go their separate ways, Nicole hugged Carol and said good night.

"Wait a minute. I want to tell you something, Nickie," said Carol. "Go ahead, Phil, I'll be a few minutes. I'll see you in the suite."

He nodded and walked away.

"I'm going in too," said Arthur, "if you don't mind?"

"No, Ah'll be right along," said Nickie.

When the men were gone, Nickie said, "What's up?"

"I'm a little embarrassed about this, but I need to know what is going on between you and my husband."

"Goin' on? Wah, nuthin' is goin' on. Why did you think there was? What Ah said tonight about bein' a flirt an' all? Ah didn't mean anythin' by it with Phil."

"I saw you together in the Barista coffee bar. It looked to me like you were having a personal conversation, and Phil's never told me a thing about it."

"Let me explain all that. It's a lot simpler than it looks. I think your husband is great, but I don't have any interest in him or any man except Arthur. Phil didn't say anything to you because I asked him not to. I asked him if I could talk to him in private because I thought he could help me with Arthur."

"With Arthur, how?"

"Phil has something that Arthur doesn't, and I wanted his advice."

Carol didn't reply, so Nicole went on. "Phil is open and easy for everybody to talk to. Arthur keeps his feelings to himself, and I want to break through that, so we have the kind of communication that you and Phil have."

Carol almost choked. "Open communication?" she thought. That was the problem she was having with Phil and the reason she was going to divorce him. How ironic. "Have I gotten so good at putting up a front that people can't see through it?" she wondered.

"So I asked Phil how I could get Arthur to open up and express his true feelings to me. I love him so much, but there is a barrier between us. I don't know why. I don't demonstrate my true feelings for him in public because that's the way he wants it."

"This makes things a lot clearer," said Carol. "Thank you. My big problem is jealousy; it always has been with him. So I know it's not you and it's not even Phil, although he could be a lot more sensitive to my feelings. It's my problem, and I've got to get over it. Let's pick up the conversation another time. We're both tired and should get some rest. I'll talk to you tomorrow, okay?"

"Yeah. We're good, then?"

"More than good," said Carol, smiling. "We're great."

They hugged and said good night.

————

Stateroom 735

At the door to their room, Eddie smiled at Melissa and held the door open for her. She smiled back and said, "Thank you. I guess this seminar is about a whole lot more than retirement. Let's go to bed and start fresh tomorrow."

As he prepared for bed, thoughts of the evening's conversation churned through Eddie's mind. "Good night, my love," he said as he turned off the light.

————

When Phil crawled into bed, Carol turned away from him, full of her own thoughts about the evening's events. Phil lay awake for a long time thinking about his revelation to the group and wondering how much more damage he'd done to his already fragile relationship with Carol.

———

"I'm sorry, Schatze," said Don as he crawled into bed next to Inga. "I'm so embarrassed. I shouldn't have broken down like that in front of everyone."

"Don't be," she said. She put her hand on his shoulder. "I think it's the best thing you could have done. You've been holding on to that pain for a long time. It's better that you let go of it."

"*Danke,*" he said, patting her hand. "*Ich liebe dich.*"

"Ich liebe dich *auch.* I love you too," she said, smiling as she turned over to go to sleep.

———

"I guess we all got pretty naked in there tonight," said Nicole. "I didn't think I'd ever confess those feelings to anyone, but they just poured out."

"I love you for being so honest and willing to be vulnerable," Arthur said.

"Thank you," she said, cuddling up to him. "And I want you to know that wherever you go, I will follow. If you decide to chuck it all and do something crazy, I'm your girl."

Taking her in his arms, he kissed her. They held one another and drifted off to a peaceful sleep.

———

Day Eleven

April 17

Eddie and Melissa sat in the red velveteen-cushioned seats, silently fidgeting, waiting to hear the assistant cruise director call their group color. They hadn't spoken during their brief, hurried breakfast.

Finally, Eddie spoke. "We should probably talk about last night."

"You mean about my gambling or your poor attempt at lying to me about your book?"

"Ouch. That hurt," he winced. "We need to talk about both issues. I'm not concerned about your gambling because I know you've always used your own money. If you decide to quit, you will. You are the most disciplined and self-directed person I've ever known. As far as my confession about my moral flabbiness," he said, grinning, "I suspect you've known all along what a fraud I am."

She snuggled closer and hugged him. "That's beautiful," she said, laughing. "You have a real talent and a writer's soul."

"What?" he said. "What do you mean?"

"When you use phrases like 'moral flabbiness' and 'you've known all along what a fraud I am,' your innate honesty shows itself and you endear yourself to your readers. Just keep using that kind of language in your writing and you'll have that *New York Times* best-selling book published in no time."

He leaned over and kissed her just as their group was called to proceed to the gangway to depart for their tour.

It was a short transfer from the ship to Pico dos Barcelos, a wonderful viewpoint overlooking the city and the surrounding bay. They visited a lovely fishing village before driving to the highest cliffs in Europe, followed by a scenic drive back to the pier.

"I don't tell you often enough how much I appreciate you for being patient with me," Eddie said, hugging her.

She smiled at him. "It's only taken forty years."

"For me to tell you?"

"No, for me to develop the patience."

———

8:00 a.m., Suite 1145

The phone rang just as Nickie stepped out of the shower and walked into the bedroom.

"I'll get it," she called. "Hello? Oh, hi! No, we don't. Uh huh, Ah see. Oh, that would be nice. I'll check with Arthur. Just a moment."

Placing her hand over the receiver, she said, "It's Carol. She wants to know if we would be available for lunch today with her and Phil."

"She and Phil," he said, correcting her. "Why?"

"She didn't say. What should I tell her?"

"Why not? We're free."

"We'd love to, Carol. What time and where? Oh, okay. We'll see you then."

"What did she say?" he asked.

"At noon in their suite. Executive suite number one."

———

12:00 p.m., Executive Suite #1

When Carol opened the door at precisely twelve noon, she noticed that Nickie was dressed conservatively in a loose-fitting blouse, linen slacks, and open-toed pumps. She wondered if it was intentional.

"Hi. Come on in," she said. She gave Nickie a warm hug. "Hi, Arthur."

"Welcome," called Phil from the living room. "Is it too early for a glass of Prosecco?"

"Never too early." Arthur grinned.

They seated themselves on the plush sofa and accepted glasses of the chilled wine.

"Room service will be bringing some lobster bisque, Caesar salads, and warm baguettes in about thirty minutes. I noticed that you both have ordered that for lunch before, so I took the liberty of ordering it for all of us. I hope I wasn't too presumptuous," he said.

"No, not at all," said Arthur. "You are right, we both like the bisque."

"Did anyone else have a bit of a hangover this morning?" asked Phil.

"Ah sure did," drawled Nicole. "That was a lotta drinkin' last night."

"And a lot of honesty," said Arthur.

"That's why we invited you today," said Phil, filling their glasses. "We both wanted to talk to you about some of the things that we said. I think the whisky loosened our tongues a bit too much."

"Well, it sure did myun," said Nickie. "And Ah'm not sure Ah wanted to say all that Ah did."

"Let me go first," said Carol. "I've never told anybody about that dreadful business of my father's suicide until last night. I know that everyone in San Francisco knows about it, and they talk about me behind my back. I think that's one of the reasons I never tried to leave the safety of working with Phil in his business, so I wouldn't have to be exposed to the criticism that goes with a public scandal of that nature. I have no idea what you and the others are thinking about me now, but I want to let you know how embarrassed I am and apologize for my outburst."

Nickie's eyes filled with tears. She put her arms around Carol and said, "You don't have anything to be embarrassed about, dahlin'. You didn't do nuthin'. Ah jist luv yer honesty and trust and openness. Ah jist luv you more."

Carol was crying now too. Phil and Arthur sipped their wine, not knowing where to look. Finally, Phil did the only thing he knew to do; he opened another bottle of Prosecco and refilled everyone's glass.

Just then there was a knock on the door, and Phil opened it to the room service waiter. The women went to the bathroom to dry their tears.

"Are you all right?" asked Nickie after Carol washed her face.

She nodded. "Yes, I'm okay now. I didn't think I would cry. I'm glad I had a chance to apologize, but that's not the only thing Phil and I wanted to talk to you about."

"Oh, ah know," said Nickie. "It's what ah said about bein' a flirt an actin' all sexy an ever'thin'. It musta looked lak ah wuz cummin' on to Phil, but ah wuzn't, honest."

"Oh, honey, we know. You are such a sweetheart," said Carol. "Don't worry about our not understanding. Phil and I had a long talk about what you said and what he said, and it cleared a lot of things up for both of us. Actually, he should be here with us while we discuss this."

"What, here in the bathroom?" laughed Nickie.

"No," laughed Carol. "I mean we should all be talking about this together, including Arthur."

"I guess they're going to be a while," Arthur said, after twenty minutes had gone by.

"The soup will stay hot with that burner under the pot," said Phil. "What you said last night about not wanting to do what other people expected of you; you meant you want to play the sax and follow your love of music, right?"

"What?" said Nickie, as she and Carol walked unnoticed into the room. "What sax?"

"Your guy's first love, other than you, is the saxophone and playing jazz," said Phil.

"You nevuh told me about that. When? Ah'm hearin' this for the first time. Ah nevuh knew," she stammered. "Y'all woulda thought he'da said sumthin'," she said, to no one in particular.

"I never discussed it with you because I thought you'd just think I was being foolish and frivolous," he said.

"What? Oh no, Ah luv it. Is that what you meant last night when you said that thang about the direction you wanted to go?"

He nodded, smiling sheepishly.

She took his hand and said, "Ah said it lass night. If you want to go off and do some crazy thang, Ah'm with you. Oh my god, music. Ah luv it. Ah grew up in Cajun country. We're all about music."

By this time Arthur and the others were all grinning, and the feeling in the room was upbeat and happy.

"We'd better have lunch now," said Phil. He brought the salad bowl to the table. "Have a seat, everyone. I'm afraid the bread is not going to be warm, but the soup is fine."

"It doesn't matter," said Carol. "It'll be fine because we're enjoying it with friends. Is there more Prosecco?"

Phil took the bottle from the ice bucket and refilled the glasses. "Let's drink to Arthur's musical career."

"Does that mean I don't get to drink because of the absent friends thing?" laughed Arthur.

"No, because we're drinking to your career and not to you," said Carol. "Arthur, Nickie and I started to talk in the bathroom about last night."

"Let me jump in here," said Phil. "I don't know what possessed me to say those things about being attracted to beautiful women."

"Was it the truth?" asked Arthur.

"Well, yes, but I want you to know that it wasn't personal. I wasn't attempting to, like I said last night, act on it."

"Yes," said Carol. "We had a long talk about it this morning, and for the first time in our marriage, I understood what that was all about and why I was so insecure about it."

"Ah jest told Carol kinda the same thang about me tryin't to be sexy an' all not bein' a personal thang."

"Both of you can relax," said Arthur. "Those are perfectly natural feelings and thoughts. We studied compulsions and drives in medical school, and they are not unnatural. Frankie Laine was one of my favorite male vocalists when I was in college. I had every one of his albums. One of his songs that helped me understand those drives was 'It's a Necessary Evil.' I listened to it over and over while we studied Freud."

Then Arthur surprised everyone. His inhibitions loosened by the Prosecco, he jumped to his feet and launched into an off-key Frankie Laine impression, complete with hand gestures. He sang, "A man must sometimes take a sip of the grape or cast his eye on a lovely shape. If a man says he don't, he's not a man, he's a liar. It's a necessary evil, my friend."

"Oh, fab-yoo-lus," shrieked Nickie, applauding vigorously. "Not only are we going to go on stage playin' his hatchet but he can sing too! You see? You see? That's what I was talkin' about when I told you about his wild side, when he did his Cary Grant thing."

"It's an axe, not a hatchet," said Phil, "And I'm not sure he's ready for the vocals just yet."

"I'd agree with that," said Arthur. He was more than a little embarrassed by his slightly tipsy, impromptu outburst. "I'm not a singer, but I wanted to make the point as dramatically as possible."

"You're saying that a wandering eye is normal, right?" said Carol. "That all men do it?"

"Right," said Arthur. "In varying degrees; some more overtly than others. Nickie, I know from being with you for the last ten years that you are a person of unswerving integrity. I've had a chance to watch you and listen to you in all kinds of situations, and I know you are a person I can trust.

"Phil, even though we've only known one another for a short time,

I can tell you that people who have achieved your level of success, worked as hard as you, and made the contributions to society that you have don't have the time or inclination to burn up energy on frivolous pursuits."

Nickie, again with tears in her eyes, said, "I luv you," and kissed Arthur tenderly.

Carol's eyes glistened too. She could see that Phil was moved by what he heard.

"Hey, way too heavy. Let's have another glass of bubbly and finish our lunch," said Nickie.

They agreed and enjoyed the balance of their meal, talking about the morning activities and plans for the rest of the afternoon.

"It's nice to have a free afternoon," said Carol. "Nothing to do until cocktails at six."

"Time for our afternoon nap?" she asked Arthur.

Arthur, a little sleepy from the Prosecco, nodded. As they said their goodbyes, the earlier tension was totally gone.

6:00 p.m., the Porthole Bar

Arthur and Nickie were already seated on the couch in the corner when Eddie and Melissa arrived.

"Hey, where's the rest of the gang?" asked Eddie.

"Haven't seen them yet," said Arthur. "How was your day? We didn't see you around the ship."

"It was great," said Melissa. "We took an interesting tour."

"We had a great one too," said Don. He and Inga walked in just in time to hear Melissa's comment.

Phil and Carol were right behind them. Phil signaled Sven to bring their usual drinks. "We want to hear all about it. We stayed on the ship, so we didn't see any of the island," he said.

For the next thirty minutes, the two couples shared their adventures of the day, bolstered by frequent specifics from Inga's notebook.

"I have to tell you again, Inga, how impressed I am with the completeness and accuracy of your notes," said Carol.

"Yes, and if there is a way you can share them with us when the cruise is over, I'm sure we'd all like to have a copy of them," said Melissa.

"I'd be happy to share them, but I'm not sure how useful they'll be. I've used a lot of shorthand, and many times I reverted to writing in German when I couldn't think of the English words."

"I could help you put them in useable form if you like," said Carol.

"How could you do that?" asked Inga.

"I've been using voice recognition software to write the monthly newsletter for my college sorority, and it is efficient. We could sit down together and transcribe it."

"Ja, we can do that. When?"

"What if we get started right after breakfast tomorrow morning? If it takes more time, we can schedule it then."

Inga nodded in agreement.

"What about the rest of you?" asked Don. "What did you do today?"

"Well," said Nicole, "after being hosted to a gourmet lunch, including gallons of Prosecco, in Carol and Phil's suite, I just lay around the pool and read and slept."

Arthur smiled and said, "I did pretty much the same thing except for the pool and the reading part. I took a long, relaxing nap until the cocktail hour."

"I'm jealous," said, Melissa. "I wish I'd known that the Butlers were entertaining; I'd have canceled my tour."

Phil laughed and said, "We'll do it another time, Melissa. Actually, Carol and I felt that after our outburst of honesty last night, we had a need to clean up some things with the two of them. That was the purpose of the get-together."

"How did it go?" asked Eddie.

"That's none of our business," said Melissa sharply, glaring at her husband.

"In a way it is," said Phil. "Since we were all part of it, it is all of our business."

"What do you mean?" asked Melissa.

"In the almost two weeks we've been together, we've developed a level of intimacy that people who've known one another for years do not have. The honesty that we all displayed last night revealed a lot of personal stuff. So I think the things we talked about at lunch today affect the four of you as much it does us."

"I agree," said Eddie. "The openness and raw honesty we shared last night is ideal for anyone who wants to have deep and significant relationships."

"What *is* a significant relationship?" asked Arthur.

"I think a significant relationship is one in which mutual trust and caring exists; one in which two or even more people have an affinity for one another," said Don.

"This is an important discussion for us to have in retirement," said Arthur. "Our relationships are changing. Old friends are moving away, or we are. Work relationships tend to wither rather rapidly. Some old friends are dying. We're meeting new people, and I don't think the kind of closeness we've developed here is the norm."

"Don, your definition of a significant relationship would be an ideal condition to have in anyone's life," said Melissa, looking at Eddie. "But I think those kinds of relationships are rare, even in a marriage."

"That's true, but the rewards in that kind of relationship are so great that it is worth pursuing," said Carol.

"How do y'all do that?" asked Nicole quietly.

"I think the simple, clichéd answer is: to have a friend, you must be a friend," said Eddie.

"It might be a cliché, but it's true," said Arthur. "The dynamic that exists in this room now has been made possible by the willingness to risk that each of us demonstrated in our openness with one another. Trust begets trust."

"So if y'all were going to advise someone on how to make new friends, what would y'all tell 'em?" asked Nicole.

A long pause followed, with everyone thinking seriously about the question.

"I'd say, if you meet someone that you'd like to have as a friend, tell them," said Eddie.

"I'd say find some common ground and start by talking about that. If you both like to read, talk about books," said Melissa.

"Good idea," said Phil. "Birds of a feather share the same interests. Good places to go to meet potential close friends are clubs or organizations that are interesting to you."

Sven came from the bar and said, "Your table is ready, folks. Here are your checks."

They signed their bills and went to the dining room.

―――――

7:00 p.m., the Grand Dining Room

Bruno the sommelier asked, "What would delight your palates this evening, *mesdames* and *messieurs*?"

"What would delight my liver would be a two-month respite from all the alcohol I've been running through it," said Don. "But my palate would find a glass of chardonnay a delightful complement to the sole almandine I'm having."

"Would a Napa Valley chardonnay please your palate?" he asked.

"Do you have a bottle of 2010 Far Niente from Oakville?" asked Melissa, reading from her wine-tasting notes.

"We do," he said. "Would you like a bottle?"

"I sure would," said Phil. "I'd rather have a bottle in front of me than a frontal lobotomy."

Everyone groaned loudly. "You've already used that one," said Arthur.

"More than once," said Eddie.

"Everyone okay with the chardonnay?" asked Don. "Better make it two bottles, please, Bruno. I'm not much of a drinker myself, but these lushes will go through that before the salad course is finished."

"Lushes," laughed Phil. "Isn't that a case of the kettle calling the pot black?"

The bantering and frivolity continued throughout dinner with an obvious outpouring of affection for one another. At one point, Carol, feeling the glow of friendship and the chardonnay, grew teary. She said, "Hey, you guys," slurring slightly, "I gotta tell you something. I've never felt so loved or so safe in my life as I do with you. You are the family I've wanted and needed for a long time. I love you."

Phil leaned over and put his arm around her. She snuggled into his shoulder and smiled.

"I'll tell you, there's a lot of love in this room," said Arthur. "It feels good to me too."

Natalia came by and asked, "Would anyone like a last cup of coffee?"

They all laughed at her subtle message. "No, I think we'll say good night," said Don.

9:45 p.m., Elevator Lobby

"See you about nine," said Carol to Inga. "In our suite, okay? It will be quieter there. Phil will be out doing some kind of exercise thing. Right, dear?"

"Uh, yeah," he said, smiling. "That was my plan all along."

"Is there any way I can help?" asked Melissa. She wanted to be invited to see Carol's suite.

"Absolutely," said Carol. "It should be a collaborative effort. Nickie, are you available?"

"Ah wouldn't miss it for the world. Ah don't want y'all writin' anythin' in those notes about me that I didn't say. Ah'll be there."

"Well, all right then, see you all in the morning."

———

Day Twelve

April 18

The clock read seven-thirty when Melissa rolled over in bed. Eddie was sitting at the desk in front of his computer.

"What are you doing?" she asked.

"Quiet, woman. I need coffee in order to move this masterpiece along."

She smiled, crawled out of bed, and gave him a kiss on the back of his head. She looked over his shoulder at the computer screen.

"Wow, you are cooking," she said, seeing how much he'd done. "I'll get on the coffee detail at once."

She put the coffee on and went into the bathroom to get herself awake. When she came out, she poured two cups of coffee and brought them to the desk. "What have you written so far?" she asked.

"Sit back, relax, and enjoy," he said, grinning.

Sipping his coffee, he began to read from the computer screen:

"*Fulfillment after Fifty: How to Retire Happy.* A fast-moving, inspirational, and practical guide for successful living in the second chapter of life.

"What do I do now that I've retired? Now what? This is the question I ask myself as I contemplate my future after my own retirement. I've since discovered that most people are asking the same question, in one form or another. Some have found the answer and are enjoying a happy, joy-filled life after work.

"The purpose of this book is to help you answer that critical question and make your retirement a full, rich, and rewarding experience."

He looked up to see her reaction. "Don't be so damn needy," she said. "Just read."

He went on. "On many occasions, I'd sit with my wife, Melissa, and friends, enjoying a glass of wine, watching the sun set over the lake from the front deck of our home. More than once, I observed that none of us know how many sunsets we have left. I don't always wax that philosophical, but a good glass of Oregon Pinot Noir will do that to you.

"I never intend for that observation to be dismal or lugubrious but rather as a reminder of the specialness of the present experience. My golfing buddy, Charlie, always says, 'Life is too short not to do the things we enjoy doing.'

"I did find that most people can only play golf or go fishing for just so long before it becomes a habit or a routine, and like any other, it loses its allure. It becomes no different than having a job. It is like work.

"Work: 'anything you are doing when you'd rather be doing something else.'

"Humor: One retiree says to another, 'I go fishing in a well in my backyard every day.'

"Retiree #2: 'Do you ever catch anything?'

"Retiree #1: 'No, but it sure is convenient.'

"So unless that activity is an absolute passion, aside from the convenience of not having to think, you might not be getting the most that life has to offer.

"Like many people, I thought retirement was the idyllic condition of living the good life. I planned, worked for, and achieved this good life by using the tools I learned during my career, attending management and leadership training programs. I observed failures, so I knew what success was not. It was not Thoreau's life of quiet desperation, going to the grave with one's song unsung. It was living fully, using all of one's talents to live a worthwhile life. Hadn't I done that? Hadn't I paid my dues?

"I'd found my purpose. I'd sung my song, or so I thought. But there was a quiet nagging in the back of my mind during my reveries on those wonderful evenings watching the magic of the setting sun. I heard a little voice repeating the lines of 'The Spell of the Yukon':

> I wanted the gold and I sought it;
> Came out with a fortune last fall.
> Yet life's not what I thought it,
> and somehow the gold isn't all.

"We will explore the meaning of this poem. What I've learned from my own experience and that of others. This book will provide you with the richness of life to which I'm referring.

"You no doubt picked up this book, or it was given to you by someone who cares about you and your happiness. The fact that you are reading it tells me that you are success minded. By success minded I mean that you have a desire to make your life satisfying and meaningful.

"Now I knew something, something, something ...

"Well, what do you think, my love?"

"What's that something, something, and something part?"

"Well, that's where I ran out of ideas for now, but it'll come to me," he said.

"Oh, well then, it shows a lot of promise," she said. "You're off to a good start. Congratulations."

"Thank you, my love. You're my muse, you know."

"Well, your muse is off to get ready to see that suite of Phil and Carol's," she said. She carried her coffee toward the bathroom. "Can you manage on your own for breakfast this morning?"

"Writers of my caliber don't need food for sustenance," he said. "We are nourished by the inspiration in the ether."

"Yeah, yeah, yeah. Order room service when the ether stops supplying you with enough energy to keep writing," she said playfully.

———————

9:00 a.m., Executive Suite #1

When Carol opened the door, Melissa saw that the other women were already there.

"My God, did you all sleep together?" she asked.

"No, but that might be a great idea for another time," said Nicole.

"Come on in before my neighbors hear that kind of talk," she said, linking her arm with Melissa's.

"Have you had breakfast yet?"

"No, I was too excited to see your suite after hearing Nickie's description of it," said Melissa.

"Well, good. I have some fresh fruit, warm croissants, and coffee."

"Let's sit around the table in the dining room."

"The dining room! Oh my God," said Melissa excitedly, being decidedly uncool.

"Ja, this is nice," said Inga, noticing that the dining room was bigger than her whole suite.

"Sit here, Inga," said Carol, indicating the chair next to hers where she had set up her computer.

Inga opened her notebook and started to read into the computer's voice recognition software. Carol looked at the computer's interpretation of what Inga had said. "Uh oh, we've got a problem." She turned the computer screen to the others. It read, "aklgper rjg=satuirer fpgjojur pjgpoiurts psjgruhg,girj."

"What happened?" asked Melissa.

"It doesn't understand your accent, Inga," said Carol.

"Why, y'all, maybe Ah should read Inga's notes, and y'all be able to read them from there."

The other three burst out laughing. "No offense, but do you think the computer is going to understand you any better than Inga?" laughed Melissa.

"Ah guess not," she said. "Ah don't s'pose y'all could lay yer hans on a more intelligent computer in time to get this done by Sunday, do yuh?"

"Prolly not, Blanche, honey," said Carol, using her imitation southern accent.

"Well, that just leaves you or me," said Melissa to Carol. "Which one should do it?"

"I'll do it," she said. "The computer is already familiar with my voice, so it will be quicker if I do it. Okay with you?"

"No problem," said Melissa. "Just so we get it by Sunday morning before we all disembark."

"Okay, then. Inga, you translate your shorthand and the stuff you've written in German, and I'll read to Violet."

"Who's Violet?" asked Nicole.

"The computer. That's what I call her when I'm talking to her."

"You're even weirder than I thought," joked Melissa.

"Let's get to work then," said Inga. "Do we need Don to translate, so you can understand me?" she asked.

"Oh, I'm sorry," said Carol. "I didn't mean to offend you."

"It vashn't you. It vash that damn machine," she said, with a laugh.

They all laughed, and Carol said, "Now if you two have finished snooping around the suite, get out so Inga and I can get to work."

1:00 p.m.

After Pat's announcements and another interesting reporting period, he called the group together and introduced the day's presenter.

1:45 p.m.

"May I have your attention?" announced Pat Higgins. "We're ready to start our program in fifteen minutes."

Some people stayed at their tables, deep in conversation, while others left for the restrooms and the water table. Most returned to their seats on time.

2:00 p.m.

"The topic of the day is, Your Spiritual Life in Retirement.

"Our speaker will be talking about the role a spiritual—not religious—life plays in retirement. She will share the latest findings in the field and what they have revealed to us about living a healthier life during retirement. She draws from her studies, work, and research at the Center for Spiritual Living in Almador, California, where she is the senior minister. Please join me in welcoming Reverend Diana Morgan."

"Thank you, Pat, and good afternoon, everyone. There are so many different faiths, religions, and philosophies represented here, and I believe they all have merit and validity. For this reason, I am not going to talk about church or religion but rather about one thing we all have in common: consciousness. Consciousness and the way in which understanding it and using it can enrich our lives."

Reverend Morgan's talk bridged from quantum physics to additional thoughts about religion and spirituality.

Inga was able to capture most of the quantum physics material as well as her other ideas during Reverend Morgan's sixty-minute talk. The following are her notes:

- Everyone has different beliefs about their religious or spiritual life.
- As we mature and evolve we become more sensitive to others and more accepting.
- We tend to practice gratitude more frequently.

- Gregg Kreech, author of *Naikan: Gratitude, Grace, and the Japanese Art of Self Reflection*
- Seven principles of gratitude:
  - Gratitude is independent of one's objective life circumstances
  - Gratitude is a function of attention
  - Entitlement makes gratitude impossible
  - When we continue to receive something on a regular basis, we typically begin to take it for granted
  - Our deepest sense of gratitude comes through grace—the awareness that we have not earned, nor do we deserve, what we have been given
  - Gratitude can be cultivated through sincere self-reflection
  - The expression of gratitude (through words and deeds) has the effect of heightening our personal experience of gratitude
- Ervin Laszlo's book, *Quantum Shift in the Global Brain: How the New Scientific Reality Can Change Us and Our World*

3:00 p.m.

Pat Higgins asked everyone to regroup and, using the same reporting format, answer the question, 'How will you use one idea from today's talk?'

After the think-and-write exercise, Carlos asked his group, "Who'd like to go first?"

"I would," said Frank. "When she spoke of gratitude, it struck me like a blinding flash of the obvious. I've been taking everything that Marilyn does for me for granted and not appreciating it, or her."

Dean said, "I never thought about maturity and spiritual evolution being so closely related. I grew up in the Catholic Church and stopped attending when I thought I'd outgrown it. I think now that I just didn't keep up."

"This is a lot like our dinner conversation last night," said Karen.

"We need to pay more attention to one another and appreciate one another more if we are going to have a happier life."

The others nodded, and the conversation continued until Pat announced that time was up. He reminded everyone that there would be no meeting the next day. "We'll be docking in Tangier, so I'll see you for our final meeting on Saturday."

Eddie heard his name as they walked toward the elevators. He turned and saw Ron Champion standing at the door. "Hi, Ron. Wasn't that great stuff today?"

"Yeah, mate. I liked what she had to say. I was wishing I had a tape recorder to capture it all."

"It'll be in our seminar notes this evening," said Eddie.

Melissa cleared her throat. "Oh, excuse me. Ron. This is Melissa, my wife. Melissa, meet a fellow writer, Ron Champion."

"Lovely to meet you, Melissa. How's your writing coming, Eddie?"

"Smashingly," said Eddie. He delighted in adopting a British accent when he met someone from the UK. "I've been writing uh, uh, ..."

"Up a storm," interrupted Melissa.

"Is that so, old bean?" said Ron, mockingly overlaying a posh accent on his Cockney. "I'd love to see what you've done."

"I'd like to get your opinion," said Eddie.

"Why don't you two boys go to the room and talk? I'm going to meet Carol to see how the transcribing of Inga's notes went after I left this morning."

"Sounds great," said Ron. "Do you have any lager in your room?"

"We can order some," said Eddie. "Let's go."

Melissa leaned over and kissed him on the cheek. "So needy," she whispered in his ear.

Stateroom 735

"This is it, be it ever so humble," said Eddie as he unlocked the door and gestured for Ron to enter.

"Yeah, life on a cruise ship is tough, ain't it, mate?" he said with a laugh.

"Have a seat. I'll show you what I've got so far," Eddie said, opening his computer.

Ron said, "What about the lager, mate?"

"Oh, yeah," said Eddie. "Heineken okay?" Ron nodded. He picked up the phone and called room service for a couple of bottles of beer, knowing that Melissa was going to have a fit about his extravagance.

Ron settled back on the couch as Eddie started to read.

"'Now that I am in this stage of my life, what do I do to achieve happiness and satisfaction?'

"I should tell you," he said, interrupting himself, "that I've already written the first chapter, where I laid the foundation. I used a quotation from 'The Spell of the Yukon' and a funny joke about a retired guy."

He went on.

"As I researched the question of what makes for a successful retirement, health was the most important issue and the one that came up most frequently. I learned some important lessons from people who are doing some things right, and, unfortunately, some who have made poor choices.

"One Valentine's Day I had a wonderful phone conversation with my daughter Courtney. What I inherited from her is her great sense of humor. We laugh and joke as well as talk about our more serious issues. I believe that a sense of humor has an impact on our health. The fifty trillion cells in our bodies love it when we program them with laughter. They respond to any and all of the positive vibrations they pick up from us.

"Courtney told me that she and her boyfriend are faithful to their aerobic and weight-lifting program. Those kinds of activities also promote health. We know that our attitude is positively affected by the release of endorphins in our brains that produce the sensation of happiness. Anything we can do, whether exercising, laughing, or engaging in positive conversations or activities, has the desired healthy effect on our total being.

"I have the acronym HEAL – Health, Energy, Appearance, Longevity – posted on the treasure map on my office wall to remind me of the positive results I accrue from the healthy activities that I engage in. It gives me the motivation to go for a walk or to the gym or watch my diet."

Just then there was a knock on the door. The room service waiter came in with the beer, which he set up on the table with chilled glasses. Eddie looked at the bill, winced, and signed it. He thanked the waiter and gave a beer to Ron.

"Thank you, mate. Cheers," Ron said, lifting his glass in a toast.

Eddie picked up where he left off. "As you know from your own experience, these activities have a positive influence on our self-esteem and self-image. Why is that important? An enhanced self-image enables one to take on and master greater, more satisfying challenges.

"Here are some actions you can take today:

- Take inventory of the things you are currently doing that promote the HEAL objectives.
- Congratulate yourself for being the positive self-directed person you are.
- Look at yourself with constructive discontent. What can you do more of, less of, or eliminate to be even healthier?

"Let's remember what Arthur Schopenhauer said: 'With health, everything is a source of pleasure; without it nothing else, whatever it may be, is enjoyable. Health is by far the most important element in human happiness.'

"So why do we want to take care of our health? To add years to our lives and to add life to our years, right? To live to a ripe old age, perhaps to one hundred and beyond.

"I've already got my answer ready for the question, 'What do you do in order to live to be a hundred years old?'

Health is an important part of living fully and abundantly.
Energy is needed to pursue and achieve ambitious goals.
Appearance enables us to feel good about ourselves.
Longevity is essential for attaining long-range goals.

"I still have a long way to go before I reach a hundred, but I know I'm going to need all the time I can get. I suspect that you do too.

"Here are some suggestions for us to follow to improve the odds of our being here to answer those questions:

1. Find your purpose in life. What have you been put on this earth to do?

2. Study and follow the diet and exercise recommendations that are appropriate for your age.

3. Get busy and do something that you deem to be important for the world. Make a difference.

4. Act as if your life matters, because it does. The world needs you.

5. Select your ancestors carefully. They make a big difference. (Just kidding about that, although we can learn from their health history the things to guard against.)

"C. C. Colton said, 'The poorest man would not part with health for money, but the richest would gladly part with all their money for health.'

"That's all I've got so far," he said, closing the computer. "What do you think? Do you have any suggestions to improve it?"

"It's great, mate. Brilliant." He finished the second bottle of Heineken and stood up. "I believe you've got a real talent for writing. You might want to cut down on some of the verbiage, and I'd use more stories to illustrate your points."

"Thank you," Eddie said. "I appreciate your feedback." He leaned forward to hug Ron.

"No problem," said Ron, stepping back and offering his hand.

6:00 p.m., the Porthole Piano Bar

The women arrived ahead of their husbands, who had stopped at the casino on the way to win some drink money. Just as they entered, Sammy stood up from his piano stool, nodded to them, and sat down on a chair in the corner.

"I notice that Sammy takes his break just as the guys come in, so he doesn't have to listen to their terrible singing while he's playing," said Melissa.

"You know what would teach them a lesson? If they come in and we all was standin' up there and singin'," said Nicole.

"That would be fun. Let's do it," said Carol.

"How can we?" said Inga. "He's not playing."

"Oh, he will," said Nicole. "Come on." The others followed her to the piano.

She leaned on the piano and started to sing, doing a burlesque imitation of one of the guys. Sammy looked at them curiously.

"Blue moon, y'all saw me standin' alone."

"Y'all di'n't know what ah wuz doin' there," chimed in Carol, posing drunkenly.

Sammy laughed and came back to the piano. He began to purposely play off key, enjoying the joke.

"Yah, because Ah di'n't have a dream," sang Inga, off key. Carol wasn't sure if it was on purpose, but it didn't matter; they were having fun.

Melissa thrust her arms out like a cabaret singer, just as the men walked in. "And then there suddenly appeared before me ..."

"The only one my arms would ever hold," the other three chimed in.

"What the hell?" said Phil. Their bewildered husbands stood in the doorway, staring disbelievingly. The women continued to sing. When they stopped, the men applauded and headed for the piano. Sammy stood up, looked at his watch, shook his head, and said, "Break time."

The women burst out laughing and sat down on the couch.

"You were having a lot of fun there, weren't you?" said Arthur with a smile.

"A ton," said Nickie. "We just wanted y'all to git a taste of your own medicine an' see how bad y'all sound."

"Bad? I thought that was good," said Eddie.

"I couldn't agree more," said Phil, going along with the joke.

"I wonder if Sammy will have you back for an encore after his break," said Arthur.

"I'd pay plenty to hear first-rate entertainment like that every night," said Don.

"Y'all are spoil sports," said Nicole. "We wuz jist havin' some fun."

"More than that," said Carol. "That spontaneous demonstration of the coming-together of our exquisite talents was an example of how close we've become during this cruise."

"We have become closer, especially in the past two days," said Arthur. "And it's not just you womenfolk." He laughed. "We are more trusting and loving."

"It's what our speaker was talking about today," said Don. "It would be desirable to have that closeness in our friendships at home."

"That's right," said Melissa. "That's why she suggested that finding a group of like-minded people to bond with can be psychologically healthy."

"She made a good point about the disintegration of the nuclear family in so many communities and the mobilization of people around the country. These conditions are the major cause of many people's renewed interest in belonging to a church, not religious so much as a need for community," said Carol.

"That's true," said Eddie. "I've been a member of the same Rotary

Club for over twenty-five years, and we have a special bond based on shared values."

"Yes, and I also like the point she made that it is each person's responsibility to contribute to creating the kind of loving community they want rather than just finding it already in existence," said Don. "I think that is especially true for people like Inga and me, who have moved away from the city in which we were born."

"There are new opportunities appearing all the time, too," said Phil, with a grin, "especially for this group. We could start a barbershop quartet."

"It's time for dinner," said Don as he signaled Sven to bring their drink checks. "I'm looking forward to trying the French restaurant."

———

7:00 p.m., Jacques's Bistro

When they were seated, there was a slight wait before the waiter came to the table. When he arrived, Pierre said, "*Bonsoir, mesdames et messieurs.* Pardon me for the wait. We just got a little rushed."

"*De nada,*" said Phil, with his usual display of his "mastery" of foreign languages. "What's special this evening?"

"We have a special dinner for you this evening." From memory he rattled off a description of the delicious menu. The French chefs outdid themselves with another spectacular meal with excellent wine pairings.

After they all ordered and settled back in their chairs, Don said, "I'm eager to talk about today's presentation. That Reverend Morgan is a bright woman."

"I'd agree with that," said Arthur. "She inspired me to think about the role of consciousness if I'm to characterize my life as being well lived. For many years, I've associated consciousness with just being aware or awake. What she said today about the new developments and discoveries in quantum physics made a lot of sense. I have an increased understanding of what consciousness is and the ways in which it affects every area of our lives."

Francois, their waiter, brought their food, and the sommelier brought the perfect wine to accompany it.

"I especially liked her recommended reading," said Melissa. "Laszlo and the Deepak Chopra book, *Creating Affluence.* I've got that on my list to download on my Kindle."

"I like that too," said Carol. She read from her notes. "The universe literally means 'one song'—*uni* equals one; *verse* equals song. Chopra goes on to say that in this song, in this harmony, there is peace, laughter, joy, and bliss. Those are wonderful values to embrace. Reverend Morgan said Chopra gives a us a lucid and comprehensive explanation of the application of thought to create matter, using the principles of quantum physics. She also recommended Lynn McTaggart's *The Field,* to deepen our understanding of quantum physics."

"That's just old-fashioned positive thinking *a la* Napoleon Hill," chimed in Phil. "For centuries people have advocated the use of prayer and meditation to achieve their goals and outcomes in their lives."

"What kinda prayer could you use to create matta?" asked Nicole.

"Well it's not actually prayer but more like affirmations," said Phil. "Something like, 'I know, feel, and envision my life the way I choose to be. My desires are filled with good. I am abundantly prosperous, possessing all I desire, and more. I have wonderful relationships with my family and friends, and I bring good to others. My career is rewarding and fulfilling. I love what I do, and I allow it to increase in blessings. I am in wonderful health and feel energetic, healthy, and happy. I am all I dream of being.'"

"Is this the type of affirmation Chopra and others are saying will bring reality into being? And how does that work?" asked Inga.

"As I understand it," said Carol, "it works by focusing our attention on certain probability amplitudes in the field of infinite possibilities and bringing them into material existence. Recognizing the unity of all things, as the physicists and the metaphysicists are now doing, opens up the portals of a great new life. Let's act on this knowledge to create true affluence for ourselves and others."

"I liked the closing Deepak Chopra quotation that Reverend Morgan used, which summarizes her talk and this conversation," said Inga, reading from her notebook. "Affluence or wealth means that one is easily able to fulfill one's desires, whatever they may be, whether they apply to the material realm or to our emotional, psychological, or spiritual needs or to the realm of relationships."

The timing was perfect, as François and his assistants cleared the table and brought coffee and dessert. Their conversation turned to lighter topics as they enjoyed one another's company and the chocolate mousse.

9:00 p.m., the Lobby

"Good night, everybody," said Arthur. "Oh, is anyone going into Tangier tomorrow?"

"Not me. I'm going to spend the day writing up a storm," said Eddie.

"We're going," said Carol. "We've never been to Morocco, and we want to see what it's like."

"Can I tag along with you since 'Hemingway' is going to be creating high winds or whatever happens when he writes up a storm?" asked Melissa.

"You bet," said Phil. "It'll be fun to have you along. Don't worry, Eddie, I'll take good care of her and have her back safe and sound—unless I get a good offer for her in the market. I was planning on seeing what they would give me for Carol, but now that I have two to sell, I'll probably get a better price."

"We've been there before, so we want to stay on board and read and relax," said Don.

"See y'all for cocktails tomorrow," said Nicole as she and Arthur turned toward the elevators.

A chorus of good nights from everyone ended another stimulating day.

Day Thirteen

April 19

When Phil walked into the fitness center, he heard someone call his name. There was Arthur on the treadmill with a big smile on his face. "What are you doing here at this ungodly hour?" he asked.

"Getting in shape," said Arthur, as he climbed down and wiped the sweat from his face.

"What? For more heavy drinking and dinner tonight?"

"I thought you were going to Tangier today."

"We are. I'm meeting Carol and Melissa at ten o'clock, but I wanted to get a workout in before we go. So what's with you in the gym? I haven't seen you here before."

"Meet me for a quick cup of coffee after your workout, and I'll tell you all about it," said Arthur.

"Okay, give me a half hour, and I'll be there."

———

8:00 a.m., Barista Coffee Bar
Arthur was hunched over writing in a notebook and didn't see Phil right away. "Hey," said Phil, "can I get you a coffee?"

"Oh, hey, dawg. 'Sup?"

"Dawg? What's up with that?"

"It's part of my new image. I want to have a more modern, up-to-date, hip persona," Arthur said, smiling.

"Don't do that," said Phil, "Retirement-aged people don't call one another dawg or dude or brother or any other street-lingo names. What's this all about anyway?"

"Let me buy you a coffee, and I'll tell you the whole story."

"You don't have to buy the coffee. It's free," said Phil. "But I'll have a *doppio.* How about you?"

At the counter Arthur said to the barista, "Give me a double cappuccino, and give my friend here anything he wants. I'm buying."

"There'll be no charge," said the barista.

"What I told you," said Phil. "A doppio, please."

They chose a corner table, and the barista brought their coffees.

"Well?" said Phil.

"The seminar has been an eye-opener for me," said Arthur, his eyes shining.

"How do you mean?" said Phil, taking a sip of coffee. He watched Arthur closely for a clue to his unusual behavior.

"As soon as I get home, I'm resigning from the hospital board and the presidencies of both the country club and the Rotary Club. I'm going to devote all my time to my music."

"What?" gasped Phil. "Don't you think that's a little rash? What does Nickie think of your decision?"

Taking a drink of his coffee, he said, "Don't know. I haven't told her yet."

"What caused this radical decision? You said the seminar has been an eye-opener for you. Specifically, what happened to initiate your decision?"

"All my life I've been preprogrammed to do what others expected of me. I never stopped to ask myself, 'What does Arthur expect of Arthur?' I've heard so many stories in our small-group discussions from people saying they regretted and even resented the time they spent on their jobs and how glad they are to be out of them. I could see that happening to me in the time I have left. I just don't want it to happen. Do you know what I mean?"

"Absolutely," said Phil. "Have you heard that Thoreau quotation about most men leading lives of quiet desperation?"

"Yes, and go to their graves with their music still in them," said Arthur, finishing the quotation. That's exactly what I'm talking about. I've never heard of a surgeon who said on his deathbed, 'I wish I could have done one more surgery.'"

"So that's it then," said Phil. "If that's what you want to do, then I support you. What can I do to help you?"

"I thought of that, and I want to ask you about a quality you possess that I envy."

Phil felt a rush of pleasure from the compliment, then immediately chastised himself for still needing so much approval from others.

"Oh? What's that?" he asked.

"You are so disciplined with your exercise and fitness program that you put the rest of us to shame. Eddie and I were talking about the fact that you are in the fitness center every morning no matter how late we were up the night before. You seem to control your eating and drinking better than the rest of us. So my question is, 'How do you do it?'"

Phil laughed. "I haven't always been so disciplined. I was like a lot of people trying to get ahead. Working long hours, I ate too much and used alcohol to relax. Until ten years ago, I was forty pounds heavier than I am now, and I was chain-smoking two packs of cigarettes a day."

"Wow, how did you make all those changes, dawg?" said Arthur, laughing at his own joke.

"In a word: habit."

"Habit? What do you mean? How?"

"I changed my habits a little at a time. See, when I celebrated my fortieth birthday, I looked in the mirror and I didn't like what I saw. I looked like an old man. I didn't like the way I felt. I was tired too much of the time. A sharper, faster group of young lions were showing up in the business arena, and I had to either get myself in shape to compete or get out of the game."

"But you were in business for yourself, right? You weren't competing with anyone, were you?"

"Oh, I was doing all right in the scrap business, but to make big money, you need to invest and be aware of the opportunities when they come up. There is an unspoken rule in the business and social world. The players want to hang with the people who look and act like winners, and I wanted to be one of them."

"What do you mean?" asked Arthur, leaning forward. He'd never heard anyone in the medical field talk like that.

"When you are at the country club or the athletic club, it's easy to spot the people who know from the ones who don't have a clue. I knew that those were the people I wanted to associate with, so I did. I'm sure you have those same kinds of people in Des Moines, right?"

"I guess so. I've never thought about it though, and it never occurred to me that I should consciously cultivate those types of friendships."

"Because you were at a disadvantage," said Phil with a smile. "You were part of a highly respected segment of society where your family and your education automatically earned you a seat in the game, so you never had to put out any extra effort to fit in."

"Well, maybe ..."

"No maybe," Phil interrupted. "You didn't have to learn to go after something with all your might." He let that sink in for a minute before adding, "Now you do."

"What?" asked Arthur, looking puzzled.

"You'll have to use the same strategies and tactics to achieve success in your musical career that every successful person has used to achieve success in any field."

"I'm afraid it's too late in life for me to take on something as demanding as excellence in music," said Arthur, with a dejected look on his face.

"I don't believe that," said Phil. "You have the desire, so you'll do whatever is necessary to achieve it. Besides, all that love and passion for jazz has never left you. It is a part of the fabric of your being. There is one other reason for going all out to pursue your passion."

"What's that?" asked Arthur.

"Your success doesn't depend on achieving a particular goal as much as it does the satisfaction you'll feel every day you are moving forward. Forward toward your ideal of the kind of musician that you aspire to be, this century's Charlie Parker. In other words, it is not the destination but the journey."

Arthur's eyes were glistening as he absorbed Phil's words.

"Look at the time," said Phil. "I'm meeting Carol and Melissa to go ashore. We'll be back in time for cocktails at six. Let's continue our conversation then, okay?"

"Yeah, fine," said Arthur. "Be there or be square." They both laughed at their corny joke. Phil put his coffee cup down and hurried back to his suite.

9:30 a.m.

Carol was sitting on a sofa in the living room, nervously flipping through the pages of a *Vanity Fair* magazine.

"Where have you been?" she asked sharply. "We have to be downstairs to meet Melissa in thirty minutes."

"I thought she was meeting us here," said Phil.

"She *was* here and left thirty minutes ago to check us in for the tour."

"I'm sorry. I got tied up talking to Arthur. He was at the gym this morning and had something important to talk to me about, so I met him for coffee."

"What did he have to talk to you about?" she asked, her voice softening.

"I'd better get ready. I'll tell you later," he said with a grin.

"Tell me now. Don't keep me in suspense, you tease." She laughed.

"Get me a quick something to eat while I change, and I'll tell you on the way down."

Twenty minutes later they left the suite. "Well?" she asked. "What did he say?"

"Who?" said Phil innocently.

She punched him on the arm. "Arthur. What did he say?" It was the most playful she'd been in a long time.

"It's almost the way it used to be with us," thought Phil. He put his arm around her. "Okay, but you can't breathe a word of this to Nicole. Promise?"

"I promise. Now dish. What's the dirt?"

He gave her a brief description of his conversation with Arthur as they rode down to the fifth level.

Melissa was nervously standing at the entrance to the theater.

"Where have you two been? They called our color fifteen minutes ago. I told them you were on your way down and would be here any minute."

Phil rushed to the front of the room to let the crew member know they were there.

"So what kept you? You said when I left that Phil was going to be back any minute."

"Well, you know," said Carol suggestively, "it can get pritt-tee—how can I say it? With Phil coming back all sweaty and everything—well, we better get checked in."

"What, what?" begged Melissa. "Pretty please, what? We've got time. Does that mean you've come to a decision about the divorce?"

"Oh, here's Phil," said Carol. "We better get moving. All set, honey?"

"Yeah, she radioed the purser to let him know we are on our way."

"I guess you had to be pretty quick when you got back from your workout to get down here in time, didn't you?" said Melissa impishly.

"Well, yeah, I got back a little late, but I'm used to being able to move fast, so I had no trouble getting here in time."

To Phil's confusion, Carol and Melissa burst out laughing. They hurried down to the fourth deck to disembark.

10:00 a.m.

They showed their identification cards to the purser and rushed ashore to board the waiting bus. They were eager to take in the sights of the exotic city of Tangier.

"What do we know about this place?" asked Phil. As usual, he had done minimal advance studying about the ports they visited.

"Well," said Melissa, reading from the issue of the ship's newspaper, "Morocco became a French protectorate in 1912. It wasn't until 1956 that Tangier would finally be reunited with the rest of Morocco. In recent years, looking for new ways to encourage foreign investment in Morocco, the government established Tangier as a free-trade zone."

"We have an interesting six hours ahead of us," said Carol. "From what I've read about this place, we're going to see the lifestyle of the Moroccan people."

———

6:00 p.m., the Porthole Piano Bar

"Hey, the world travelers are back," boomed Don when the Butlers and Townsends walked into the piano bar.

"I see you weren't able to sell off those two women in the Kasbah," joked Arthur.

"I tried," said Phil, "but there were no takers. The head buyer said there's no one in all of Morocco who could afford merchandise of this quality."

"Aren't you sweet," cooed Melissa.

"That's why he's such a good salesman," said Carol. "He has a real gift of gab. He can make anything sound good. His customers used to say he is skilled at 'putting lipstick on a pig.'"

That brought a laugh from the group as everyone settled into their seats. Sven brought their usual round of drinks.

Phil said, "How did the writing go today, Eddie? Did you get a lot done?"

"I can answer that," said Melissa. "When I came back to our room, he was asleep on the couch with two empty beer bottles on the table and the TV blaring away. So I don't think he wrote up the storm we were all expecting."

"You know not from where you speak, woman," said Eddie. "The beer and the nap were my rewards for having created golden prose for the better part of the day."

"Golden prose is another euphemism like 'writing up a storm.' I've learned to interpret it as 'not much happened,'" said Melissa, with a laugh.

"Never mind that," said Arthur. "How did the tour go?"

"It was great," said Carol. "We began with a drive past some beautiful villas—the governor's residence and the king's summer palace. We got some good photos."

"We visited the Kasbah and had a guided tour of the walled medina and the old town; tiny streets with fabric shops with the colorful souks," continued Melissa. "They gave us free time for shopping, but a guide was always escorting us to be sure we didn't get our purses snatched or pockets picked. Neither Carol nor I bought anything."

"That's when I tried to auction them off, Eddie," laughed Phil. "But the best offer I got for the two of them was one crippled old camel."

"Right," said Carol. "No way would we support their economy after that insult."

Melissa jumped in. "You said it, girlfriend. Imagine! One camel."

"Yeah," said Carol. "A crippled old one at that."

"I wouldn't mind if he was crippled *or* old. One or the other, but not both. And by the way, I thought Phil was the silver-tongued salesman who could make anything sound good, even us."

"Oh yeah, that," said Carol. "What I didn't tell you is that he'll say smooth stuff like that and then spoil it all by putting his foot in his mouth."

"I guess once you understand that, he's more tolerable, huh?" said Melissa, looking at Carol to see her reaction.

"Yeah," she said, smiling at Phil. "It took twenty-five years, but I get him now."

"Was that it, then?" asked Inga.

"Pretty much," said Carol.

"Wait, wait," said Phil. "I want to give part of the report."

"Go ahead, honey," said Carol. "What do you remember about the tour?"

"Well, not about the tour, but when we got back to the ship, I took a nap."

"That brings us up to date then," said Don, laughing. "It was worthwhile?'

"Oh yeah," said Carol and Melissa in unison.

"Your table is ready," said Sven as he put their drink checks in front of them.

"Great," said Don as he picked up his bill and signed it. "I'm hungry."

7:00 p.m., the Grand Dining Room

The maître d' seated them and handed them their menus. "I'd recommend the salmon tonight, or the pork loin also looks good."

"Thank you, Carlos," said Eddie. "Would you please ask the sommelier to come over right away? I've worked hard today and have a tremendous thirst. I deserve a good bottle of wine."

"Right away, Mr. Townsend. It sounds as though you wrote up a storm again today," he said, with a straight face.

As he turned away, the whole group broke out laughing.

"You've developed quite a reputation," said Arthur, wiping the tears from his eyes. "Even the maître d' knows your famous line."

"Well, all I can say is that there are going to be some pretty embarrassed people around this ship when they read that *Fulfillment after Fifty: How to Retire Happier* made the *New York Times* best-seller list," he said sternly.

"Happier? I thought it was going to be 'happy,'" said Melissa.

"Well, I changed it so I don't offend my readers."

"Y'all are too sweet to offend anyone," purred Nicole as she sensed the mounting tension between Eddie and his wife.

"Thank you, Nickie. I appreciate those words of support and encouragement," he said.

Alberto, the sommelier, came to the table and recommended a bottle of 2010 Far Niente chardonnay from Oakville in the Napa Valley. "This is one you've had before, and you all enjoyed it very much," he said.

"Everyone agree?" asked Phil.

"Bring it on," said a subdued Eddie. He did not want to bring on another round of jokes about celebrating his writing success.

Istvan, one of their favorite waiters, took their orders while Regina, his assistant, brought water and bread and butter.

"Ladies," asked Istvan, "What will it be?"

"Salmon for me," said Melissa.

"Me too," echoed Nicole.

"I'll try the pork loin," said Carol, "and a small salad."

The men all ordered sirloin steak with pommes frites accompanied by Caesar salads.

Alberto returned and, based on their orders, suggested a French burgundy to pair with the steaks and another bottle of the chardonnay to complement the fish.

They agreed and started on their salads. They chatted about the day's happenings on the ship while the Butlers and Melissa were ashore.

When their entrees arrived, Arthur said, "I had an interesting conversation with Phil this morning after our morning workout at the fitness center."

"What?" said Nicole in mock horror. "Ah thought you were jist goin' down to the bar to drink. I didn't know you was sneakin' off to go to the fitness center. Oh, the deceit! What's to become of us?"

That brought a laugh from the group as Arthur smirked at Nicole.

"You don't know everything about me," he said.

"Probably not and it's probably best that way," she said. "Tell us about your conversation with Phil."

"Okay, here goes," he said. "You know what we talked about in Carol and Phil's suite at breakfast the other day?"

"You mean about us blurting out all that personal stuff the night before?"

"No, I mean about my playing the saxophone. There's more to it. I want to give up all the phony baloney stuff I've been doing and seriously pursue a career in music."

"What does 'seriously pursue a career in music' mean?" she asked.

"Well, not actually a career. I don't know if there is enough time to become good enough to actually get paid for playing, but I want to give up all the committees and other activities that are getting in the way of my going after being a professional musician."

"Like what?" she asked.

"Everything that is not being a professional musician."

"Everything?"

"Everything. The country club, the Rotary Club, the hospital board, everything. I want to practice and hang out with other weirdoes like me and talk jazz, and maybe I'll even smoke pot again."

"You smoked pot?" laughed Carol.

"Yeah, sometimes, when I was in medical school in Chicago hanging out with other musicians."

Arthur looked at Nickie, searching her face to see what her reaction would be.

"Hot day-um," she said, as she lifted her wine glass. "Let's drink to that. We all are gonna be on the road playin' and havin' fun."

"Does that mean you're okay with it?" said a relieved Arthur.

"Okay? Ah tole you, whatev-ah crazy-ass thing you wanna do, Ah'm yer girl." She leaned over and kissed him on the mouth.

The others were grinning as if they'd just witnessed a major and dramatic change in what had been a staid and conservative relationship.

"Bravo," said Phil, lifting his glass. "Congratulations, Arthur. Let us know where you'll be playing, and we'll be there to support you."

"Don't you go getting any wild ideas now, Schatze," said Inga to Don.

Everyone laughed at the incongruity of that coming from Inga.

"We've gotten way off track here," said Arthur. "What I started to talk to Phil about this morning affects all of us."

"You talking about that habit thing, dawg?" laughed Phil.

"Yeah, my brotha'," said Arthur, smiling.

The others looked at them quizzically.

Phil said, "Arthur asked me about my fitness routine, and I told him that it is due to the habits I developed. I told him I had to develop them out of necessity. I was out of shape and I needed to make changes in the way I was eating and exercising, or I should say, not exercising."

"So what did you do?" asked Eddie, leaning forward.

"I knew I needed to find out how successful people did it. I learned early in my career to ask financially successful people what their secrets were and adapted their answers to my business. I just did the same thing with my health, wellness, and fitness goals."

"What was that?" asked Melissa, obviously interested in what he had to say.

"There's a saying I heard a long time ago: 'Successful people form the habit of doing the things that failures don't like to do.'"

"Albert E. N. Grey, right?" said Eddie.

"Right. I knew all I had to do was look at the people I admired, pick their brains, and use the tactics they were using to get the results I wanted."

"And it worked, obviously," said Don.

"Yeah. It was simple, but it wasn't easy."

"How so?" asked Nicole.

"Well, the common denominator I found in healthy, physically fit people was habit. They all developed the habits of eating right and exercising. They reminded themselves that the chief cause of failure and unhappiness is trading what they wanted most for what they wanted at the moment. That's when I decided to develop a new set of healthier habits."

"Like going for a run at six o'clock in the morning?" asked Eddie.

"That came later. I knew if I tried to change too much too soon, I'd get discouraged and give it up, so I started small."

"What do you mean?" asked Don.

"Well," grinned Phil. "How do you eat an elephant?"

"Eat an elephant?" asked Inga, with a confused look." I don't know."

"One bite at a time," chorused Eddie, Melissa, and Carol together.

"Right, and that's what I did. I literally started one bite at a time. I started by making a commitment to myself to eat an apple every day instead of a morning sweet roll, which I used to buy at 7-Eleven on my way to the office. I created an image of how I wanted to look and feel. Then I substituted one positive habit for one counterproductive one."

"That makes a whole lotta sense," said Nicole.

"And y'all thought he was just another pretty face," teased Carol.

"There's got to be more to it than that," said Arthur.

"No," said Phil. "If we were to set out to build a house or a garden, the first thing we would need is a clear vision of the final outcome. This is true when designing any phase or aspect of our lives, including retirement."

"So that's it then," said Eddie, interested. "Just get a vision, and you are guaranteed success."

"No, the vision by itself is not enough. We need to set goals along with actions to make our vision a reality. All we need to do is take one step at a time. In my case that was literally true. My vision for the future was to be well, healthy, and physically fit during my later years. So I set goals in the areas of health, wellness, and fitness. It started out as a walking program, then when that got too easy, I started jogging. I needed a way to be held accountable, so I asked Carol to keep me on track by asking me if I walked or jogged the two miles a day I said I would do."

"That was what, ten years ago? Does he still do that Carol?" asked Melissa.

"Oh yes. Sometimes I forget, but he'll tell me he's going for a run or I'll wake up, as I did this morning, and he'll be gone. Then I remember that he had to get his two miles in for the day."

"Also," said Phil, "I remind myself that my happiness is a result of not trading what I want at the moment for what I want most."

"I imagine you could do the same thing in other areas, couldn't you?" asked Don.

"Sure, why not? Focus on any area that is important to you, that you feel would give you increased satisfaction."

"Do you think that's so important once you're retired?" asked Don.

"No, I don't think it is *as* important, I think it is *more* important because there is a tendency on the part of some people to get lazy, not put out as much effort, and not live their lives fully after they are no longer working."

"Why do you think habit is so important?" asked Inga.

"I think I can answer that," said Don. "There has been a lot of research done on that topic, most recently Charles Duhigg's book, *The Power of Habit*. It gave me a lot of insight on the subject."

"Have you changed any of your habits as a result of reading it?" asked his wife.

"No, but I've been meaning to," he laughed.

"Isn't that the problem with just reading or hearing about something?" asked Arthur.

"Absolutely," said Eddie. "When I was in charge of training for our company, we wasted a lot of money on knowledge-only programs. It wasn't until we started using vendors who provided experiential training that we started to see behavioral change in our employees."

"Yes," said Carol. "That makes a lot of sense. We've heard all our lives that knowledge is power, but I learned that is not always the case. I took a lot of courses and learned a plethora of useless information at Stanford that hasn't given me any power."

Don said, "I agree. Knowledge is power but only if it is intelligently applied. I have known many people who have a great deal of knowledge but don't know how to put it to use. They're called educated derelicts. We learn some useful or not-so-useful tidbit of information, then leave it behind, never to be called on again.

"I once quoted Herbert Spencer's famous observation on learning—'The great aim of education is not knowledge, but action,'—to a professor friend. He immediately took exception to that statement. He said, 'When I go to a historical site and read the plaque describing what took place there, I don't expect to take any action.' I didn't have a snappy retort at the time.

"What I should have said is, 'Spencer said it is the *great* aim of education, not the *only* aim.' There is nothing wrong with reading informational plaques at state parks or light entertaining novels or, for that matter, *People* magazine. We don't always have to be watching Nova or the Discovery channel on TV. Those activities serve different purposes."

"Right," said Phil. "When you and I are in pursuit of our own goals, goals that we deem worthwhile, we should connect our learning with activities that move us in the direction of attaining those goals. When reading, studying, and in conversations, we should ask ourselves, 'How will this help me achieve my goal?'"

By the way they were nodding and smiling as he spoke, Melissa observed that the entire group was obviously listening to him with respect. She also noticed that Carol was looking at him with pride, her eyes glistening and her expression softer than Melissa had seen it before.

"So," said Arthur, getting back to the subject of habits, "how do we go about developing new habits?"

"Okay," said Phil. "I'm not an authority, and this is a complicated subject, but I'll do my best to answer that. The first thing I found when I started to make positive changes in my life was the importance of understanding what payoff I was looking for when I engaged in counterproductive behaviors."

"What do you mean by counterproductive behaviors?" asked Inga.

"My definition of a counterproductive behavior is any activity or action you take that keeps you from being the person you want to be. As an example, in my own case, I wanted to be energetic and youthful looking, so I could compete in the world of business."

"How would that apply to me in my musical career, homey?" asked Arthur.

Phil laughed at Arthur's continuing efforts to be hip. He said, "It's pretty simple. Just ask yourself, 'Is what I'm doing, or getting ready to do, helping me to play my 'axe' like the Bird?'"

"What?" asked Nicole, confused again.

"Got it, dawg," said Arthur.

"What the hell are you two talking about?" asked Eddie.

"What we're saying," said Phil, "is that to change your habits, you need to start with a strong enough reason to change; that is, a desire for a more positive outcome in a specific area of your life. Arthur has decided that he wants to go back to playing his saxophone and is willing to do whatever it takes to become good at it. Right, my man?"

Arthur grinned broadly and said, "Right, brother."

Phil went on. "Then you need to find out what's getting in the way of accomplishing your goal. Once you figure that out, you only have to change your unproductive behavior. That's the hard part, because what causes us to be negative and not positive are triggers. Triggers are those things that either consciously or unconsciously cause us to automatically default to counterproductive behavior."

"What can we do about it if it happens to us unconsciously?" asked Melissa.

"All you have to do is substitute a more positive behavior to get the same reward or to achieve the goal."

"That sounds like an awful lot of work," said Don. "Is it worth all that effort?"

"I don't know," said Phil. "What is it worth to play the sax as close to the way that Charlie Parker played it, Arthur?"

"If I could play one riff that was even a little like Yardbird's, I'd die a happy man."

"I think we all know the reason for that," said Eddie. "We've talked about psychology and Eastern philosophy. We know that when we get totally lost in any kind of activity, we are the most fulfilled, satisfied, and the happiest.

"I read a comment by Abby Wambach of the USA Women's Soccer team, after she scored the winning goal against France in the semi-finals of the World Cup. 'It's as if no one else is in the stadium when a soccer ball is sailing through the air, coming straight toward my head.' She said, 'I have this sixth sense in which I can read the flight of the ball and just put my body there. Sometimes, though, it seems like it takes forever for the ball to get to me. It's like time stands still.'

"This is a kind of Zen or peak experience, and I think it is the kind of experience Arthur has when he is playing the sax."

"Yes," said Phil. "It is a feeling of being one with the experience. It is the best reason I can think of for any of us to find our mission, calling, or purpose in life."

"Well, we're talking about happiness," said Melissa, "and I once read that the writer Willa Cather said, 'That is happiness; to be dissolved into something complete and great.'"

"There's your answer, Don," said Phil. "What we all want is to be able to say at any point in our lives, especially in retirement, that my life has been well lived, and I can die a happy person."

"That is the main lesson for today," said Don. "I don't know if I can say I found an important enough goal to devote myself to, like Arthur's music, but I think the reward that I want now is a good night's sleep. I think I'll turn in."

Just then Istvan appeared and asked if they would like more coffee, which was the signal for the group to end their evening.

———

As they stood in the hallway, there was an unspoken feeling of melancholy in the air. The group of friends sensed that their journey together was coming to an end.

"Tomorrow's our last day together," said Eddie. "We've covered a lot of ground in two weeks."

"Schatze, I hope you were able to capture all this stuff in your notes," said Don.

"Ja, thanks to Carol, we've got everything except today in pretty good shape."

"We can add today's material if you can come up to our suite in the morning. It shouldn't take us more than an hour," said Carol.

"Ja, *das is gut.* What time?"

"Ten thirty work for you?"

"I'll be there or be square," she said, causing a burst of laughter from the others.

"Hey, I've got an idea. Why don't you all come up? We can have lunch and review Inga's notes," said Phil.

"Not until we finish adding today's notes and editing what we already have," said Carol.

"Okay everybody, how about noon? There will probably be some chilled Prosecco about that time."

———

DAY FOURTEEN

April 20

"Hi," said Carol, as she opened the door at exactly ten thirty and greeted a smiling Inga. "I'm not surprised that you are right on time. You are the most precise and prompt person I've ever known. Come on in."

"And don't forget predictable, square, and uptight too," replied Inga.

"I've got some coffee, and the computer is turned on and ready to go."

Carol stopped and did a double take. She squinted at Inga and said, "Something's different. What have you done to yourself?"

"What do you mean?" asked Inga, smiling.

"You look, ah, I don't know, younger? Your hair, your clothes—what's up?"

"Oh this," she said casually. She gestured to her red blouse, white shorts, and sporty jeweled sandals. "I went to the salon this morning and had my nails and my hair done. Then I stopped in at the boutique and bought this outfit. I've been admiring it all week."

"But what brought that on? It's not like you."

"Ja, it's not like I was. I've learned this week that we become what we think about, and I've been thinking like a mousy person, not colorful. I've been inhibited in everything I do, including the way I dress. I've held back from speaking up and expressing myself for too long. When Arthur and your husband talked about being hip and 'with it,' talking like they were all young and everything, I decided to act and do some being young myself."

"I love it! You look fabulous. What did Don say when he saw you?"

"He hasn't seen me yet. I suspect he's going to have a fit, especially when he sees what I paid for all this. But I don't care; let him." She laughed.

Carol clapped her hands and laughed along with her.

Just then Phil walked in. He looked at Inga and said, "What the hell?"

"It's Inga's new look," said Carol. "Isn't it great?"

"Yeah, she does—you do," said Phil, smiling. "What did Don say?"

Before Inga could answer, Carol said, "He loves it. It was his idea."

"Ja," said, Inga. She and Carol had another outburst of laughter.

"Whatever," said Phil. "I'm going to the fitness center to work out. I'll be back in time for lunch. I've already asked Alphonso to bring it at twelve thirty."

He gave a still-giggling Carol a hug and a kiss and left.

The two women sat at the dining room table, and Inga took her notebook from her new patent leather tote bag. They began to read and copy her notes from the day before.

When they finished, Carol called Violin and asked him to make eight copies of all of Inga's compiled notes.

12:00 p.m.

"Hey, y'all," said Nicole when Carol opened the door. "Is this the raht place to git mah grits? Ah'm askin' cuz Ah'm hongry."

"You kinda turn that Blanche Dubois thing on at will, don't you?" said Carol, smiling.

"Yas, Ah do if it'll git me some grits, honey."

"Well it'll work here anytime," said Carol. "Come on in."

"Mah Lord, what happened to you?" She gaped at Inga.

"I decided to get with it," she said.

"Well, you certainly did. You look amazin'."

"What? What?" said Don, pushing past Nicole to see what the fuss was all about.

"Oh *mein Gott in Himmel*," he said. "*Vas ist los?*" Turning to Carol, he said, "What did you do to her?"

"She didn't do anything to me. I did it myself. Do you like it, *Schatze*?" she asked. "It's my new look."

"Do I like it? Do I like it?" he sputtered. "Uh ... uh ..."

"You better," she said, "because I'm going to keep it."

Inga surprised everyone with her uncharacteristic assertiveness—most of all Don. He said, "Well then, yes, I guess I do like it. I've never seen you look like this before."

"Hubba, hubba," said Arthur, peering around Don to catch the excitement. "You look great, Inga."

"Hubba, hubba?" said Phil. "Is that more of your be-bop lingo, dawg?"

"I thought you two were going to work on Inga's notes, not her, her ... whatever," said a surprised Eddie, following Arthur into the room.

"Have a seat, everyone," said Phil. "Lunch is coming, and we are all eager to hear Inga's notes."

"Just a reminder, everyone," said Melissa. "We have a two o'clock meeting in the Celebrity Theater to wrap up the seminar."

Just then Alphonso wheeled the dining cart into the room and served the clam chowder, baskets of warm bread, grilled ham and cheese sandwiches, and fresh fruit cups.

"Mmm, mmm," said Nicole. "Mah favorite."

They began enjoying lunch, chatting about the woes of packing and preparing to disembark in the morning.

Just as they finished, Violin arrived with printed copies of Inga's notes.

"Thank you once again, Violin, for everything you've done for us on this voyage," said Phil.

"What I'd prefer to do is study these this afternoon and discuss them at dinner this evening, after I've had time to digest them. How do the rest of you feel about that?"

They murmured their agreement.

Looking at his watch, Don said, "We'd better leave to get ready for the afternoon meeting. It's already one thirty, and I need to change."

"I don't need to change. I've already changed," said Inga.

––––––––––

2:00 p.m., the Celebrity Theater

The BCGT number-one group arrived together ten minutes early, as they had agreed, so they could sit together for the final presentation.

Right on time, the ever-ebullient Pat Higgins bounded onto the stage and yelled, "Good afternoon, everybody! Are you ready for an exciting wrap-up of our journey into the next chapter of our lives?"

"Yes!" The room echoed with the cheers of the participants. By this time, they were used to his over-the-top enthusiasm.

"Let's give it up one more time for Mr. Enthusiasm, Doug Carson!"

Doug took the microphone and shouted, "Good afternoon, everybody! We're ready to wrap up this seminar and cruise. Have you enjoyed it?"

The group applauded and cheered loudly to show him their enthusiasm for the program.

"I agree. What's not to like? The food, the hospitality of Captain Manzini's crew and staff, the amenities of Imperial Cruise Lines' beautiful ship?"

The participants cheered and applauded even more enthusiastically than before.

"We'll be leaving it all behind tomorrow morning when we reach Barcelona. We'll also be leaving behind something else. We'll be leaving behind the old selves that we brought on board in Miami, and we'll be taking something with us: memories, new friends, and our new selves with a new outlook on life and a new future ahead of us. You'll also probably be accepting some things about yourself that you want to keep.

"A case in point: A guy is walking down the road carrying all his problems in a big sack on his shoulder. Finally, he can't take it anymore, so he throws down the sack and says, 'Man, I wish I was dead.'

"Just then the angel of death appears and says in a deep voice, 'You called?'

"'Yeah,' he says, 'Give me a hand and help me get this sack back up on my shoulder.'"

This brought another round of appreciative laughter from the group.

When the laughter died down he went on to say, "I'd be willing to bet that if we all threw our problems down in a pile in the middle of a field and sorted through them, we'd end up taking our own back. Right? At least we're familiar with them.

"We need to gain perspective on how fortunate we are. This poem by Joy Lovelet Crawford always does it for me:

Today upon a bus I saw a girl with golden hair.
She seemed so gay; I envied her, and wished that I were half
   so fair.
I watched her as she rose to leave and saw her hobble down
   the aisle.
She had one leg and wore a crutch, but as she passed, a smile.
O God, forgive me when I whine, I have two legs; the world
   is mine.

Later on, I bought some sweets; the boy who sold them had
   such charm.
I thought I'd stop and talk a while; if I were late t'would do
   no harm.
And as we talked he said, "Thank you sir, you've been so kind.
It's nice to talk to folks like you. Because, you see, I'm blind."

O God, forgive me when I whine, I have two eyes; the world
    is mine.

Later, walking down the street, I met a boy with eyes so blue.
But he stood and looked and watched the others play,
It seemed he knew not what to do.
I paused, and then I said, "Why don't you join the others, dear?"
He looked straight ahead without a word; then I knew he
    could not hear.
O God, forgive me when I whine, I have two ears; the world
    is mine.

Two legs to take me where I go,
Two eyes to see the sunsets glow,
Two ears to hear all that I should know.
O God, forgive me when I whine.
Why I'm blest indeed, for the world is mine.

"I hope, during the past two weeks, you've gained some of that
perspective and have found some answers for the question, 'What's
next?' And also, have the answer to Mary Oliver's question, 'What are
you going to do with this one wild and precious life?'"

Doug read a passage from his new book, *Retire Successfully*, emphasizing the importance of embracing satisfaction and joy.

"Wow, that strikes home," whispered Phil to Carol. "I feel as
though I've been caught in a trap of earn, spend, and consume for a
long time." Carol smiled in agreement.

"That is what this seminar has been about," Doug continued.
"Reprioritizing and redefining who we are and who we want to be.

"I know you've dreamed some new dreams and set some new
goals. I hope they are big and ambitious and that you are confident
in your ability to manifest those dreams and achieve those goals.

"It's only appropriate, then, that we remind ourselves of the words of Henry David Thoreau: 'I learned this, at least, by my experiment: that if one advances confidently in the direction of his dreams, and endeavors to live the life which he has imagined, he will meet with a success unexpected in common hours.

"'He will put some things behind, will pass an invisible boundary; new universal, and more liberal laws will begin to establish themselves around and within him; or the old laws be expanded and interpreted in his favor in a more liberal sense, and he will live with the license of a higher order of being.'

"So the rest of today is designed for you to spend some time with yourself and answer these five questions on the evaluation forms being distributed now:

"One: What is the most important realization or insight I had about myself, as a result of spending the past two weeks here?

"Two: What baggage did I bring to the seminar?

"Three: What baggage am I discarding as a result of being here?

"Four: What action am I going to take when I leave here?

"Five: What qualities do I and the other members of my group have in common?

"When you get together with your groups for dinner this evening, share your answers with one another and say your goodbyes because there won't be time in the morning.

"I'd like to close with a quotation from an old southern preacher who said to his congregation,

"'Lord, we ain't what we oughta be.
And Lord, we ain't what we wanna be.
And we promise you, Lord,
We ain't what we're gonna be.
But we wanna thank you, Lord; we ain't what we usta be!'

"Thank you. God bless, and good luck."

Cheering, the crowd gave Doug an extended standing ovation and then began to file out.

There was little chattering as each person took Doug's assignments seriously and wanted to be alone with their thoughts.

6:00 p.m., the Porthole Piano Bar

"Hey, that was a good farewell party the captain gave, wasn't it? What's happening with the women?" asked Eddie of Arthur and Phil, who stood at the bar, talking.

He and Melissa saw Carol and Nicole sitting on the couch in the corner, crying.

"They're just a couple of crybabies," said Phil. "They're all broken up because they think they're never going to see one another again after tonight."

"Or something like that. The truth is, we don't exactly know what's going on," said Arthur.

"You men," said Melissa. "I can never figure out if you are stupid or just insensitive."

"I can answer that. Both!" said Inga, who overheard the conversation as she and Don followed the Townsends. She and Melissa sat down with the other two women and joined their conversation.

"Nice going, guys. You've upset them; now we'll have to stand here and drink while they all have a cry," laughed Don.

"Yeah, I don't know what's wrong with you two," said Eddie, signaling Sven for a Dewar's and water. "I don't know why you can't be more like Don and me."

"I'll tell you what's wrong with us. We're stupid," said Phil, taking a drink.

"Not only that, we're insensitive," said Arthur. He clinked his glass against Phil's in mock pride.

"That's right. Your wife told us," said Phil.

"You know, Inga could be right," said Eddie. The women were now engaged in what appeared to be a serious conversation. "They are expressing real feelings about our time together coming to an end, and we're acting like it's no big deal."

"Come here now and give me a big kiss," laughed Phil, as he moved toward Eddie.

Eddie backed away. "You're not my type. Go kiss Don."

"Hold on," said Arthur, "I don't know why, but it's true. We men bottle up our feelings and don't tell one another what's going on with our emotions."

"It's true," said Don. "I'm already starting to miss this experience, and that includes the closeness I feel for all of us."

The women rose from the sofa and joined them at the bar. Melissa asked, "What are you Neanderthals talking about?"

"Surprisingly, the same thing you girls were talking about," said Eddie.

"Ve haven't been girls for a long time," said Inga.

"Well then, you ladies," said Arthur. "And we're not the emotional dwarfs you think we are. We've been talking about how empty it is going to seem without being together every evening."

"Yeah, and our solution is we're going to buy a big house and all move in together," said Phil.

"Can't you be serious?" asked Carol. "This has not been just a casual get-together. Nickie and I were talking about how close we've all become, and we are going to miss one another."

"You all remember we've got reservations in the Sienna dining room in ten minutes, so we better get on up there," said Arthur.

7:00 p.m., the Sienna Dining Room

"It's great to have the private dining room for our final dinner together," said Melissa.

"Hey," said Nicole, laughing. "This isn't our final dinner, the one just before we die. Let's make this one our 'penalternate' dinner."

"Sven," said Eddie. Their favorite waiter brought a bottle of Dom

Perignon and filled their glasses. "I'm delighted to see you. How do you happen to be here this evening?"

"I told Mr. Higgins that I would like to have the honor of serving you on your last night aboard, and he agreed. You've all meant so much to me, and Mr. Townsend, your encouragement has helped me with my writing. Thank you."

"You're welcome. You have a real talent; keep working on it."

"So this is it," said a teary Carol as she lifted her glass to toast absent friends.

"None of that, now," said Melissa. "If we start getting weepy this early in the evening, we won't have any tears left for our goodbyes later."

"We don't need any tears," said Arthur. "Let's make this a celebration of our friendship and enjoy the evening. What are you serving this evening, Alfonso?"

"We have a special surf and turf with lobster and filet mignon, Dr. Gibson. We'll be serving a cup of clam chowder laced with brandy and a green salad with oil and chardonnay vinaigrette dressing."

"That sounds like a perfect penalternate meal to me," laughed Don.

"Me too. Medium rare," said Phil. "Carol?"

"Perfect," she said, and the others agreed.

"Sven, what kind of swill should we drink with the surf and turf?" asked a laughing Phil.

"I'm recommending a chardonnay and a pinot noir, both from Mi Sueno in the Napa Valley. You'll find them to be a perfect complement to those dishes."

"Everybody okay with that?" asked Phil.

They all agreed, and Carol was pleased to see that her husband had become more considerate.

Since everyone consented, Phil said, "Bring it on, Sven. This is our last night, so we'll be drinking more than usual. You may want to have a couple more servers help you haul away the empties. Okay, Inga?"

Inga laughed and said, "Ja, that should do it."

After the servers brought salads and baskets of warm bread, Don asked, "Well, did you figure out what we all have in common?"

"That was a no-brainer," said Melissa. "All they had to do was find out which group of men consumed the most alcohol in the past ten years, divide that by the amount of patience and forgiveness on the part of their wives, and *voila!*—you guys were a shoo-in."

"Bravo, right on," said Carol.

"I'll bet she spent all afternoon thinking up that little speech," said Arthur.

"Ja, and it was true," said Inga. "I didn't see any other table where it took three extra servers to carry away the empty wine bottles after dinner every night."

"And I'll bet the two of them got together this afternoon to rehearse that skit," said Eddie.

"No matter, now that you have finished with the biting sarcasm, what do you think?" asked Don.

"I partially meant that," said Melissa. "I'm sure we've all noticed that we share an appreciation of good wine and good food. Our meals together have been punctuated with *wows* and *mm, mm, mms.*"

"It is true that there were a lot of food and drink-related questions on the application," said Carol, "and I answered them in depth."

"I did too," said Eddie, "especially the essay part. It is also worth noting that not every group in this seminar imbibes to the degree we do. Melissa and I were in one small group with a guy from Cincinnati who told us he was an alcoholic and that he was in a group made up of AA members."

"We met a bridge player whose group plays every day," said Carol. "That would bore me to death."

"That's the point of grouping us with like-minded people, isn't it?" said Don.

"Well the other common denominator is that we are all talkers," said Arthur. "There were a lot of questions on the application about our verbal interests, and I answered them positively."

"Way-al, Ah sure enuf did say Ah luvd mah food on mah application," drawled Nicole. "Ded Ah menshun Ah'm from Cajun country an' we all are all about good food?" she said in her best Blanche Dubois accent.

"Y'all did menshun that afore," said Carol, mimicking Nicole.

"Ah swear, Ah bulleve she mita menshund that once or twice," said Melissa, playing along with the gag.

"Y'all just stop that. Ah don't sound that horrible," said Nicole.

Phil teased, "That's not as bad as the Louisiana girl visiting up north in Connecticut. She saw a group of young women carrying textbooks and asked them, 'Where do y'all go to school?'

"'Yale,' one of them said.

"So the southern belle said in a loud voice, '*Ah sed, Where do y'all go to school?*'"

"Y'all just keep on gettin' worse and worse," laughed Nicole.

"We have food and drink in common for sure," said Don, "but what else? There must be other foodies on this ship."

"That's true. There must be. We must have other common denominators," said Arthur.

"Reflecting on our conversations over the past two weeks, we share an uncommon interest and familiarity with good books and ideas," said Don.

The group nodded in agreement. "Mostly," said Carol, "I've observed that we are analytical. By that I mean that we think about life and the issues in our lives."

"Yes, and we not only think about those things, we talk about them," said Melissa.

"I agree," said Eddie. "I read once that you can judge the intellectual capacity of an individual by the subject matter he talks about."

"I've heard the same thing," said Arthur. "Small minds talk about people, average minds talk about events, and great minds talk about ideas."

"In our attempt to separate ourselves from the great unwashed masses, let's not get too full of ourselves," laughed Don. "During a typical day we talk about all three of those things at different times."

"No question about that," agreed Eddie. "But we were looking for commonalities that bound this particular group together, and I do think that as a group we are intellectually curious, not necessarily more so than any other group on this cruise."

"Well, yes, I do feel especially fortunate that I didn't get thrown in with the stupid group," laughed Phil.

"Saying that, based on your behavior in the bar earlier, you guys would all have fit in with that group quite comfortably," teased Melissa.

"Well said, my dear," said Carol.

"I wrote those ideas about subject matter down in my notes from an earlier day. Do you remember, Carol?" said Inga.

"Yes, one of the speakers talked about the level of our conversation being related to the level of our intelligence. As I recall, he also said that a lot of that conversation is internal."

"Right, I remember," said Don. "That was in the same talk that emphasized that we become what we think about."

"Vell, vell, I think we've pretty much come to the conclusion that ve are schmart people who talk about important subjects," laughed Inga.

"Yes, and another one of our common qualities that we should be proud of is our humility," laughed Arthur as the others joined in.

"Don't forget our level of sophistication," said Don, lifting his glass in a salute to his fellow male companions.

"We are certainly 'swave and deboner,'" said Phil, toasting Don in return.

"Seriously," said Arthur, "another quality we have in common is a sense of humor. I've laughed more in the past two weeks than I have in years."

"Not all of the jokes were funny though, were they?" said Melissa, to no one in particular.

"No, not at all," said Carol, laughing and looking at Phil. "Some of them were downright bad. Not naming any names, but I'm sure the perpetrator of the groaners knows who he is."

"So there we have it. The qualities we seem to have in common. We'd be hard-pressed to find a group of friends back home with this degree of compatibility."

"Right. It would take time, but it would be worth looking for such people and cultivating relationships with them," said Eddie.

By this time, they had finished dinner and were enjoying chocolate mousse, coffee, and ruby port.

Sven and his server cleared the table. The group enjoyed the glow of their friendship and the feeling of satisfaction from another perfect meal.

8:00 p.m.

"What about the questions Doug assigned to us to answer this evening? Did any of you give any thought to them?" asked Don.

"Ah did, an' I answered all of them," said Nicole, holding up her evaluation form.

"Well then, let's hear what you had to say," said Carol.

"Before she answers, tell us what they were again," said Phil. "I didn't bring my evaluation form."

Inga opened her ever-present notebook and began to read.

As she did, Melissa and Carol both took notice of her new dress, which was a garish red and yellow striped, off-the-shoulder jersey, which did not fit quite right. She was also wearing makeup—eye shadow, lipstick, and a touch of rouge—which she had never worn before. Along with a recently acquired permanent smile, the look produced a new, more attractive person. Melissa caught Carol's eye, smiled, and winked as they both appreciated the new Inga.

"Number one, 'What was the most important realization or insight I had about myself as a result of spending the past two weeks here?'

"Number two, 'What baggage did I bring to the seminar?'"

"Number three, 'What baggage am I discarding as a result of being here?'"

"Number four, 'What action am I going to take when I leave here?'"

"And number five, we already discussed, 'What qualities do I and the other members of my group have in common?' Remember, this is the one where we all agreed that the men in the group were a bunch of fun-loving drunks," she laughed.

"Okay, Nickie, you're on," said Carol.

"Ah wanted to be first, so that y'all didn't take all the good stuff," she laughed.

"Ah told y'all before that I realized I was bein' a flirt and tryin' to look all sexy and everything because Ah'm afraid of gettin' old."

They nodded and smiled encouragingly.

"Ah think it's more than that," she went on. "Ah think Ah'd been afraid of bein' alone and dyin' alone," she said, eyes welling with tears.

"You said that you had been afraid," said Melissa, handing over a tissue. "Is that in the past?"

"Yas," she sniffed. "That wuz mah baggage, and Ah don't need it anymore, so Ah'm throwin' it overboard raht now."

"What caused you to come to that conclusion?" asked Carol.

Now Nickie was seriously weeping. She pointed to Arthur, "H-h-him," she stammered. "Ah nevah knew how much he loved me and how much Ah meant to him until now."

Soon, Carol was crying. Melissa and Inga were teary-eyed and caught up in the emotion of the moment.

The guys just didn't know what to do, so they sipped their port.

"So vat are you going to do now?" asked Inga.

Nicole read the notes she had written on her evaluation form. "Ah'v ben puttin' up a false front. The way Ah dress, the way Ah act all the time, everywhere, in front of Arthur, in front of the whole city of Des Moines. Tryin' to be what Ah thought everybody wanted me to be. So Ah'm gonna stop that raht now. Ah'm gonna drop my act, Ah'm gonna be real! Ah brought a poem I found in the library that says what Ah wanna say to mahself. Can I read part of it?"

"Yes, by all means," said Melissa.

"It's called, '*Please Hear What I'm Not Saying*,' by Charles Finn."

As she started to read, her eyes misted over with tears again, so she said, "Carol, would you read it for me? Ah don't think Ah can make it through to the end."

"Yes, of course," Carol said, and read:

"Don't be fooled by me.
  Don't be fooled by the face I wear
  For I wear a mask, a thousand masks,
  Masks that I'm afraid to take off,
  And none of them is me.

"Pretending is an art that's second nature with me,
  But don't be fooled,
  For God's sake don't be fooled.
  I give you the impression that I'm secure,
  That all is sunny and unruffled with me, within as well
     as without,
  That confidence is my name and coolness my game,
  That the water's calm and I'm in command
  And that I need no one,
  But don't believe me.
  My surface may seem smooth but my surface is my mask,
  Ever-varying and ever-concealing.
  Beneath lies no complacence.
  Beneath lies confusion, and fear, and aloneness.
  But I hide this. I don't want anybody to know it.
  I panic at the thought of my weakness exposed.
  That's why I frantically create a mask to hide behind,
  A nonchalant sophisticated facade,

To help me pretend,
To shield me from the glance that knows."

"That's beautiful," said Don. "That applies to all of us. To live life successfully, we need to be real."

"I agree," said Arthur. "It's easier to be real when we are no longer working. A certain amount of role-playing is expected of us. Who would have had confidence in a surgeon who confessed just before operating that he was a musician at heart?"

Everybody laughed at that and nodded in agreement.

"So specifically, what are you going to do, Nickie?" asked Eddie.

"First off, Ah'm gonna start dressing more like Inga, or at least the way you did before today. No offense, Inga."

"None taken," replied Inga. "I know I dressed too conservatively."

"Then," Nicole continued, "Ah'm gonna replace mah sexy act with a lifestyle and behavior that is more appropriate for a woman mah age. Finally, Ah'm gonna try to give this hippy-dippy crazy-ass saxophone player all the support, encouragement, and love he deserves. Ah'm gonna folla him where evah he wants to go."

Arthur put his arms around her and kissed her tenderly. His tears mingled with hers, and the rest of the group cheered and applauded.

"Let's hear from another one of you gals," said Don.

"First of all, we are not gals," said Inga forcefully, in her newfound assertiveness. "And secondly, it doesn't have to be one of us *women*. Let's hear from one of you men next."

Silence. They looked around the table at one another. No one wanted to follow Nicole's raw, honest disclosure.

Don, Eddie, and Phil looked expectantly at Arthur, since it was Nicole who had created the mood in the room. They obviously felt it was up to him to be next.

"All right, I'll be next," he said, with his arm still around Nicole.

"It's pretty obvious to everyone here that I'm one lucky guy to have a woman like this in my life. Although I did tell Phil, I haven't told the rest of you that Nickie and I are not married. Everybody in Des Moines thinks we are. We told them that we'd been married at Nicki's house in Louisiana. I told her we had to do that because Iowans were stuffy and conservative, but that's not the truth. Well, they are, but that's not the reason we didn't get married. I never wanted to because I was afraid that I was being unfaithful to Doris."

"What do you mean? Who's Doris?" asked Melissa.

"His wife," said Nicole. "He still has her pictures all over the house."

"That's crazy," said Eddie. "You can't live in the past. She's been dead for what, ten years?"

"Eleven and a half. I know you're right, but it was the way I was brought up, and I feel guilty every day I'm with Nickie because of it."

"You have a house and a car and other possessions, right?" asked Don.

"Yes, obviously," said Arthur, unsure where Don was going with this line of questioning.

"I'll bet you take care of them or have people who take care of them for you, right?" Without waiting for Arthur to answer, Don went on. "Nickie is far more precious than any of those possessions. We must take better care of our loved ones than the material things in our lives."

Arthur wiped a tear away from his eye, looked at Don and said, "Thank you. I needed to hear that."

Nicole squeezed his hand and said, "Ah love you."

"That triggered an important thought that's been going through my mind since we started on this journey," said Melissa.

"Wait," said Arthur, "I have one more thing before you go on, Melissa. I have something I want to throw overboard." Looking at Nicole, he said, "When we get back to the house, would you help me box up those old pictures around the house? That was another lifetime ago. You are my life now."

"Yas, yas," she said, throwing her arms around his neck and kissing him.

The room was filled with the sounds of the women sniffling, and the men were wiping their eyes, trying to avoid one another's gaze.

After a pause, Melissa leaned over and squeezed Arthur's hand and continued. "As I started to say about this journey—not the cruise, but the inner journey of self-exploration we've been on for the past two weeks—I didn't want to admit it to myself, but I've been a control freak all my life. I've tried to control myself and everyone around me."

"We know," said Carol.

"I didn't realize it's so obvious. Eddie, I want to apologize to you, my love. I've tried so hard to get you to conform to what I think is right for you, I've not nurtured you. I've been so petty and nit-picky that I've lost sight of all the reasons I love you, honor you, and value you."

Phil and Carol glanced at one another.

Eddie looked at Melissa as if seeing her for the first time. He took her hand and said, "I got it, my love."

There was a heavy silence in the room; no one seemed to know what was coming next.

Then Don spoke up, "Melissa, that sounds like a major insight, and you've identified the baggage you brought on board. What are you going to discard?"

"Isn't it obvious from what I just said?" she said defensively, trying to control the emotion in her voice.

"I think it is," said Don, "And there is real value in verbalizing it. When you hear yourself say it, it becomes more concrete, more real."

"Okay," she said. "My insight and my baggage are my need to control because I become afraid when things don't go the way I want them to or think they should go. I know it's because I'm afraid of what will happen if they don't. So I'm discarding the artificial protective barrier I've wrapped around myself. Let's see, what's next?"

"The action you're going to take," said Don.

"Right. I'm going to keep a journal and do that thing Nickie told us about. Ah'm glad Ah did, and Ah wisht Ah hadn't," she said, smiling at her Blanche Dubois impression.

More laughter and applause.

Nickie said, "Y'all do the worst southern accents of anybody ev'ah."

————————

"I vant to go next," said Inga. "I know something about myself, thanks to all of you. I have power. My baggage was a low opinion of myself and thinking that I wasn't as good as everybody else. I thought that because I have an accent, people think less of me. I realize now that it is actually an asset. It makes me different in a good way. I am unique. So I'm getting rid of that self-limiting attitude. Not that I'm going to lord my superiority over other people," she said, laughing.

The others, enjoying her new show of self-confidence and ability to laugh at herself, joined in and laughed along with her.

Looking down at her notes, she read, "The action I'm going to take is to look for opportunities to step out of my comfort zone and do more risky things," she said with finality and slammed her notebook shut.

The group applauded. Carol laughed and said, "Riskier than changing your hairstyle and dressing more va-va-voomishly?"

"Ja," she said.

"I hope that doesn't mean you are going to use up our nest egg on a whole new wardrobe," said Don, laughing.

Putting her fists on her hips, she said, smiling, "I might, so don't try to stop me."

The group gave her a new round of applause. The mood in the room was light, with a smile on everyone's face. The love in the room was palpable.

"Va-va-voomishly?" said Melissa. "I don't think there is such a word."

"There wasn't until now," said Carol, "but it fits, so we'll allow it into the lexicon, and I'll take credit for coining it."

"May I add something?" said Arthur.

"Yes, if you promise not to sing," said Phil, laughing.

Nicole and Carol laughed along with him.

"What?" said Melissa. "What's this about singing?"

"You had to be there," said Carol. "Never mind. Arthur, whatcha got?"

"A lot more sensitivity and better manners than the rest of you," he said with mock indignation. "But I think everybody knows what's going on with me. My insight was I'm not what I've been pretending to be, a surgeon or now a retired surgeon with a lot of the impedimenta that came along with it. That was also the baggage I brought with me and have been struggling to carry around for the past forty years. I hereby cast it off for all time and am going to reveal to the world my true identity, that of an ass-kicking tenor sax player. My action I've already started. I've drafted letters to the organizations back in Des Moines who are going to have to muddle along somehow without my less-than-competent leadership."

"Bravo, a bit dramatic, but well said," said Don, applauding along with the rest of the group.

"Aren't you afraid?" asked Carol. "That's a lot of dramatic change all at once."

"It's been coming for some time. This seminar ignited it and gave me the clarity to see what I needed to do. It was like that Anais Nin quotation one of you mentioned the other day. He looked at his notes and read, 'There came a time when the risk to stay tight in the bud was more painful than the risk to blossom.' I just don't want to not be me. 'I gotta be me, I gotta be me,'" he sang.

"Stop. You promised," said Eddie. "*No mas, no mas.*"

"See, y'all, that's what Ah wuz talkin' about," said Nicole excitedly. "He's got a wacky side to him that he doesn't go 'round showin' everybody."

Still laughing at Arthur's impromptu musical, the group laughed even harder at Nicole's bubbling pride.

"Let's hear from you, Eddie," said Don, sneering at Arthur. "We know you have enough respect for the group to not sing."

"Whether I'm right or whether I'm wrong, I gotta be me—something—something—something," sang Eddie, off key. "Hey, Arthur, do you think you might be able to use me when you get your first gig?"

"Absolutely, dawg, you'll hear from my agent."

"Good," he said. "My deal is pretty obvious. I believe I mentioned to you that I'm a writer?"

"What? No, I had no idea," said Phil. "Did he mention that to anyone else?"

"The first I heard of it," said Inga, playing along.

"I'm personally shocked," said Arthur. "I thought you were a plumber or something like that."

"Hey, this is supposed to be the serious part of the seminar. If you guys aren't going to take it seriously, it's not too late for me to find a new group."

"I'm afraid it is," said Don. "We tried to trade you last week and got no offers, so you're stuck with us. Whatcha got?"

"Well, okay, my discovery about myself is that I lack self-confidence, true self-confidence. On my job I always had to appear like I had it all together, but deep down I was faking it. That's why your poem meant so much to me, Nickie. My baggage is not being real. What I've discovered from all of you during the past two weeks is that it is okay to be me, to be authentic. So I'm discarding those unwarranted, senseless insecurities. My action is to approach my writing from that place of authenticity and not try to impress people. I'm going to go back home, and you'll never guess what I'm going to do."

"Write up a storm," they all said in unison.

"That's right, and I'm going to let the chips fall where they may."

"What about you, Phil?" asked Don. "What happened for you? Did you pick up any new jokes on this trip?"

"No," he said, unsmilingly. "In fact, that was an insight I had about myself. I use all that joking around as a cover for my insecurity about my lack of depth, my shallowness. I sit back in awe when I hear you men and women with college degrees talk about stuff I don't know anything about. My baggage is my phoniness. I've built a big ego, which is just a defense mechanism to cover up my insecurities. I've found that I do genuinely care about people, but I put up a false front. My action plan is to stop and think before every meeting and be sure that the real Phil shows up."

Once again everybody broke into applause, from habit now.

"Wow!" said Eddie. "That's honest. That's the kind of authenticity I was talking about.

"Don, it's your turn. We haven't heard from you yet," said Melissa.

Don said quietly, "I realized a couple of things. One, I am smart, but I am not always wise. The difference between the two is that smart is having knowledge, but being wise is knowing how to apply that knowledge. Phil, you are wise. You've learned how to sort useful, practical gems out of the plethora of information with which we are bombarded daily. I want more of that for myself. I've watched you during the past two weeks, and under all of that humor and great personality is a keen interest in other people and an ability to ask them questions and listen to the answers. That's the source of your wisdom. So my baggage is that I talk too much and listen too little. In fact, if I were to objectively evaluate someone else doing what I do all the time, I'd call them a windbag. I want to stop that. Not only is it not an endearing quality, it prevents me from taking advantage of the wisdom that others possess. My action is to listen to others and glean the knowledge they possess. I have a golden opportunity with the people who attend my lectures at the Smithsonian. I know they are not only interested in what I have to say, but they would like an opportunity to let others know what they think. Starting with my next series of lectures, I'm going to invite any of them who are interested to join me after the lecture for coffee and a discussion of the topic. I'll give them an opportunity to talk, and I'll listen."

The others applauded, smiling and giving him approbation with thumbs-up signs and verbal approval and encouragement.

"I know that revelation comes as somewhat of a surprise to many of you," he said, smiling at his own self-deprecating sarcasm.

"Oh, yeah, it did for me," said Phil, still feeling the warmth of Don's compliment.

"Not for me," said a laughing Arthur. "I noticed it at once, and I was going to point it out to you, but I couldn't get a word in edgewise."

Turning to Carol, he said, "Carol, you are the only one we haven't heard from. What did you write on your questionnaire?"

"All right," she said hesitantly, looking at her worksheet. She read, "I am lovable. I haven't always been sure of that. My most important insight, however, is that I'm afraid. I always have been. I always needed my parents' approval because I was afraid of disappointing them. Then when they died, I transferred that need to Phil. I don't know what I'm afraid of—the future, the unknown, I guess. That's my baggage, all the attitudes that fearful people have and especially me. I'd like to throw it overboard, but I don't think I can. So my action is to look for some way to get over this fear. I guess like you, Arthur, I gotta be me. So my action," she said, looking at Phil, "is to do whatever it takes to become my own person."

At that, everybody supported her with their applause; Phil's a little less enthusiastic than the rest.

9:00 p.m.

"Well, that's it then," said Don. "I know we have to wrap up early because we need to have our bags in the hall by ten o'clock. Before we end it for this evening, does anyone have any comments or concluding thoughts?"

"Yes, a comment," said Arthur. "Don, you will be an effective discussion leader at the Smithsonian. The way you've been asking questions, listening to our answers, and keeping us on track has been impressive."

"I agree with that, in spades," said Eddie, "and I do have a concern in retrospect. I told you what I hope to do, but I don't know if I can pull it off. It's one thing to sit here and bask in the warm spirit of the group and believe that we can change, but what happens when we get back on our home turf?"

"Amen to that," said Don. "That is a concern we all have."

"What is that?" asked Nicole.

"Fear. I believe that is what traps us all into continuing to engage in counterproductive behaviors and prevents us from breaking loose."

"There is a way out of that trap, though," said Phil.

"Do tell," said Arthur. "What is it?"

"The reason we are able to gather the courage to make these bold commitments is the environment of support and encouragement we've developed in an incredibly short period of time. What we need is a way to take that home with us, short of all moving in together."

"Yeah, it wouldn't take long for that to wear thin, would it?" said Melissa.

"You would all love living with me, but some of you have some bad faults, and you know who you are and what they are, so I don't have to name names," said Phil, laughing.

"How can we transfer the best of what we've developed here back to our home turf, as Eddie calls it?" asked Inga.

"I think we need to be accountable to one another," said Arthur.

"Good idea. But how can we do that?" asked Don.

"We need a way to stay in touch, as we have here every day at six o'clock."

"Great idea. At six o'clock we can all start drinkin'," said Nicole.

"Or we could do a weekly email to keep our commitments at the conscious level," said Melissa.

"That would work for me," said Arthur. "I don't know one person in Des Moines who will support me or even understand what I want to do. It will take a group of weirdoes like you to be able to keep me on track."

"Now there's the pot calling the kettle black," said Don.

"I like it. How do we set up the email thing?" asked Nicole.

"I can do it, and I would like to," said Melissa. "I'm only working part-time, so I have the time and all the equipment at my office."

"All in favor of turning the 'keep everybody accountable' project over to the lawyer, say aye," said Don.

A chorus of 'ayes' rang out. "It's settled then. You're in charge, Melissa. Tell us what to do next."

"Okay, everyone give me the best email address to dependably reach you and the best time of the week to communicate with you, and I'll take it from there."

"There is one other thing before we leave," said Arthur. "It would be fun to see what happens to all of us in a year."

"I've been thinking about that too," said Phil. "Why don't we get together at some central location in one year? I'll organize it, and Melissa can check everybody's schedule to make it work."

A chorus of "great idea" and "count me in" followed. "It's set then," said Phil.

"Look at the time! I must get packed and get the suitcases out in the hall," said Carol.

"*Mein Gott in Himmel*," said Inga. "I do too. I didn't realize it was so late."

They gathered in a circle and, with tears in their eyes, spontaneously hugged one another. They knew there would never be another time in their lives quite like this.

———

EPILOGUE

Six Months After

Middle Bass Island, Lake Erie, Ohio

Eddie leaned back in his chair, scratched his six-month growth of beard, smiled to himself, and looked at the last word he had written on the computer screen:

FINIS

The surge of satisfaction that pulsed through him was unlike anything he'd ever felt during his years at Amalgamated Global Insurance Company.

He poured himself a cup of coffee from his thermos and allowed his mind to reflect back on the events of the last six months. The weekly email exchanges and encouragement from the seminar group gave him a lot of help, but the big breakthrough came later.

It started when he called Charlie, his best friend since grade school, and told him about the cruise and the seminar and his nonstop thinking about the book from the time he got off the ship and how he couldn't wait to sit down and "write up a storm." They both laughed at his overused expression of nonproductivity. After a serious discussion, Charlie told him about his vacation home on the island in Lake Erie that they were not going to be using this year, saying that it would be a perfect place for Eddie to write up his storm without interruption.

Melissa, who underwent her own epiphany of sorts, thanks to the positive support from the group, took him seriously for the first time. She was supportive of the idea, so two weeks later he drove to Sandusky, Ohio, and got on the ferry to Middle Bass, settled into Charlie's place, and almost immediately started writing.

As he looked at the screen and reread the 250-page manuscript, he was satisfied that he had followed his intention of having said what he meant to convey. He knew that it needed copy and content editing, but he felt that the ten thousand baby boomers reaching the age of retirement every day would have in their hands a valuable resource with the techniques, strategies, and attitude needed to ensure theirs would be a life well lived.

He'd already received an email from author Ron Champion's publisher. Ron had liked what he read before they disembarked and had forwarded the concept to his publisher. That was a valuable contact he'd made on the cruise. He had immediately emailed Ron and thanked him.

Eddie sat back and reviewed the table of contents one last time to be double sure he'd covered all the essentials of *Creating Well-Being in Your Bonus Years*. That was the title he'd decided on. He'd subtitled it *Finding Happiness and Fulfillment in Retirement*. He knew he might have to negotiate that with the publisher, but that was okay. They would know better than he would as to what would sell.

Introduction: What you can expect to gain by reading this book

1. You'll alter your view of yourself in retirement.

2. You'll redefine what retirement is and set some new goals for yourself.

3. You'll gain the techniques and strategies that will help you move forward in the second chapter of your life.

4. You'll be able to find purpose in retirement.

5. You'll be able to do the things that make life memorable and to create *a life worth living.*

Whether you are already retired or approaching retirement, you'll find this book to be one of the most valuable and enjoyable educational experiences of your life.

How to get the most from this book.

I suggest you read one chapter per day and put the principles into practice.

Table of Content

Day One: Getting Acquainted
Learn how to meet new people in a new community or deepen relationships in your current one.

Day Two: Identifying the Challenges of Retirement
Explore and identify your specific barriers and challenges to happiness in retirement.

Day Three: The Role of Money in Retirement
Plan on making the most of your money.
Get the most satisfaction from what you have.

Days Four and Five:
Review what you've read so far and reinforce the techniques.

Day Six: Healthy Living
Increase physical fitness and energy as we age.

Day Seven: Making the Most of Life
Develop planning and goal-setting tools for the new reality.

Day Eight: Attitudes of a Successful Retiree
Find your purpose after retirement.

Day Nine: To Work, Not Work, or Volunteer?
Clarify your values in retirement.

Day Ten: The Challenge of Change
Find the things that contribute to joy in your life.

Day Eleven:
Review and reinforce what you've gained so far.

Day Twelve: Your Spiritual Life
Examine your spiritual beliefs.

Day Thirteen:
Summarize your benefits.

Day Fourteen:
Set goals and make a plan for the future.

After he reviewed it, Eddie felt confident that he had a winner on his hands. He hit the print key and got up to pack and head back to Muncie.

———

acknowledgments

No book is ever the work of one person. This one is no exception. The many thousands of people I worked with in my thirty-five-year career all contributed to my understanding of the components for successful living.

As a Dale Carnegie instructor and business owner, teaching men and women the principles of success, I became intimately acquainted with their struggles and triumphs as they planned for their futures.

The reading and studying during the research on this book has enabled me to bring the best of current wisdom on the components of a life worth living. The hundreds of interviews I conducted with retirees has informed me as to what does and does not work in attempting to create well-being in the second chapter of life.

But, by far the most valuable contributors were my beta readers, the group who read, tested the validity of the ideas, and gave me feedback on the ideas contained in the book.

Thanks to them: Doug Carter, Alan Hutton, Loree Johnson, Cindy Monro, Marcia Sherman, Stacy Stack, Leslie Miller, and Jackie Peterson.

Thanks also to Wheatmark and Project Manager Lori Conser for her dedicated and professional service in publishing and editorial advice.

Special acknowledgement goes out to Daughter Michelle who, once again, as she did with my first book, did the lion's share of organizing and scheduling the beta readers' reports.

Jay Westrom, good buddy and longtime Dale Carnegie colleague who knew what I wanted to say right from the beginning. Also, Adella Macdonald whom I could, again, rely on for professional as well as accurate observations as we progressed. Fellow author and bff, Pati Hope, whose feedback kept me on track. Greg "Bunkie" Berg, PhD, a good friend who provided a great sounding board and words of encouragement throughout the entire process and fixed my numerous typographical errors as he reviewed the work while in process.

Thanks also to daughter Ana for ongoing inspiration and my life partner, best friend, and my wife, Patricia.